SO-AFV-298

Managing
Public Programs

𐄷𐄷𐄷𐄷𐄷𐄷𐄷𐄷𐄷𐄷𐄷𐄷𐄷𐄷𐄷𐄷𐄷𐄷𐄷𐄷𐄷𐄷𐄷𐄷𐄷𐄷𐄷𐄷

Robert E. Cleary
Nicholas Henry
and Associates

Managing Public Programs

Balancing Politics,
Administration,
and Public Needs

 J o s s e y - B a s s P u b l i s h e r s

San Francisco   •   London   •   1989

MANAGING PUBLIC PROGRAMS
Balancing Politics, Administration, and Public Needs
  by Robert E. Cleary, Nicholas Henry, and Associates

Copyright © 1989 by: Jossey-Bass Inc., Publishers
                     350 Sansome Street
                     San Francisco, California 94104
                           &
                     Jossey-Bass Limited
                     28 Banner Street
                     London EC1Y 8QE

Library of Congress Cataloging-in-Publication Data

Managing public programs.

   (The Jossey-Bass public administration series)
   Includes bibliographies and index.
   1. Public administration. I. Cleary, Robert E.
(Robert Edward), date. II. Henry, Nicholas,
date. III. Series.
JF1351.M35 1989   350   88-46089
ISBN 1-55542-143-1 (alk. paper)

Manufactured in the United States of America

The paper in this book meets the guidelines for
permanence and durability of the Committee on
Production Guidelines for Book Longevity of the
Council on Library Resources.

JACKET DESIGN BY WILLI BAUM

FIRST EDITION

Code 8916

The Jossey-Bass
Public Administration Series

Contents

Preface

The purpose of this book is to present information and approaches that can assist managers of public programs and services in the United States in improving their administrative abilities. Programs and services are the products of government—the "goods" delivered by the polity to the people. These include such diverse services as education, police and fire protection, road construction and maintenance, postal delivery, cleaner air and water, nuclear plant regulation, and national defense. Some are provided by one level of government only, as, for example, postal service is by the national government. Some are delivered by all three levels—for example, road construction, which, depending on the road, might be financed by local government with local funds, local government with state funds, state government with state funds, state government with federal funds, or some other combination of these.

The difficulties of managing and delivering public programs are enormous, but so are the rewards: service to one's fellow human beings is the ultimate reward of a public service career. *Managing Public Programs* aims to provide public managers with background information, ideas, techniques, and approaches, and also with a perspective on the forces that affect their official functions. The book is designed to help managers develop skills in hands-on program management for today's complex environment. The chapter authors present what they have learned from research, scholarship, and practice, in order to illustrate how a manager in this setting can provide maximum service to the public. We stress the relationship between public service administration and politics and the need for managers to consider the political forces that structure their environments as they implement and maintain programs.

Managing Public Programs presents a way of viewing government programs that is quite different from the typical approach. Chapters focus on managers and their problems, viewed in a broad—even societal—context. The chapter authors address issues of process and function that are of concern to program managers; these range from the problems of operating in a political setting to how such matters as ethical dilemmas, program retrenchment, privatization, relations with political superiors, and the changing nature of U.S. federalism affect managers' jobs and programs.

The authors develop and explain concepts and approaches that will enhance public servants' understanding of the relationship between the workplace and the larger political system. At the same time, the volume includes nuts and bolts commentary and advice for current and aspiring program managers. Substantive examples are drawn from all levels of government to explain approaches and illustrate problems. After all, not only is managing public programs increasingly an intergovernmental—and, indeed, intersector—matter, but each level of government (federal, state, and local) has supplied unique solutions to vexing public problems. Often these solutions have not been transmitted to or understood by other levels of government. We hope that this book will serve, among other things, to let each level of government know what the others are doing.

Organization of the Book

The Introduction sets the stage for the remainder of the volume by detailing the fundamental differences between public administration and private sector management in the United States. Parts One and Two situate the role and tasks of public managers in an organizational and conceptual framework. Part One, comprising Chapters One and Two, analyzes the political and organizational environment within which public administrators operate. Part Two—Chapters Three, Four, and Five—

examines key personnel issues and outlines some human resource skills and perspectives that contribute to successful public management. In Part Three, which encompasses Chapters Six through Ten, we explore public budgeting, computing, strategic management and planning, contracting out, and program evaluation— additional key areas in which basic skills and concepts are essential for effective public program administration. Finally, in the concluding chapter we present an analytical, integrative summary of the strategies, techniques, and skills of effective public management that have been set forth in the various chapters of the book.

Overview of the Contents

The Introduction, by Nicholas Henry and Robert E. Cleary, focuses on the realities of public program management. The authors emphasize the distinctions between public administration and private management, examining such matters as how the values and goals that guide private organizations differ from those that guide public management—and how these values and goals affect the ways in which the two sectors function and are evaluated. Henry and Cleary also pose the basic question of what impact public managers can have on the delivery of public programs and services.

In Chapter One H. George Frederickson discusses the political context of public program administration, concentrating on the interrelatedness of politics and administration of public programs and services. In this context, Frederickson argues that "if government is to be well executed, public servants must be both technically expert and politically wise."

In Chapter Two David B. Walker analyzes the changed role of federal program managers in the 1980s and 1990s. Although he deals with a wide variety of intersecting relationships in intergovernmental management, Walker particularly emphasizes the importance of relationships between federal fiscal and regulatory managers on the one hand and program administrators at the state and local levels of government on the other.

In Chapter Three Robert E. Cleary examines the role that specialists play in U.S. government—their conflicting obligations and resultant dilemmas, the role of personnel policy in attracting and retaining quality professionals in government, and the central importance of education to the career development of professional managers.

Chapter Four, by Ralph Clark Chandler, focuses on the importance of ethics as a guide to behavior for public administrators. Chandler argues that time-tested internal norms that guide private conduct should also be applied to administrative practice. He concludes that "professionalism rooted in moral reasoning is the most practical management consideration of all."

N. Joseph Cayer examines, in Chapter Five, the qualities that tend to identify the successful program manager. Cayer discusses *positive management* and the importance of various practical skills, people skills, political skills, and leadership skills to good program administration. He also analyzes such current aspects of public personnel policy and development as equal employment opportunity and affirmative action, employee organizations, the increasing legal regulation of employer/employee relations, and the impact of the human resource development (HRD) movement on public management and organizations.

Chapter Six, by Frank Sackton, deals with financing public programs in a time of fiscal constraint. He emphasizes the importance of such tools as performance budgeting, productivity management, cutback management, forecasting, and performance auditing for managers attempting to maintain effectiveness, equity, and agency cohesion in a period of budgetary austerity.

In Chapter Seven Alana Northrop, Kenneth L. Kraemer, and John Leslie King assess the impact of computers on public program management. These authors emphasize the crucial importance of managers' understanding the possibilities and limitations of the computer. The results of computerization are conditioned by the organizational context, they argue; public administrators need not be expert at using computers, but they do need to be knowledgeable about the impact computers can have on their organization.

In Chapter Eight Jerry L. Mc Caffery applies to public organizations the tools of strategic management and planning developed in the business world. After outlining the methodology and techniques of strategic management and planning, Mc Caffery argues that they provide "a good tool for keeping the organization in balance with its environment; for determining an agency's critical tasks, operational policies, and programs; and for making optimal use of its human capital and resources."

John Rehfuss discusses the "contracting out" movement (Chapter Nine). He examines the difficulties of maintaining quality, avoiding corruption, and ensuring accountability in a time of increasing privatization. He discusses the repercussions for public managers and concludes that despite its problems, contracting out is, in the final analysis, simply another tool for providing efficient, effective public services and that it should be used if the situation seems to warrant it.

In Chapter Ten Sharon L. Caudle explores how to evaluate public programs in political settings. Caudle points out that managers involved in program evaluation must take into account not only program considerations that promise improved performance but the overall political setting, as well, if the evaluation is to prove really useful. Administrators therefore need to gain a clear understanding of the techniques of evaluation.

The Conclusion, by Robert E. Cleary and Nicholas Henry, recapitulates the chapter authors' recommendations for managing effectively in a political context. As H. George Frederickson argues (Chapter One), "effective political skills . . . make good public administration possible." If managers want to be effective politically, we believe they should be familiar with the skills and techniques outlined in this volume. Moreover, public administrators who understand and put into practice the concepts presented here will be more successful managers. The concluding chapter presents an integrative summary of the following skills and techniques set forth in *Managing Public Programs:* personnel management, financial management, computing skills, strategic management and planning, contracting out, and program evaluation.

Cleary and Henry also discuss in the concluding chapter

additional capabilities required for effective public program
management, including the ability

- To deal fairly and competently with others
- To operate in the current framework of intricate intergovern-
  mental relations
- To understand the political context that surrounds public
  program decisions
- To understand, when making public program and organi-
  zational decisions, the importance of the public interest
- To act in a professional manner
- To act ethically
- To understand the fundamental civic duty inherent in public
  service

Audience

Managing Public Programs is written primarily for civil servants who are or who aspire to be program managers at the
federal, state, or local level of government; but political supervisors will also benefit from reading it, as will all those wishing
to acquaint themselves with the fundamental systems problems
plaguing administrators of government programs. Finally, the
book can serve as a primary or supplementary text for upper-
division and beginning graduate courses in public administration, political science, and public policy.

Practitioners will find that the book offers specific, concrete information and advice on the processes and concepts of
management. It deals with major issues of public management
in a way that demonstrates how managers can develop the skills
necessary to improve both processes and procedures.

Academics will find that *Managing Public Programs* offers
a perspective different from the prevailing view in literature on
public administration programs and issues, which are only occasionally presented in the larger political or organizational
context. We focus on understanding managers and their problems in the political/organizational setting. As noted earlier,
Managing Public Programs can serve as a textbook, and it should

prove especially useful in courses that deal with management, human resource development, the relationship between organizations and their managers, or the interface between politics and administration.

The principal authors, Robert E. Cleary and Nicholas Henry, take this opportunity to acknowledge their debt to the other authors of *Managing Public Programs,* each of whom is a specialist in his or her field. Working with the contributing authors has been a distinct pleasure for both of us; the virtues of this volume are largely due to their efforts.

December 1988   Robert E. Cleary
                                                  Washington, D.C.

                                                  Nicholas Henry
                                                  Statesboro, Georgia

The Authors

Robert E. Cleary is professor of public affairs at American University. He received his B.A. degree (1953) from Montclair State College in social science, master's degrees from Montclair State College in social science (1957) and from Rutgers University in political science (1959), and his Ph.D. (1962) from Rutgers in political science. His scholarly interests center on the interrelationships among politics, administration, and education. He is a past president of the National Association of Schools of Public Affairs and Administration and of the Society for College and University Planning. The first executive secretary of the Harry S Truman Foundation, he has also served as dean of the College of Public and International Affairs, provost, and acting president of American University. His most recent publications are *The Role of Government in the United States: Theory and Practice* (1985) and (coauthored) "Why Can't We Resolve the Research Issue in Public Administration?" (1984).

Nicholas Henry is president of Georgia Southern College. Before accepting that post, he was professor of public affairs and dean of the College of Public Programs at Arizona State University. He received his B.A. degree (1965) from Centre College in government and English, his M.A. degree (1967) from Pennsylvania State University in political science, and both his M.P.A. (1970) and his Ph.D. in political science (1971) from Indiana University.

Henry is the author of several books on the management of public programs, including *Public Administration and Public*

Affairs (1975), *Governing at the Grassroots* (1980) and *Reconsidering American Politics* (1985, with John Stuart Hall). He also is editor of *Doing Public Administration* (1978), a workbook in the field of public management. His book *Public Administration and Public Affairs* is the only American book on public administration to have been translated and published in Japanese. Currently Henry serves as president of Pi Alpha Alpha, the national public administration honor society.

Sharon L. Caudle is assistant professor of information resources management at Syracuse University's School of Information Studies. Previously, she worked at the Center for Governmental Services at Auburn University and the National Academy of Public Administration and held positions as specialist and manager with the Nevada State Welfare Division, the U.S. Department of Agriculture, and the U.S. Office of Management and Budget. She received her B.A. degree (1971) from the University of Nevada, Reno, in social services and corrections and her M.P.A. and Ph.D. in public administration from George Washington University (in 1985 and 1988, respectively).

N. Joseph Cayer is professor of public affairs in the School of Public Affairs at Arizona State University. He received both his B.A. (1964) in political science and his M.P.A. (1966) degrees from the University of Colorado and his Ph.D. (1972) from the University of Massachusetts in political science. His main research activities are in public personnel management and labor relations, with a particular emphasis on equal employment opportunity and affirmative action.

Ralph Clark Chandler teaches public administration and constitutional law at Western Michigan University in Kalamazoo. He is the author or editor of eleven books, including *The Constitutional Law Dictionary: Individual Rights* (1985), which won the American Library Association's Outstanding Reference Book award for 1985, and the recently published *Centennial History of the American Administrative State* (1987), called by Luther Gulick "the New Testament of public administration for America today."

Chandler holds five academic degrees, including a B.D. (1965) and Th.M. (1966) in ethics from Union and Princeton Theological Seminaries, respectively, and a Ph.D. (1970) from Columbia University in public law and government. He won his university's excellence in teaching award in both 1982 and 1986.

H. George Frederickson is the Edwin O. Stene Distinguished Professor of Public Administration at the University of Kansas. He is a past president of the American Society for Public Administration and is a member of the National Academy of Public Administration. From 1977 to 1987 he was the president of Eastern Washington University at Cheney and Spokane. Among his publications is *New Public Administration* (1980). Frederickson received his B.S. degree (1959) from Brigham Young University in political science, and both his M.P.A. and his Ph.D. in public administration from the University of California, Los Angeles (in 1961 and 1967, respectively).

John Leslie King is the chairperson of the Department of Information and Computer Science and an associate professor in the Graduate School of Management and the Department of Information and Computer Science at the University of California, Irvine. King received his B.A. degree in philosophy and his M.S. and Ph.D. degrees, both in administration, from the University of California, Irvine (in 1972, 1974, and 1977 respectively).

Kenneth L. Kraemer is the director of the Public Policy Research Organization and a professor in the Graduate School of Management and the Department of Information and Computer Science at the University of California, Irvine. He received his B. Arch. (1959) from the University of Notre Dame, his M.S.C. and R.P. (1964) from the University of Southern California, and his M.P.A. and Ph.D. in public administration from the University of Southern California in 1965 and 1967, respectively.

Jerry L. Mc Caffery is professor of public budgeting at the Naval Postgraduate School. He received his B.S. (1959), M.A. (1969), and Ph.D. (1972) degrees from the University of Wisconsin in political science with a concentration in public administration. Mc Caffery's research activities have focused on budget system innovations and strategic planning for resource allocation. His current interests center on computer-assisted budget decision making and on the resource allocation process within the Department of Defense. Mc Caffery has taught at Indiana University and the University of Georgia and served the state of Wisconsin as a budget analyst.

Alana Northrop is professor of political science and coordinator of the master's program in public administration at California State University, Fullerton. She received her B.A. degree (1971) from Smith College in government and her M.A. (1974) and Ph.D. (1975) degrees from the University of Chicago in political science.

John Rehfuss is professor of public management in the School of Business and Public Administration at California State University, Sacramento. He has written four books—*Public Administration as Political Process* (1973), *Urban Politics in the Suburban Era* (1976, with Thomas Murphy), *Contracting Out in Government* (1989), and *The Job of the Public Manager* (1989)—as well as forty articles on urban government and public administration. He received his B.A. (1956) from Willamette University in political science and his M.A. (1958) and D.P.A. (1965) degrees from the University of Southern California. Before entering academe, he served in California local government, including a stint as acting city manager of Palm Springs.

Frank Sackton is professor of public affairs at Arizona State University, where he has also served as deputy director of athletics, acting dean of the College of Public Programs, and vice-president for business affairs. He received his B.S. degree (1970) from the University of Maryland in Turkish language and his M.P.A. (1976) from Arizona State University. Before entering academe, he served in the U.S. Army for thirty years, retiring as a lieutenant general. His last assignment, of four years' duration, was as comptroller of the army.

David B. Walker is a professor of political science at the University of Connecticut, where he is also director of the Institute of Public and Urban Affairs and the Master of Public Affairs program. He currently serves as chairperson of the Connecticut Advisory Commission on Intergovernmental Relations. From 1966 to 1984 he was the assistant director of the Government Structure and Function Section, U.S. Advisory Commission on Intergovernmental Relations, in Washington, D.C.

He received his B.A. (1949) and M.A. (1950) degrees from Boston University, both in government, and his Ph.D. (1956) from Brown University in political science.

⊡⊡⊡⊡⊡⊡⊡⊡⊡⊡⊡⊡⊡⊡⊡⊡⊡⊡⊡⊡⊡⊡⊡⊡⊡⊡⊡

Managing
Public Programs

Introduction:
The Realities
of Public Program Management

Nicholas Henry
Robert E. Cleary

Managing Public Programs is aimed at the practice of public management and the practitioners of public administration. In addressing this theme and this audience, *Managing Public Programs* necessarily illuminates the differences between public administration and private management. Not only are public administration and private management different beasts, but public administration clearly is the beastlier of the two. The public sector is, in short, simply a tougher, meaner, nastier, and ultimately more rewarding animal when tamed than is the creature of corporate America.

What makes public administration different? Paramountly, the difference lies in the milieu in which public organizations find themselves. Organization theorists call this milieu the "task environment." Most of us as citizens, however, simply call it "politics."

But the dilemma of the manager of public programs runs deeper than mere politics. The real dilemma, the ultimate problem, for the public manager is that the world beyond the boundaries of the program that he or she is charged with managing intrudes deeply and profoundly into those very programs—their inner workings, their impact on their clients, their efficiency, their effectiveness, and even their directions. Few observers bring out these realities more vividly and more clearly than do the contributors to this volume.

What do we mean when we contend that the outside world interferes more strongly in the management of public programs than in the management of private ones? One problem is that public programs are far more difficult to plan coherently than private ones are. Planning and setting priorities can be substantially more difficult in the public sector than in the private sector because of less focused organizational goals and higher turnover among top executives (Buchanan, 1975; Gawthrop, 1971). Granted, planning in the private sector is no mean chore, but consider the teeming phenomena with which public planners must contend. Not only must they develop projections for future economic performance (as do private planners), but they must consider how legislators might react to such economic performance and take into account a variety of other variables, including constituency pressures, the performance of microeconomies in contrast to macroeconomies, the wishes of campaign contributors, community interests, the interpretation of statutes as they apply to campaign contributions and a variety of other areas, the interaction of legislative committees, and a plethora of prospective social changes that virtually no one can hope to predict. Planning in the public sector therefore bears little, if any, relationship to what planning means in the private sector.

Similarly, programmatic objectives in the public sector are characterized not by their definition, but by their lack of it. Unlike the private sector, the public sector has only a vague understanding about what it really wants and what causes its goals to be realized. As a consequence, measuring productivity and success becomes inordinately difficult when compared to the private sector.

Few scholars have addressed this problem of ill-defined goals in the public sector more lucidly than James D. Thompson, in his classic work, *Organizations in Action* (1967). Thompson observed that programs and organizations may be categorized as to how "crystallized" their standards of desirability are and according to whether they have members who believe that they fully comprehend the relationships between causes and effects.

Thompson observed that in those organizations that had highly crystallized standards of desirability *and* firm beliefs among its members as to causality, relatively straightforward performance criteria could be applied in the form of what he called "efficiency tests." For example, executives in a private corporation typically have a solid notion of what they want to do and how to do it: They want to make as high profits as possible (in other words, their standards of desirability are quite crystallized), and they believe that manufacturing their product line as cheaply as possible is what causes higher profits.

By contrast, public organizations must use either an instrumental test or a social test to determine adequacy of organizational performance, and by any accountancy-based definition of "management," such tests of performance are unsatisfactory indeed.

The instrumental test is a test of productivity used in organizations that have a crystallized standard of desirability but only a poorly understood concept of causality. For example, the Department of Health and Human Services may have a concrete idea about what it wants: the reduction of poverty. On the other hand, how poverty can be reduced and what "causes" the reduction of poverty become problematic. Is poverty a question of "life-style," or is it a question of simply not having enough money? Depending on how one answers that question alone, policymakers would emphasize the training and hiring of more social workers or, by contrast, not hiring social workers and instead implementing the controversial idea of a negative income tax (Moynihan, 1969). Ultimately, public managers must attempt to address these questions.

Even more vague are the social tests explained by Thompson. The social test is applied to those organizations that have neither crystallized standards of desirability nor agreed-upon perceptions of causality. Organizations that must rely on social tests to determine their level of performance are found almost exclusively in the public sector. No one can even attempt to pinpoint the performance goals, or even the operational goals, of such agencies—indeed, the operational goals of public organizations are so sprawling, at least as described by the statutes that establish them, that to attempt to match such cosmic legislative views with "green-eyeshade" performance criteria is not merely difficult but often absurd.

Social tests come to the rescue of organizations facing these dilemmas. A social test is the determination of whether an organization is making society feel good or bad about itself. How one measures this dimension is usually determined by the agency's success in acquiring a budget. Thus, unlike the private sector, where success is determined by how little an organization spends as a means of maximizing its profits, success in the public sector is determined by how much money an organization garners from the legislative process. The most common way of acquiring such legislative largesse is by building the organization's status and prestige in society or, perhaps more accurately in the case of public organizations, creating a constituency. The more status (or constituents) an organization has, the more resources it will acquire from society. This is the essence of the social test.

Because public organizations must often be evaluated in different ways from private ones, it follows that public managers must also be evaluated in different ways from private managers. Research indicates that not only do managers in the two sectors behave differently, but even what constitutes effective management can be entirely different in each sector. When the executive work behavior of managers in city governments was compared with that of managers in industry, it was found that public managers believed (and quite accurately so) that they had little control over how they used their time; hence, they did not spend a great deal of effort on time management relative to managers in the private sector. City managers were considerably more at the mercy of forces in their organizations' task environments than were their counterparts in private industry. Public administrators spent less time alone in their offices and less time on planning, they were more rushed to get things done, and (significantly) they spent nearly twice as much time on the telephone as private executives did (Porter and Van Maanen, 1970).

Disconcertingly, effective managers displayed entirely different work behaviors depending on whether they worked in the private or public sector. The more effective public administrators were more flexible, planned less, and had less control over their time than the managers in industry. Indeed, the less effective public managers spent more time on planning their time than did the more effective public managers, while quite the reverse held true in the industrial sector: The *less* effective private administrators spent *less* time planning their time than did their more effective colleagues (Porter and Van Maanen, 1970).

These realities of public life are brought out by the contributors to this book. Looming implicitly throughout their writings is the theme of the growing complexity of the public bureaucracy. It is a theme worth keeping in mind because the bureaucratization of the public sector is likely to develop rather than diminish over time. This development, too, is a result of the easy access that politics has to the inner workings of the organization and to the management of public programs.

Normally, the bureaucratization of any organization would be viewed with alarm, and, indeed, alarm is the typical response from observers of the public sector. Anthony Downs was among the first to describe why the public sector is more likely to bureaucratize than the private sector. In *Inside Bureaucracy,* Downs (1967) suggested that organizations that do not work in free market conditions (in other words, government agencies and nonprofit groups) are inexorably pushed into devoting more time to internal communications and the development of internal control mechanisms than are private organizations, because government agencies have no easily recognized criterion of performance that private corporations have in the form of the profit margin. To compensate for this lack of accurate feedback, those charged with the management of public programs must develop (and spend a great deal of time and effort in developing) internal rules to control spending, assure that "customers" receive public programs efficiently and effectively, and coordinate activities that often are massive in scale (Downs, 1967).

Most observers find this kind of dynamic horrendous and offensive (Warwick, 1975), but not all do. For example, Marshall

W. Meyer (1979) argues that the bureaucratization of public program management is a response by the public bureaucracy not merely to *control* the delivery of these services but also to deliver these services more effectively. Meyer suggests, unlike more mainstream scholars in this literature, that such bureaucratization is not a sign of resistance to new demands on the public bureaucracy but rather one of eagerness to accommodate those demands: "Increasing the bureaucratization of public agencies through additional rules and layers of hierarchy results, in part, from their openness to their environments" (p. 5).

No one, of course, has justified the bureaucratization of the public sector more directly—even confrontationally—than Max Weber, the famous theorist of the late nineteenth and early twentieth centuries. Weber thought that bureaucracy was essential in achieving the goal of rationality dominating chaos and that it was vital to the achievement of social justice. As Weber put it (1946, p. 260), "bureaucracy is a means of carrying 'community action' over into rationally ordered 'societal action' . . . [T]he individual bureaucrat cannot squirm out of the apparatus in which he is harnessed. . . . If his work is forcefully interrupted, chaos results, and it is difficult to improvise replacements from among the government who are fit to master such chaos. This holds for public administration as well as for private economic management."

Today, the assessment of the role of the public program manager has switched from one of Weberian autonomy of bureaucrats to one of Meyerian victimization of bureaucracy by the forces of politics. Whatever the cause, however, it appears that decision making and program management in the public sector are different from those in the private sector. Again, the contributions to this book tease out these differences in a way that no academic treatise can, but some scholars have helped us understand these differences as well. Some observers, for example, have called the process by which public programs are managed, "organized anarchies." Organized anarchies are characterized by three phenomena: Members of the organization charged with the administration of programs and the delivery of services do not define their preferences about policies and goals very precisely (and when they do, the policies and goals are often in conflict); what the organization actually does is unclear; and decision making in the organization is extraordinarily fluid. Organized anarchies use a decision-making process consisting of four streams: problems, solutions, participants, and opportunities to make choices. These streams rarely combine, but when they do connect, major decisions often result. Hence, the structure of organized anarchies is a flow of separate processes throughout the organization, and decisions rely almost exclusively on the joining of these processes at some unpredictable time (Cohen, March, and Olsen, 1972; Kingdon, 1984).

Increasingly, observers are describing this reality of organizational life in the public sector as the question of "determinism versus choice." The descriptors are ours, and not necessarily those found in the literature. But we think that these descriptors convey more concretely what the dilemma is: Do "outside forces" determine the destiny of public program management, or does individual human choice do so? This question will pose an interesting intellectual dilemma for academics for many years to come, and it involves far more serious concerns for those practicing the art of public program management.

Nowhere is this dilemma brought out more amply than in this volume.

References

Buchanan, B. "Government Managers, Business Executives, and Organizational Commitment." *Public Administration Review,* July-Aug. 1975, *35,* 339-347.

Cohen, M., March, J. G., and Olsen, J. "The Garbage Can Model of Organizational Choice." *Administrative Science Quarterly,* 1972, *17,* 1-25.

Downs, A. *Inside Bureaucracy.* Boston: Little, Brown, 1967.

Gawthrop, L. C. *Administrative Politics and Social Change.* New York: St. Martin's Press, 1971.

Kingdon, J. W. *Agendas, Alternatives, and Public Policies.* Boston: Little, Brown, 1984.

Meyer, M. W. *Change in Public Bureaucracies.* London: Cambridge University Press, 1979.

Moynihan, D. P. *Maximum Feasible Misunderstanding: Community Action and the War on Poverty.* New York: Free Press, 1969.

Porter, L. W., and Van Maanen, J. "Task Accomplishment in the Management of Time." In B. Bass (ed.), *Managing for Accomplishment.* Lexington, Mass.: Lexington Books, 1970.

Thompson, J. D. *Organizations in Action.* New York: McGraw-Hill, 1967.

Warwick, D. P. *A Theory of Public Bureaucracy.* Cambridge, Mass.: Harvard University Press, 1975.

Weber, M. *From Max Weber: Essays in Sociology.* (H. H. Gerth and C. W. Mills, eds. and trans.) New York: Oxford University Press, 1946.

One

᠁᠁᠁᠁᠁᠁᠁᠁᠁᠁᠁᠁᠁᠁᠁᠁᠁᠁᠁᠁᠁᠁᠁

The Politics
and Complexities
of Meeting Public Needs

Government is a different phenomenon than business. It is different for many reasons, but certainly one of the most important derives from the all-encompassing environment surrounding performance of the public's work. In one way or another, everyone is interested and involved in what those who deliver public programs and services do and how they do it. The result for public managers is a need to appreciate and understand the intricate context within which they must carry out their tasks. Consequently, Chapters One and Two of *Managing Public Programs* focus on the environment in which public administrators in the United States, no matter what their level of government, must operate. The authors of these chapters attempt to outline those appreciations and understandings necessary for a public manager to function well in the midst of substantial political and organizational complexity.

In Chapter One, H. George Frederickson emphasizes the overall political context that surrounds public management. The classic dichotomy between politics and administration, if it ever existed, certainly does not exist in American politics today. Program expertise is found in a variety of executive offices outside of program offices, as well as on legislative staffs. Privatization, or "government by proxy," has substantially complicated program

9

delivery. Politicians are deeply interested in the outcomes of public program management—that is, public programs and services. Frederickson argues that public administrators must understand all this and, as a consequence, realize the importance of working actively with the political leadership of their organizations whenever possible to help formulate program mandates and goals in the interests of better performance. Public administrators, he declares, cannot ignore politics and political implications.

In Chapter Two, David B. Walker describes the interlocking network that now binds American federal, state, and local program managers together. An explosion in the field of intergovernmental relations in the 1950s and 1960s led to intricate arrangements across levels of government for the financing and delivery of public programs and services in program area after program area. The emphasis on deregulation and fiscal stringency in the 1980s, accompanied by vigorous verbal attacks on the competence of federal bureaucrats, led to substantial delegation of program authority to states and localities within the framework of severe budgetary limitations. The result was a need to rewrite and rework existing administrative arrangements for intergovernmental cooperation under less than ideal conditions. Fallout from these reorganizations was finally settling at the end of the 1980s. Federal managers were not as directly involved in the delivery of state and local programs and services as they had been a generation before, but they were still quite involved in the basic financing, auditing, and oversight of dozens, even hundreds, of such programs.

1

𝄢𝄢𝄢𝄢𝄢𝄢𝄢𝄢𝄢𝄢𝄢𝄢𝄢𝄢𝄢𝄢𝄢𝄢𝄢𝄢𝄢𝄢𝄢𝄢𝄢

How Politics
Affects Public Programs

H. George Frederickson

When asked why the prison riot had happened, the warden replied, "Politics. The citizens wanted stricter law enforcement and longer prison sentences. The police and the judges responded, filling the prison to overflowing. Yet the budget of the Department of Corrections has not kept up with inflation. The crowding got worse; so did the food, the educational and counseling services, and the quality of the staff. A riot was certain to happen and it did. The reason was politics." Shortly after these comments the warden was replaced and the governor appointed a task force to study the possibility of contracting out prison services.

Presidents Jimmy Carter and Ronald Reagan both favored the deregulation of business, including the airlines. The Federal Aviation Administration's responsibilities for schedules, fares, and service regulations were discontinued and the airlines were left to compete. By late 1987 there were, due to airline mergers resulting from deregulation, fewer than half the major airlines that were in service in 1977. Some major airports, such as St. Louis and Minneapolis–St. Paul, are now served primarily by only one major carrier. Persons flying from one major urban center to another now have lower air fares and more flights available, but persons flying to or from smaller locations have diminished service and higher fares. Traffic delays at large urban airports are no longer discussed in terms of numbers of minutes but in terms of numbers of hours. Since the firing of the air

11

traffic controllers early in 1980, the air traffic control system
has not returned to earlier levels of quality. And now midair
collisions and near-misses are increasing.

What accounts for all of this? Politics. Elizabeth Dole,
as U.S. Secretary of Transportation, answered citizen complaints
about deteriorating airline services and safety concerns by saying that significant improvements are expected in air traffic control and that airlines have agreed to operate an "honest" schedule. Airlines are to make available to customers information on
the actual delays experienced by particular flights and on "or-
dinary" norms for baggage loss. Yet Secretary Dole also indicated that the Reagan administration was not interested in further
regulating the airlines but only in making them more efficient
and safe.

In 1977 the U.S. Food and Drug Administration (FDA)
announced a ban on saccharin because research indicated that
it may have cancer-causing properties. After a protracted political battle Congress delayed the ban for eighteen months to
mid-1979, and it has been delayed in consecutive two-year periods to this date.

The prison warden, the secretary of transportation, and
the FDA were all experiencing the single most consistent and
significant phenomenon in American public administration:
Public administration is embedded in politics. It follows, therefore,
that effectiveness as a public administrator is predicted on both
an understanding of politics and of the political process and an
ability to manage public programs in a political context.

Understanding Politics and Public Administration

Politics, at its best, is a noble expression of the human
capacity to cooperate in the operation of anything collective:
a village, a business, or a nation. It is through politics that the
particular interests of diverse individuals are brought together
to fashion a common or general view.

At its worst, however, politics is the utilization of power
to advance the interests of some at the expense of others. Politics
is the perfect venue for the person who wishes either to receive

extraordinary attention or to exercise unjust dominion over others.

Politics, good and bad, as Webster tells us, is the art and science of government. It is the context in which public administration works. Politics takes many forms, each affecting public administration in different ways. There are partisan politics, interest group politics, bureaucratic politics, media politics, and many others. In the United States all forms of politics are carried on according to the political agreements of the Founders in the U.S. Constitution and state constitutions. Therefore, to understand the relationship between politics and public administration one must begin with the Constitution.

The Constitution. The U.S. Constitution and the state constitutions established democratic governments based on popular sovereignty; that is, they established government by the consent of the governed. Sovereignty, though, does not mean that we are self-governing. Ordinarily this sovereignty is expressed through the selection of representatives—senators, members of Congress, state senators and representatives, county commissioners, city councils. Pursuant to the constitution(s), these representatives set up laws, establish rates of taxation, and provide for public services. In almost all cases, the selection of representatives is by the majority of voters, as is the passage of most legislation. In American representative government, majority rule is the basis of the concept of popular sovereignty, but the sovereign majority cannot legislate away the constitutionally protected rights of individuals. The Bill of Rights guarantees freedom of the press, of assembly, and of religion, and it guarantees privacy and other freedoms, to protect the individual from government in a general sense and protect minorities from the tyranny of elected majorities.

Because of long experience with despotic governments in Europe, the framers of the U.S. Constitution and state constitutions designed a system of limited government. Not all governmental power was to be placed in the hands of one person or even one group of persons. The first principle of limited government is the separation of powers. Legislators pass laws and control the budget, elected executives carry out the laws, courts protect individuals and provide judicial review of the actions of the other branches of government. The second principle of limited government is that the three branches are to be balanced so that possible excesses in one branch can be checked by the other branches. Justice Louis D. Brandeis once noted that "the doctrine of separation of powers was adopted, not to promote efficiency but to preclude the exercise of arbitrary power" (Seidman and Gilmour, 1986, p. 28). The third principle of limited government is federalism, a decentralized form of government kept close to the people. All powers not expressly given to the national government are reserved to the states. The states follow suit by providing for the creation of counties and cities and other local jurisdictions to carry out governmental services.

The constitution(s) provides for the rights of citizens to organize to advance their individual and shared interests.

Over the years the U.S. Constitution has been amended, and many state constitutions have been completely revised. For example, sovereignty, generally expressed through the right to vote, has over the years and as a result of protracted political struggles been extended to women and minorities. As far as public administration is concerned, the most critical development in national constitutional change has been the Fourteenth Amendment and its "equal protection of the law" clause, which extends equal rights to minorities. It is important to note, however, that many state constitutions have been revised in the last two decades to strengthen the power and authority of governors.

No mention is made in the Constitution of political parties, interest groups, or administration—and yet all three obviously have become significant in the practice of contemporary American government. Because administration is not mentioned in the U.S. Constitution (it is mentioned in most state constitutions), it should not be assumed that public administration lacks a legitimate role in government. Governmental power can be legitimized either through a constitution or directly through the political process. It has been through the political process that public administration has developed and become a legitimate part of American government. Indeed, not only has public administration managed the daily affairs of government effectively, it has made ''a significant contribution to the process of self-government in the United States by providing oportunities for groups of citizens to be more intimately involved in government decision making than the traditional election system permits'' (Rourke, 1987, p. 230).

In a thorough and persuasive assessment of the role of public administration in the constitutional order, Francis Rourke (1987) describes the legitimate place of public administration as correcting a defect in the Constitution. The founding document ''does not make adequate provision for public participation in government decision making. The role of bureaucracy in government opens an opportunity for many people to become actively involved in the work of government. They may do so as civil servants, as citizens attending public hearings, or by taking advantage of other opportunities to participate in the many activities of administrative agencies'' (p. 230).

Legislative Politics. In the practice of politics in the constitutional order, legislators pass enabling statutes and delegate to administrative agencies and administrators the authority to operate federal, state, and local programs. Once an agency is established and staffed, ordinarily through a personnel system applying standards of merit for initial appointment and promotion, the agency is funded through an annual budget passed by the legislature. The legislature also engages in routine oversight of agency functioning. The professional staff, then, is left to operate the agency on a day-to-day basis. In the classic theory of public administration this situation is described conceptually as the *politics-administration dichotomy*. In this theory, elected representatives decide politically what programs the government will operate and administrators then carry out these programs. Once an agency's mission is defined and its budget established through the legislative process, the political process stops and the administrative process starts. Partisan political interests are not expected to meddle in routine administrative affairs, nor are administrators expected to participate in partisan politics.

The politics-administration dichotomy is an ''ideal type,''

a theoretical construct or an abstraction used to differentiate between governmental processes that are *primarily* political and those that are *primarily* administrative. But, as with any abstraction used for purposes of description and prescription, a considerable difference often exists between theory and practice.

In practice, statutes are often vague. It is usually the case that governmental programs are described legislatively in overreaching ways. The experience has been that public administrators then must exercise a good bit of discretion in trying to bring definition and specificity to vague and sometimes contradictory legislative language.

In practice, budgets are seldom adequate to carry out legislative expectations. One significant task for public administrators is to align reasonable expectations with both budget realities and the overreaching rhetoric of statutes.

In practice, when government agencies are unable to meet the expectations of the legislature or meet the sometimes exaggerated expectations of the citizens resulting from political promise, it is often convenient for legislators to practice the politics of blame—blaming the amorphous bureaucracy or hinting at fraud or waste.

In practice, the national legislature, as well as state legislators and larger city councils and county commissions, has a division of labor based on committees and subcommittees organized around particular functions of government, such as national defense at the national level or law enforcement at the state and local level. These committees and subcommittees often match in a general way the organizational structure set up to administer these laws.

In legislative politics there is often a close working relationship between legislators on a particular committee or subcommittee and top-level administrative officials in the functionally connected administrative agency. Some of these connections are legendary, as in the case of state highway departments and highway committees in state legislatures, or the agriculture committees in Congress and the U.S. Department of Agriculture.

In legislative politics, higher levels of legislatures ordinarily follow the policy preference of lesser levels. Should a legislative subcommittee adopt a particular position, it is usually supported by its parent committee and by the full legislature. It is for this reason that subcommittee and committee chairpersons are especially powerful. They are ordinarily chosen on the basis of seniority and by the party in power. There is great jockeying on the part of particular legislators to find committee assignments suitable to their particular regions of the country.

Because legislators are chosen by state or by counties within a state, not only are there regional preoccupations and tensions, there is the tendency to distribute governmental services or programs on a regional basis. The most notable example, of course, is the annual funding of river and harbor "pork barrel" projects to be carried out by the U.S. Army Corps of Engineers. The Department of Defense and the Corps of Engineers participate directly in the development of these projects, testify favorably before legislative committees in the budgeting process, and support the politics of regional distribution. It is, of course, through the provision of local projects that incumbent legislators can indicate to the people who elect them that they have caused the government to effectively serve their interests.

It was once the case that the national and state legislatures were not well staffed, either in numbers or in expertise. Now, however, virtually all national legislative committees and subcommittees, as well as most state and major city legislatures, have relatively large and often expert staffs. Legislators no longer must rely entirely on public administration professionals or specialists for expertise.

One of the most common patterns in legislative politics is case work. In case work, a legislator will take up "cases" of constituents who have problems with agencies of the national government, especially the Social Security system, the Veterans Administration, and the Department of Agriculture. The same pattern can be seen at the state and local level. Ordinarily, public administrators in agencies such as the Veterans Administration find it to their benefit to work with legislators in resolving the problems of local constituents. Most of the staff in legislative offices these days are engaged in case work, and much of the time of legislators is so dedicated. Critics, of course, contend

that this emphasis on case work detracts significantly from the
ability of legislators to work on significant issues of public policy
(Fiorina, 1977). It is, however, empirically true that the number
of incumbents defeated in primary and general elections has
decreased sharply, and legislators believe that the main reason
is effective case work (Newland, 1987).

Finally, one of the most significant factors affecting legislative politics and public administration is the iron triangle. An
example of an iron triangle on highways: the legislative committees on highways work with the administrative bureau of highways, and both are supported by the highway interest groups
or lobbyists representing road construction companies, truck-
ing companies, the Teamsters Union, and sand, gravel, and
asphalt concerns. Such triangles can be found in most major
areas of American public policy.

The iron triangle metaphor as a way to describe legislative–executive–interest group politics may be changing. In many
highly technical policy fields, such as monetary policy and arms
control, the triangle has given way to "issue networks in which
highly sophisticated knowledge and expertise becomes more important than the distribution of economic benefits" (Heclo, 1978,
p. 21). In certain social service areas in which the courts have
been particularly active, such as entitlements of rights to governmental assistance for the elderly or physically handicapped, the
triangle is being replaced by a quadrilateral, with the courts constituting the fourth leg (Shapiro, 1981).

Executive Politics. Elected executives—presidents, governors,
mayors—have, in the past twenty years, reacted sharply to the
growth in government spending. Presidents Nixon, Carter, and
Reagan and many state governors and large-city mayors have
campaigned on platforms of reducing the size of government,
cutting out waste and fraud, and trimming the budget. This
political style has been highly successful, most notably in the
case of President Reagan.

Once executives are elected, they discover that they have
little command authority over public administration. They soon
learn that most agencies are not beholden to the chief executive

for their political survival and that executive leadership is a product more of political persuasion than of authority (Neustadt, 1960). As Harry S Truman was leaving office, he said that his successor, Dwight D. Eisenhower, would "say, Do this! Do that! *And nothing will happen.* Poor Ike—it won't be a bit like the Army. He'll find it very frustrating" (Neustadt, 1960, p. 9).

A chief executive usually has the high ground with respect to initiatives in the formulation of public policy. Executives can often effectively set the agenda for discussion of new policy directives. Individual administrative agencies, though, are usually specialized and are staffed with persons who have narrow sets of interests and are often resistant to change. Agency or departmental interests are usually buttressed by legislative and interest group support and are, therefore, sometimes not responsive to executive directives.

Chief excutives also quickly learn that budgets ordinarily have little flexibility. Increasing percentages of both national and state budgets are made up of entitlements such as social security, veterans' benefits, aid to farmers, welfare, and the like, which are not easily reduced. Newly elected chief executives, feeling that they have a mandate for the policies they espoused in the election campaign, are often frustrated in attempting to bring about those policies.

The political problem for elected executives is *not* primarily the bureaucracy. One problem is the separation of powers; another is the long chain of legislative policy commitments backed by significant political support—which is exceedingly difficult to change. Still, it is more convenient for elected executives to "see" the bureaucracy as the source of resistance to their policies rather than to directly face the political resistance.

In recent years there have been marked and significant changes in the world of executive politics. Because of the rapid growth of the administrative parts of government beginning in the 1930s and stretching into the 1960s, elected executives have not only campaigned against "bureaucracy," they have developed their own administrative capabilities. At one time all but the top-level positions in government administrative agencies were held by persons in the merit-appointed civil service. At the national level, cabinet members and immediate subcabinet members were appointed by the president, as were a few persons such as confidential secretaries and drivers. Each cabinet member had a few appointments. This is no longer the case. There are now thousands of political appointments throughout the administrative apparatus of the national government, and the same is increasingly the case in state and local government. As Laurence E. Lynn, Jr. (1984) indicates: "The Reagan administration appeared from the outset to embrace the notion that faithful supporters in key executive positions could be a potent tool for administrative leadership. The primary qualification for appointment—overshadowing managerial competence and experience or familiarity with issues—appeared to be the extent to which an appointee shared the president's values" (p. 340).

It was once the case that presidents, governors, and mayors were plagued by office seekers (usually for lower-level jobs) and were politically successful on the basis of their effectiveness in using the spoils system. The massive political reforms between 1880 and 1940 largely eliminated the spoils system and implemented merit-appointed civil service in most governments. But now we see a return to the politicizing of the administrative apparatus of government. Indeed, the eminent public administration scholar Chester A. Newland (1987) refers to the modern era as one of "high-level spoils." He argues:

> Experience since the late 1960s suggests that those concerns for governmental excellence are a lower priority of the contemporary presidency than are the prizes of high-level spoils. In contrast with spoils practices of the earlier era, today's appointees generally lack long-standing ties to Congress (which formerly enhanced shared powers); they owe their loyalties and access to the special interests which comprise the president's coalition and which fund elections. Playing this new form of spoils may be required of a president to sustain support in this era of weak political parties, powerful but fluid interest groups, and image projection through mass media [p. 50].

In a recent analysis titled *The Administrative Presidency,* Richard P. Nathan (1983) indicates that all of the thousands of appointees of the Reagan administration had to be approved by the White House primarily for their loyalty to the president's perspective. Indeed, Nathan quotes President Reagan as having said, "Crucial to my strategy for spending control will be the appointment to top government positions of men and women who share my economic philosophy. We will have an administration in which the word from the top isn't lost or hidden in the bureaucracy. . . . [We will bring about] a new structuring of the presidential cabinet that will make cabinet officers the managers of the national administration—not captives of the bureaucracy or special interests they are supposed to direct" (p. 72).

In addition to much stronger political control of administrative agencies, most chief executives have considerably increased their immediate staff. While they give lip service to "cabinet government," many elected executives rely less and less on their cabinet secretaries and the secretaries' staffs and more and more on their immediate staffs. The classic examples, of course, are Haldeman and Erlichman and their staffs in the Nixon administration and Meese, Baker, Deaver, and others in the Reagan administration. The result has been a marked decline in the administrative effectiveness of the agencies and governments where the chief executives have used the same strategies. On the other hand, it is likely that the ideological preferences of the chief executive have been somewhat furthered by these increased levels of political involvement in administrative matters.

But there has been a much more significant price to pay. In the Nixon administration the price was Watergate; he lost his presidency as a result of activities associated with the White House staff. In the Reagan administration, White House involvement in the Iran-Contra arms sale affair crippled the president's effectiveness. And, of course, there has been a sharp increase in instances of incompetence, graft, economic advantage taking, and lawlessness throughout the politically appointed levels of the national government. The paradox is this: Many recently elected executives have campaigned against waste, fraud, and corruption yet a marked increase in waste, fraud, and corruption has occurred in government ("Ethics," 1987).

This waste, fraud, and corruption is not primarily connected with the civil service, but it is directly connected to the political appointments by elected executives.

Interest Group Politics. Earlier, in discussion of the iron triangle metaphor, interest groups were described as being associated with particular committees or subcommittees of legislatures and their counterpart agencies in the executive branch. Interest groups are probably as old as government, and they certainly have played a significant part in the practices of American government from its beginning. In our time, the strongest warning against iron triangles was Dwight Eisenhower's speech about the military-industrial complex. If anything, the military-industrial complex is more powerful today than it was in Eisenhower's time. At one time, the two senators from the State of Washington, Henry Jackson and Warren Magnuson, were referred to as the senators from Boeing. Similar "complexes" are associated with highways, tobacco, liquor, farms, and health care, to name a few, and all exercise significant influence in federal and state politics.

At the beginning of this essay there was a brief description of the inability of the U.S. Food and Drug Administration to put into effect a ban on saccharin, although the FDA's expert researchers have determined that the sweetener has cancer-causing properties. The food-production interest groups that use sugar substitutes in low-calorie products such as diet soft drinks have worked through the legislative process to "delay" the saccharin ban for more than ten years.

An administrative agency is significantly aided in the political process if it has an interest group or two as strong allies. The prison warden described at the beginning of this essay lacked an interest group supportive of prison employees or prisoners. In fact, the primary political support for prisons in recent years has come from the courts and their enforcement of the constitutional prohibitions against cruel and unusual punishment. Without a natural clientele or an interest group for support, it takes a crisis such as a riot, a scandal, or outside intervention from the courts for an agency to improve its effectiveness.

In recent years new and significant development has occurred in the field of interest group politics. While interest groups have always provided some financial support for political candidates, we now see the development of powerful and well-financed political action committees (PACs). The number of PACs grew from 608 in 1974 to over 4,000 in 1985. In the 1984 national elections, some 3,000 PACs spent over $105 million in house and senate races. Approximately 75 percent of all PAC contributions go to incumbents, and it is now clearly the case that incumbents, more than ever before, are likely to be reelected. PAC officials, primarily fund-raising specialists working with interest groups, often receive political appointments in the administration of the new president or governor. Indeed, this is a new kind of spoils that both provides big funding to assist in the election or reelection of executives (and legislators) and secures jobs in the administration in the bargain (Newland, 1987).

Media Politics. There has always been a special politics of the media in American government. Indeed, the adoption of the Constitution depended in part on the effective pamphleteering of the Federalists. Some early politicians, most notably Benjamin Franklin, came from the media, which at the time were primarily newspapers, magazines, pamphlets, and books. The media are probably more influential in politics now than they have ever been. Many television newscasters and anchorpersons now hold or have recently held public office, including Mayor Charles Royer of Seattle and Senator Jesse Helms of North Carolina.

In the modern politics of the media, a major issue is the power of television and the relative ineffectiveness of that medium when it deals in depth with the complexity of public issues. This problem is compounded by television's remarkable effectiveness in portraying personalities. As a consequence, we are in an era of high-level personality politics, accompanied by the waning of the political parties and the lessening of our capacity to "process" the complexity of public problems and to develop policies to deal with these problems. Media politics is a double-

24 Managing Public Programs

edged sword that exaggerates the importance of the personalities and private lives of politicians, corporate executives, athletes, film and television stars, and others and punishes them for personal indiscretions or failings.

The new era of media politics requires a great deal of money, particularly money to pay for television spots. It should not be surprising that there is a close connection between the high costs of media politics and the emergence of PACs. High-profile media personalities who can command significant PAC resources are able to dominate television coverage. For example, in 1984 PACs invested just over half a million dollars on behalf of the presidential candidacy of Walter Mondale, whereas over $15 million supported Ronald Reagan's reelection (Witt and Gaunt, 1985).

The effective use of the media has long been a hallmark of good politics. In the administrative arena, J. Edgar Hoover's use of films, magazines, and early television to promote the interests of the FBI is legendary. John F. Kennedy's personal skills with reporters while he was in the Senate sharply increased his effectiveness as a presidential candidate. Ronald Reagan's live, on-camera skills are exceptional. Conversely, Lyndon Johnson's prodigious political skills were not captured effectively by television.

Washington, D.C., virtually every state capital, and most larger American cities serve as centers of governmental public relations. Public relations firms advise candidates on how to improve the effectiveness of their presentations, and they conduct political polls to determine the interests of the public and to determine how to "package" their clients. Public relations firms also work closely with administrative agencies to help them improve their public image, and, of course, interest groups make effective use of public relations firms. Business corporations not only use public relations firms to advertise their products but increasingly hire these firms to make effective public presentations so as to enhance their potential for government grants and contracts or to exercise influence on particular policy issues.

In contemporary American politics, there is a three-way intersection involving (1) the politics of the media and the expenses associated herewith, (2) interest group politics and the ability of PACs to raise large sums of money, and (3) electoral politics of both legislators and executives. It is Chester Newland's (1987) contention that these three forces have left "American national government—both the presidency and Congress generally—largely mechanisms through which special interests operate in a process of exchange. By contrast, the historical leaders termed great by James MacGregor Burns engaged in transformational leadership for 'the achievement of real change in the direction of higher values'" (p. 49). And in all of this, according to Newland, we see a significant diminution in the administrative effectiveness of government, particularly at the national and state levels.

The Politics of Government by Proxy. In the past twenty-five years a new and powerful form of politics has emerged. It is generally understood that government has grown dramatically. During this twenty-five year period there has been a sevenfold increase in the size of the federal budget and an equally dramatic growth in state and local spending. In addition, the extension of governmental regulation into such fields as environmental protection, equal employment, energy, health care, education, product safety, and economic development has been described and understood. What has received far less attention, however, has been an equally fundamental change. This change does not involve the *scope* of government action but the *form* of that action (Salamon, 1986). This new form of politics is known variously as "government by proxy," "third-party government," or "privatization" (see Chapter Nine). Government by proxy takes a variety of forms. The primary categories are (Kettl, 1988):

1. Governments (federal, state, and local) contract with the private sector (profit-making corporations and businesses such as Boeing Aircraft, nonprofit organizations such as mental health clinics, and not-for-profit organizations such as the Rand Corporation) for goods and services. In the national government the Defense Department is the largest contractor. In 1985, contracts amounted to 21 percent of all federal spending. Contracting out by government has grown significantly in recent years.

2. Grants and contracts to state and local governments now amount to approximately 11 percent of federal spending. The national government provides grants for such projects as interstate highways, management of welfare, and construction of sewage treatment facilities. States contract out road construction, counties contract out mental health services, and so on.

3. The federal tax code (as well as state tax codes) has an elaborate system of preferences, breaks, loopholes, and the like. This taxing system, in effect, enables each individual to adjust his economic behavior so as to work out favorable tax circumstances. Even with the Tax Reform Act of 1986, tax expenditures are still a significant form of privatization. For example, would the housing industry continue to flourish if deductions for interest on both primary and vacation home mortgages were not allowed? By allowing tax deductions for interest on home mortgages *and* providing low-cost home ownership loans, the federal government underwrites the housing industry.

4. The national government makes loans for everything from houses to education. More than $1 trillion in loans are now outstanding to the national government. Through these programs the government makes credit available to the individual at a lower interest rate than the private sector can offer.

5. All levels of government engage in the regulation of both business and personal activity. The costs of regulating private sector goods and services—such as insuring the safety of drugs and food or licensing businesses—constitute a significant expense to both government and business. The costs of regulation both to government and to businesses and citizens who are regulated is unknown and probably unmeasurable, but it is no doubt very large.

During the Reagan administration, the growth of government by proxy was significant. In 1982, Reagan appointed what came to be known as the Grace Commission, headed by the industrialist J. Peter Grace. The commission claimed to find billions of dollars of "savings" that would occur if the national government would do such things as sell the Tennessee Valley Authority, the Bonneville Power Administration, and even the National Parks System.

It should not be surprising that this particular perspective on public affairs would tend to be favored by interest groups and particularly by big business. As a consequence, significant political support has been generated for all the various forms of proxy and privatization. In the prison riot example used at the opening of this essay, contracting out prison services to a profit-making "prison" company would be considered a serious alternative.

An additional reason that the government by proxy perspective has been influential is the closely associated view that government employees are inefficient—that they tend to be primarily concerned with enhancing their own job security and with increasing their agency's budget and scope of authority (Tullock, 1965; Downs, 1967). Although this is a widely held view among business leaders, the evidence indicates that government employees are more often motivated by civic duty and the desire to serve others than are persons employed by businesses (Goodsell, 1985). One important reason for the growth of government by proxy is the influence of the so-called public choice economists on both the theory and the practice of public administration. The public choice theorists follow the simple assumption that human beings are rational and will maximize or favor things that are important to them. Self-interest and individual rationality are seen as desirable, and the public choice theorists would hold that:

> The desirable mode of carrying out economic and social activities is through a network of private and voluntary arrangements—called, for short, "the private market." The theory of social intervention is thus concerned with defining the conditions under which that presumption is indeed rebuttable. We think of the public sector as intervening in the private sector and not vice versa [Schultze, 1976, p. 13].

In this concept of public affairs, privatization is paramount and the government is to serve as the arena for the exchange of private interests or preferences. The government becomes a market. James M. Buchanan, one of the principal proponents of public choice theory, won the 1986 Nobel Prize in economics for his initial descriptions of the theory. The primary governmental manifestation of this theory is for the public sector to provide fewer services directly and to rely more on the private sector for achieving government's goals. Put another way, the idea is to *provide services* without *producing services*. Following this theory, privatization would transfer the actual provision of services to the private sector, where economic theorists believe the pressures of competition would improve efficiency.

In a recent analysis, Donald F. Kettl (1988) reviewed several federal forms of government by proxy. His analysis included defense department contracts for building the Sergeant York tank, the growth of federal grants to state and local government, the 1986 tax reform, the federal student aid program, the present farm loan crisis, and the deregulation of airlines with particular attention to the Newfoundland air crash in which 248 American soldiers were killed. He concluded that the values of government on the one hand and proxies on the other are usually different. As a result, more graft and corruption probably occurs under government by proxy than in more traditional forms of public administration, and deeply serious problems of accountability arise when things go wrong.

Managing Public Programs in a Political Context

Career professional public administrators understand that they must function in a political context. Ordinarily, however, they come to this understanding with some conception of the politics-administration dichotomy. In the dichotomy it is assumed that politics and administration are distinct and should be distinct. While it is understood that the dichotomy is an "ideal type" or a conceptional model and that much that goes on in government practice is neither clearly administration nor clearly politics, the dichotomy still best expresses the administrative conception of public work.

However, administrative values are not the same as political values. As set out by Woodrow Wilson (1887) a century ago, our government should be professionally managed by experts who are neutral in partisan terms. It was Wilson's contention that public executives should follow the intent of the legislature and be subject to the direction of elected executives but that politics should not meddle in the processes of administration. Administrative values include partisan neutrality; selection and promotion on the basis of merit, specialization, and expertise; the use of information and data for analysis of public policy issues; record keeping for purposes of continuity; the application of the work ethic; and justification of decisions on the basis of efficiency (achieving the most productivity for the money available) or economy (achieving a given level of productivity for as little money as possible). To put these values into effect, administrators think in terms of principles and practices such as strategic planning (see Chapter Eight), matching responsibility with authority, using hierarchy and its companions, span of control and chain of command, and requiring specialization and expertise (see Chapter Five).

Following these principles and practices, administrators assume rationality in decision making. Rationality through the use of cost-benefit analysis determines the most efficient and effective policies possible, and the administrator then proceeds to implement those policies.

Political values differ from these administrative values. In American politics, power tends to be dispersed, divided, and decentralized, whereas effective administration finds the concentration of power useful. In the political world power belongs to politicians, interest groups, and the citizenry, whereas administrative efficiency requires that power be given to experts and professionals. In the political world bargaining and accommodation are part of the democratic process, while in administrative efficiency there is a desire to keep politics out of administrative processes. In the political world, the preferences or interests of individuals and politicians are paramount, while in administrative practice the means used to decide interests is efficiency—technical or scientific rationality determined on the basis of detached analysis (Yates, 1982).

Given these contrasting values, it should not be surprising that a fragmented government operating on broadly democratic principles is often inefficient and uneconomical. Douglas

Yates (1982) suggests that these values can be reconciled by a "combination of centralized planning and goal setting and decentralized implementation and service delivery . . . " (p. 200).

While the values of administration have been stereotyped here for purposes of description, there is clearly a pattern of administrative politics and power that is fundamental to the operations of government. Indeed, Harold Seidman and Robert Gilmour (1986) suggest that "economy and efficiency are demonstratively *not* the prime purpose of public administration. . . . The basic issue of . . . organization and administration relates to power: who shall control it and to what ends?" (p. 28). And there is little doubt that an adequate theory of public administration must also be a theory of politics.

A theory of public administration that is also a theory of politics might have the following seven features.

First, most legislatures lack cohesive and continuing policy majorities able to form clear-cut mandates for administrators to follow. Administrators must, therefore, take responsibility for bringing some definition to the fuzziness and ambiguity of the programmatic intent of statutes. The wise program administrator will attempt to fashion a program mandate by carefully seeking support and understanding from critical elements in the legislature and on the staff of the elected executive; he or she will also try to find as much support as possible within interest groups and among the public. There is little doubt that effective administration requires the administrator to practice this kind of politics.

Second, legislation often calls for sweeping mandates. As Lerner and Wanat (1983) point out, "Legislators, not being technical experts, frequently write laws embodying goals that are exemplary but which lack details. Skeletal legislation, as it is frequently called, is phrased in occasionally grand and, therefore, fuzzy terms. The implementing agency is told by the legislature [in national, state, or local government] to provide a *safe* environment for workers, to see that schoolchildren are served meals with *adequate* nutritional content . . . to *assist* the *visually impaired,* to maintain *adequate* income levels, and so on" (p. 500).

Not only is enabling legislation often fuzzy, but the steps to be taken to implement that legislation are rarely clear-cut.

It is, therefore, the effective administrator's responsibility to design those steps and to make them as practical and politically feasible as possible. The administrator must then "clear them" with key elements in the legislature, with the chief executive, and with relevant interest groups.

Third, expertise and specialization are fundamental to effective administrative politics. The basis of bureaucratic power is (1) full-time attention by experts to a problem or subject matter area, giving rise to both demand and opportunity for professionalism in public service; (2) specialization in the subject matter; (3) a monopoly on information in the subject area, which if successfully maintained by only one's own staff experts makes them indispensable in any decision making involving the subject; (4) a pattern of increasing reliance on bureaucratic experts for technical advice; and (5) experts' increasing control of bureaucratic discretion (Rourke, 1984). Public administration no longer has the level of domination of expertise that it once had. Expertise is now shared with the staffs of legislative committees as well as with experts on the immediate staff of the chief executive. The effective program manager will, therefore, serve a bridging or transactional role attempting to keep all of the experts informed and working in the same policy direction.

Fourth, in the politics of government by proxy, Kettl (1988) suggests that much greater attention be given, by both elected officials and public administrators, to the "co-alignment" of goals. Because the values of government agencies and proxies differ, he suggests a mechanism for reviewing goals and for using a system of feedback to co-align goals so that government and the proxies doing government business are more closely synchronized. He further suggests a new role of leadership for program administrators. Their job is to serve a diagnostic function, to provide feedback, and to "define the situation authoritatively for the group" (Tucker, 1983, pp. 19-20).

Both elected and appointed government officials should give much greater concern to the questions of accountability and performance in the tangled web of proxy government. Government officials now have responsibility for programs that they do not really control. It is Kettl's view that

As government by proxy has grown, the success of
government programs has come to depend more
on all Americans and their sense of citizenship. All
of those responsible for the performance of government—whether part of government or not—must
recognize their broader responsibility to the public
for their behavior. Accountability thus has to extend beyond creating government mechanisms to
detect and cure problems. Whether filling out an
income tax form, taking out a government loan,
following a federal regulation or working for a
government contractor, each citizen plays an important role in making programs work [1988, p.
161].

Modern government by proxy presents a significant new
challenge to public administration theory and to program and
project administration. Our classical theory is generally hostile
to the phenomenon of third-party government because it poses
a threat to accountability. In the classical theory, political power
is to be centralized in the hands of elected officials, who exercise control over professional public administrators, who are held
accountable for what their agencies do. Third-party government
violates these principles because (1) it fragments power, (2) it
obscures who is doing what, and (3) it severs lines of control
(Salamon, 1986).

Effective program management, then, cannot rely on control through the hierarchy, the use of budgeting and personnel
techniques, or the other management approaches that emphasize
internal bureaucratic controls. Program management has spilled
beyond the borders of the public agency. The effective program
manager will understand the manipulation of "a complex network of players and institutions over which the public manager
has only imperfect control, yet on which he or she must depend
to operate an agency's programs" (Salamon, 1986, p. 20).

Fifth, although partisan neutrality is part of the professional public administrator's conception of government work,
the effective program administrator will not be expected to re-

main neutral regarding the mission of the agency with which he or she is associated. Governmental agencies, like all organizations, expect employees to be both professionally qualified *and* dedicated to their responsibilities. And the citizens who pay the bills deserve dedicated professionals.

One of the characteristics of qualified, dedicated professionals is the tendency to advocate their area of specialization (see Chapter Three). The best social workers, schoolteachers, FBI agents, and soldiers all believe in their work and expect to have sufficient resources and support to do their jobs properly. One of the biggest challenges to public servants is doing the best they can with the resources available, especially when they know that additional funding could make them more effective.

In the competition for public funding, it is unreasonable to expect the Department of Agriculture, for example, to be neutral. The department's leadership will actively seek the funding they feel is necessary to fulfill their responsibilities. So will the leadership of the other departments. Thus one should not mistake the commitment to partisan neutrality to mean that public administrators will be neutral in the competition for funding. In fact, the effective administrator will make the best possible case for his or her agency, will seek support, but will recognize when advocacy oversteps partisan neutrality and becomes the politics that can affect elections. This can require a careful balancing of advocacy and neutrality. And once the budget is passed, the effective administrator will provide the best or most services possible for the dollars available.

Sixth, public administrators are often at the point in the governmental system where the public may need constitutional guarantees. Effective public administration requires a solid grounding in the Constitution and in court interpretations of the Constitution. In fact, administrators, and especially attorneys in the administrative branch, often find it necessary to advise (warn) elected executives and legislators of the limits of majority rule in light of the rights of the individual.

Seventh, public administrators are the lubrication that makes the federal system work. Most governmental functions now involve all three levels of government. The public administrator must, therefore, understand the role each level of government plays in his or her particular function. Effective administrators know that "bargaining and negotiation, not command and obedience, appear to characterize the practice of intergovernmental programs now, as in the past" (Derthick, 1987, p. 69).

In summary, technical expertise is expected in public administration. Public servants understand that they must perform their tasks efficiently, economically, and honestly. But that is not enough, because effective political skills are necessary to make good public administration possible. While it was once popular to argue that public administration should be separate from politics, we all know that is impossible. This is especially the case in the upper levels or leadership positions in public agencies.

What politics must guide public servants? It must be a politics grounded in the constitutional order of checks and balances, federalism, and the protections of the Bill of Rights. It must be a politics in which elected officials are the primary makers of policy and where administrators carry out that policy, acknowledging that the line between making and carrying out policy is fuzzy. Therefore, both elected and appointed public officials have power in the fuzzy world of public affairs. The politics of public servants should always exercise the discretion of power prudently, with a concern for both the general good and the needs and dignity of the individual citizen. "A government ill executed," Alexander Hamilton wrote in *Federalist* No. 70, "whatever it might be in theory, must be in practice a poor government." If government is to be well executed, public servants must be both technically expert and politically wise. When this is the case, the politics of public administration becomes a noble calling and an expression of the human capacity to govern for the general good.

References

Derthick, M. "American Federalism: Madison's Middle Ground in the 1980s." *Public Administration Review,* 1987, *47,* 66–74.
Downs, A. *Inside Bureaucracy.* Boston: Little, Brown, 1967.

"Ethics: Cover Story." *Time,* May 25, 1987, pp. 14–29.

Fiorina, M. P. *Congress: Keystone of the Washington Establishment.* New Haven, Conn.: Yale University Press, 1977.

Goodsell, C. T. *The Case for Bureaucracy: A Public Administration Polemic.* (2nd ed.) Chatham, N.J.: Chatham House, 1985.

Heclo, H. "Issue Networks and the Executive Establishment." In A. King (ed.), *The New American Political System.* Washington, D.C.: American Enterprise Institute, 1978.

Kettl, D. F. *Government by Proxy: Managing Federal Programs.* Washington, D.C.: CQ Press, 1988.

Lerner, N. W., and Wanat, J. "Fuzziness and Bureaucracy." *Public Administration Review,* 1983, *47,* 500–509.

Lynn, L. E., Jr. "The Reagan Administration and the Penitent Bureaucracy." In L. M. Salamon and M. S. First (eds.), *The Reagan Presidency and the Governing of America.* Washington, D.C.: The Urban Institute, 1984.

Nathan, R. P. *The Administrative Presidency.* New York: Wiley, 1983.

Neiman, M. "The Virtues of Heavy-Handedness in Government." *Law and Politics Quarterly,* 1980, *2,* 11–34.

Neustadt, R. E. *Presidential Power.* New York: Wiley, 1960.

Newland, C. A. "Public Executives: Imperium, Sacerdotium, Colloquium? Bicentennial Leadership Challenges." *Public Administration Review,* 1987, *47,* 45–56.

Rohr, J. *To Run a Constitution: The Legitimacy of the Administrative State.* Lawrence: University Press of Kansas, 1986.

Rourke, F. E. *Bureaucracy, Politics and Public Policy.* Boston: Little, Brown, 1984.

Rourke, F. E. "Bureaucracy in the American Constitutional Order." *Political Science Quarterly,* 1987, *102,* 217–232.

Salamon, L. "The Rise of Third Party Government: Implication for Public Management." Proceedings of the National Academy of Public Administration, Spring 1986.

Schultze, C. *The Public Use of Private Interest.* Washington, D.C.: Brookings Institution, 1976.

Seidman, H., and Gilmour, R. *Politics, Position and Power: From the Positive to the Regulatory State.* (4th ed.) New York: Oxford University Press, 1986.

Shapiro, M. A. "The Presidency and the Federal Courts." In

A. J. Meltsner (ed.), *Politics and the Oval Office*. San Francisco: Institute for Contemporary Studies, 1981.

Tucker, R. C. *Politics Is Leadership*. Columbia: University of Missouri Press, 1983.

Tullock, G. *The Politics of Bureaucracy*. Washington, D.C.: Public Affairs Press, 1965.

Wilson, W. "The Study of Administration." *Political Science Quarterly*, 1887, *2*, 197–222.

Witt, E., and Gaunt, J. "Court Strikes Down Limits in Independent PAC Outlays." *Congressional Quarterly*, Mar. 23, 1985, *43*, 532.

Yates, D. *Bureaucratic Democracy: The Search for Democracy and Efficiency in American Government*. Cambridge, Mass.: Harvard University Press, 1982.

2

𝄃𝄃𝄃𝄃𝄃𝄃𝄃𝄃𝄃𝄃𝄃𝄃𝄃𝄃𝄃𝄃𝄃𝄃𝄃𝄃𝄃𝄃𝄃𝄃

The Evolving Federal Role in Program Administration

David B. Walker

A prime determinant of the roles, responsibilities, relationships, and even reputation of federal administrators, especially top managers, is the nature, scope, dynamics, and implementary approaches of the national policy process. The key challenges confronting today's top- and middle-level federal administrators are in large part the fallout from sixteen years (1964–1980) of the most exuberant expansion of federal domestic programs that the nation has ever experienced. They also stem from the subsequent eight-year period (1981–1988) of continued overall expansion, but with a curbing of the growth rate for domestic programs, notably grants-in-aid.

This national activism has been evidenced in the policy, political, representational, fiscal, and administrative areas. It has resulted in a much more heavily nation-centered system in terms of policy development than was the case a quarter of a century ago, but with a much heavier reliance on nonfederal administrators to actually implement most of the national government's lengthy program agenda.

While federal career administrators were a vital force in helping to launch this expansionist era in the sixties, the subsequent dynamics of growth and subsequent reactions to it began to erode the very foundations of their heretofore powerful place within the system. Administrators' political support in many instances dwindled, and their expertise and professionalism were

questioned. Moreover, their earlier authoritative roles in the
numerous "iron triangles" and in later "issue networks" politics
were reduced even as their tenure and political neutrality were
increasingly more threatened. In short, the transformation of
the national government's role in the overall system and the
dynamics behind it created a complex system of domestic administration and governance that challenged political and administrative leaders alike. They also generated a series of
developments that singled out the federal administrators for especially harsh treatment. These developments, this treatment, and
efforts to change it are the basic concerns of this chapter.

  To gain a better appreciation of the magnitude of systematic change, we must briefly probe the contours of what might
be called the "old system" that was ushered in with the in-
auguration of Franklin D. Roosevelt in 1933 and lasted through
the era of Dwight Eisenhower if not John Kennedy. The New
Deal, of course, achieved some striking breakthroughs in expanding the federal role as regulator and subsidizer of key elements
in the private sector and as a provider of financial assistance
to state and local governments. These actions also produced a
doubling of the size of the federal civilian bureaucracy between
1929 and 1939. They prompted the new metaphor of "cooperative" or "marble cake" federalism (McLean, 1952) in that they
constituted a body blow to "dual federalism"—the traditional,
operational approach with its almost total separation and division by governmental levels of the funding, functions, administration, personnel, and policymaking associated with domestic
governance. Yet they did not obliterate this earlier "layer cake"
model of intergovernmental relations (Walker, 1981).

  The postwar years, stretching from Truman through 1960
and even to 1963, witnessed significant additions to the federal
government's direct involvement with the private sector (especially in the promotional and, to a lesser degree, the regulatory
fields) but only incremental increases in outlays for intergovernmental grants-in-aid (Walker, 1981) and in federal bureaucratic
growth. In numerical terms, the 15 permanent grants that
emerged from the New Deal years, along with the 15 pre-1933
categorical programs and the 102 enacted between 1946 and

1960, brought the total to 132 in the latter year, compared to 140 subsidy programs for the private sector. Only a small number of categorical grants and $3 billion in outlays were added during the Kennedy period.

Fiscally, this new pattern of federal-state-local interpenetration and program implementation raised the federal aid share of state-local expenditures to a modest 14.5 percent by 1960, up to 15.4 percent by fiscal 1964 (Kennedy's last). It also increased the intergovernmental aid share of total federal domestic expenditures from 11.4 percent in 1949 to 18.1 percent by 1959, and up one more percentage point by 1964 (Advisory Commission on Intergovernmental Relations, 1983).

A basic conditioner of this newly emerging pattern of intergovernmental management was the fact that the old system was only moderately "marbleized." A full 92 percent of the aid funds in 1960 went to the states, and four programs dominated the grant picture fiscally (highways, aid to the aged, AFDC, and unemployment compensation), thus simplifying the federal grant administrators' role. Only four state agencies were heavily involved with federal grant programs. Moreover, while all the grants were categorical, their conditions by current standards were quite reasonable—again facilitating federal intergovernmental administration. Most state programs and agencies and nearly all of their local counterparts were unaffected by this expansion of the federal grant role, thus preserving a truncated form of dual federalism.

Overall, then, while federal legal authority and direct operations expanded significantly during this period, a moderate version of cooperative federalism prevailed operationally during the fifties and early sixties. This had profound implications for the federal grant managers of that era. The small proportion of the federal workforce engaged in grants administration were dealing mainly with familiar, stable, and largely distributive program assignments and mostly with only state recipients.

Conceptually, authorities such as Leonard D. White (1954) found no basic conflict between the hierarchic organizational and vertical relational principles of classical public administration and the less structured pattern of federal grants management wherein the actual implementors of the aided programs were not federal employees but members of separate (mostly state) policy, personnel, political, and governmental systems. The conditions attached to the grants and the threat of cutoffs of cash, White felt, were adequate to ensure proper direction from, accountability to, and control by the national government and its instrumentalities.

What was overlooked here was that by the fifties the broad goals of most of the grant programs had become shared ones, and a cooperative federalist approach to grants management generally prevailed at the different levels. This system concealed the headaches of an intergovernmental managerial setup involving new and controversial policy goals. Much of the interlevel cooperation of the fifties can be explained by the rise of the "vertical functional autocracies," as critics described them—groups that were and are vertically structured and share the same or similar specific program, professional, technical, and administrative goals. Some of the cooperation was a by-product of the longevity of the few larger programs, of the one-to-fifty administrative arrangements that prevailed in most grants, of the absence of cooptive conditions in nearly all of them (thanks to the strength of the state and local political forces in Washington), and of the respect accorded generally to most federal grants managers. These were the halcyon years of top federal managers, and they continued through most of the Johnson period. But all these earlier administrative traits began to be overturned by the late sixties. The authoritative role and professional reputation of federal managers were undermined as a result.

The contemporary "new system" of American governance was brought about by a series of continuing centralizing actions—statutory, fiscal, political, judicial, but not administrative—over sixteen-plus years. The volume, scope, reach, cost, and impact of these largely centralizing policy initiatives affected practically all portions of the private, quasi-public, and subnational governmental sectors—not to mention the federal bureaucracy. At the same time, the federal government relied, to a greater extent than ever before, on indirect means of implementation and on third-party providers to carry out its domestic agenda. This generated major problems of intergovernmental administration and tended ultimately to weaken the professional stature, the implementary clout, and the policy-influencing role of federal career administrators.

National Policy Development (1966–1978/1980) and the Decline of Federal Managerial Capacity

From Lyndon Johnson through early Jimmy Carter, with no letup during the Nixon-Ford years, the national government's domestic policy role expanded massively—in size, scope, depth, cost, and approaches to implementation, as Table 2.1 shows. There also was little letup in the determination of national policy-makers to avoid direct federal implementation and to hold federal administrators accountable for the actions of subnational governmental officials who were not their administrative subordinates.

Creative Federalism. While Johnson's "creative federalism" was a derivative of the earlier cooperative federalism, it, like LBJ, was quite different from and much larger than its predecessor, and one way or another it conditioned all the other federalism concepts that succeeded it.

Federal domestic policy making, intergovernmental relations, and management after LBJ would never return to the comparatively uncomplicated format and management of the Eisenhower-Kennedy years, because to a greater degree than any of his immediate predecessors or successors, Johnson got most of his creative federalism goals enacted. This, in turn, transformed the system (Walker, 1986), as the Great Society column in Table 2.1 highlights.

These historic developments under LBJ established the national government as the more senior programmatically (as earlier court decisions had done judicially) in the federal system, but they also rendered this role bigger, broader, and deeper than ever before. This latter development greatly enhanced the power, strategic position, and policy development role of top federal administrators, since these officials had become the indispensible agents for helping implement the Great Society. Moreover, the basically servicing thrust of many of the LBJ programs further strengthened the pivotal role of these federal career officials.

Table 2.1. Intergovernmental Trends, 1960-1980.

	1960 Total (FY1960)	Great Society: 1966-1968 (FY 1964-1969)	New Federalism: 1969-1976 (FY 1970-1977)	New Partnership Federalism: 1977-1980 (FY 1978-1981)	1980 Total (FY 1981)
Number of grant programs	132	379 (FY 1967)	442 (FY 1975)	492 (FY 1978)	539
Grant outlays in current dollars (billions)	7.0	10.1-20.3	24.0-68.4	77.9-94.8	94.8
Grant outlays in constant dollars (billions)	10.8	14.7-24.2	27.0-46.7	49.4-46.1	46.1
Federal aid as a percentage of state-local receipts	16.8	17.9-21.6	22.9-31.0	31.7-30.1	30.1
Federal aid (current dollars) as a percentage of total federal outlays	7.6%	8.6-11.0	12.3-16.7	17.8-14.0	14.0
Grants for payments to individuals as a percentage of total federal aid	35.7				
Form(s) of grants	100% categorical	2 block grants, 3 target grants, the rest categoricals	5 block grants, general revenue sharing, 2 target grants, the rest categorical	all previous eras plus more categoricals	all previous eras plus more categoricals
Percentage of aid bypassing the states	8%	12%	24%	29%	23%
Major IGR regulations	2	8	22	5	37

Source: Adapted from Advisory Commission on Intergovernmental Relations, 1984, 1985; Walker, 1981, pp. 100-131.

Extraordinary implementary difficulties arose, however, especially for top federal and state managers. Many resulted from the trends depicted in Table 2.1 and their side effects: the huge number of new programs, their novelty in many cases, their ambitious and sometimes unrealistic goals, their frequent statutory ambiguities, the absence of reliable information and clear regulations, their reliance on a multiplicity of subnational governments, their frequently reformist thrusts whose goals many state and local officials rejected or viewed with skepticism, the quasi- or outright regulatory nature of their conditions in some instances, and the necessity for horizontal and vertical administrative cooperation in some of the more controversial grants (poverty and model cities), to cite the more obvious.

The basic administrative challenge, however, was that Johnson adhered (to a far greater degree than FDR) to intergovernmental grants and other indirect approaches as the major methods of implementing his Great Society agenda. This strategy initially tended to enhance the position and power of federal grants administrators, strengthen the already existing functional iron triangles, and generate new triangles. The surging pressures of program expansion also tended to strengthen certain traditional attitudes of federal middle-management grant administrators—attitudes that, while commendable in many respects, exacerbated the managerial problems of political executives, top generalist administrators, and the Bureau of the Budget, not to mention state and local officials. In an extensive and complete mid-sixties survey of federal grant administrators conducted by the U.S. Senate Subcommittee on Intergovernmental Relations (1965), most of the 109 respondents indicated a strong involvement with the goals of their respective programs, a deep commitment to merit system principles and to the ethical and professional goals of their individual "guilds," a stand-pat defense of traditional administrative procedures, and a rather studied indifference to the broader and new intergovernmental administrative and fiscal problems that were beginning to emerge with Great Society program enactments. In most respects, then, these federal grants managers of a generation ago pretty much reflected the bold, balky, but confident behavior that Terry Sanford (1967) ascribed to them with his "picket-fence federalism" metaphor.

For political executives and top professional administrators at all levels, but especially at the national level, the drastically expanded management setting and the traditional professional but narrowly programmatic behavior of middle management caused the most immediate problems, since positive results were expected by the architects of the Great Society programs, beginning with President Johnson.

A barrage of criticisms from key Democratic governors, senators, mayors, and others regarding the administrative confusion caused by the novelty, numbers, and wide range of new recipients of the Great Society programs arose generally after the Democratic losses in the 1966 midterm elections. In response, LBJ launched a variety of intergovernmental management initiatives, many of which were rooted in classical public administration principles. Major reorganizations were instituted (Departments of Housing and Urban Development and Transportation). Governmental management circulars were issued by the Bureau of the Budget to help standardize and simplify various aspects of grants management (Circular A-87, for recipients' overhead costs; Circular A-74, to curb duplicate and diverse audit requirements; Circular A-80, to help reduce conflicting boundaries and institutional planning requirements of increasing federal regional planning programs; and Circular A-85, to afford representatives of recipient governments opportunities to react early to proposed changes in existing or new grant regulations). Some improvements in federal headquarter-field relations were also made, with pilot regional councils set up in some areas. All of these Johnson efforts were but a prelude to expanded intergovernmental managerial reforms in the seventies.

Nixon's New Federalism and Presidential Activism (1969–1974).
With the election of Richard M. Nixon in 1968, a new phase in intergovernmental relations seemed to have been ushered in. This phase, however, contained many confusing elements, since the goals and impacts of Nixon—the administrator, the program activist, the conservative decentralizer and devolutionist, as well as pragmatic politician—frequently conflicted, thus producing in their interactions with Democratic Congresses some ambiv-

alent, if not conflicting, administrative, fiscal, and programmatic results. Nixon rejected the broad centralizing thrust of creative federalism with its heavy reliance on categoricals and on a servicing strategy approach, its resulting strengthening of the central bureaucracy's powers, its constraining conditions and new regulations, and its implicit downplaying of state and general local governments' policy processes and politicians.

This reactive portion of Nixon's New Federalism prompted efforts to devolve more power and discretion in certain federally aided program areas through more block grants and in an essentially "no-strings" general revenue sharing (GRS) proposal, all of which raised the ire of most career federal grants managers.

Federal field operations were wholly restructured by executive order. Ten administrative regions with a single field headquarters in each were established, and federal regional councils composed of the heads of each federal field agency were launched and given the job of improved interdepartmental coordinative and intergovernmental liaison responsibilities. The Nixon decentralizing drive also included moves to delegate "sign off" authority in a range of grant programs from Washington to field agency heads, which disconcerted many headquarters officials and proved to be a short-run experiment in most program cases.

Nixon's New Federalism also focused heavily on new and old ways of improving intergovernmental administration by (1) attempting to further standardize and simplify the range of administrative requirements imposed then by over 380 grant programs, which led to the interagency Federal Assistance Review undertaking and the resulting far-reaching Office of Management and Budget (OMB) Circular A-102 as well as indirectly to Circular A-110 for nonprofit recipients of federal aid; (2) launching the Integrated Grant Administration initiative whereby twenty-seven experiments in jointly funded state, regional, and local multigrant applications were undertaken, which led finally to congressional passage of the Joint Funding Act of 1974; (3) mounting a campaign to get more states to take advantage of the substate regional Circular A-80 (and several responded positively); and (4) pursuant to the Intergovernmental Cooperation Act of 1968, issuing OMB Circular A-95, which built on the

implementing Circular for Section 204 of the 1966 model cities
legislation and extended the review and comment on grant applications procedure already required in metropolitan areas to
nonmetropolitan regions and to the states, thus producing an
explosion in the number of Councils of Government (COGs).

Nixon's intergovernmental reform program also included
efforts to decongest the federal aid system by a combination of
(1) categorical consolidations into discretionary super-block
grants (six were proposed and two were enacted in drastically
modified form—CETA and CDBG—while Congress developed
yet another: Title XX—Social Services); (2) general revenue
sharing; and (3) federal assumption of certain heretofore in-
tergovernmentally shared program responsibilities (for example, Nixon's unsuccessful welfare reform proposal—the Family
Assistance Plan—and the supplementary security income (SSI)
legislation that federalized the adult welfare categorical grants).

Despite the many difficulties and some outright defeats
(decentralizations of sign off authority, devolution of significant
program discretion, wide use of joint funding, and welfare reform) in implementing these old New Federalism basic goals,
many IGR management observers of the day were fairly op-
timistic about continuing the momentum generated by the Nixon
successes, especially in the grants management, decentralization, and devolution (with more block grants) areas. But this
assessment ignored a cluster of negative developments—some
reflected in the New Federalism record and others in areas outside the Nixon intergovernmental reform efforts.

As the New Federalism column in Table 2.1 shows, the
Nixon (and Ford) administration was unable to ward off congressional moves to undercut both of the two earliest block grants
(Safe Streets was significantly conditionalized and Partnership
in Health acquired several categorical sisters that could have
been absorbed by it); the number of categorical grants experienced
a significant increase despite the loss of over twenty-five (thanks
to block grant and other mergers); total grant outlays, despite
administration retrenchment concerns, more than doubled, and
major hikes occurred in social welfare, educational, and urban
programs; and the extent of "bypassing" ultimately doubled

thanks to the dramatic increase in the number of local governments participating directly in federal grant programs (for example, CETA, CDBG, GRS, and numerous federal-local categoricals). Moreover, when the national "rush to regulate" that gained rapid momentum during the Nixon period is considered, a new and even more centripetal trend is seen. Twelve major and several minor intergovernmental regulatory statutes were enacted between 1969 and 1973 in the nondiscrimination, environmental protection, and health and safety fields (Advisory Commission on Intergovernmental Relations, 1984).

The Remainder of the Decade and Overall Systemic Results. The optimism of intergovernmental reformers in the early seventies evaporated as the decade progressed. The centralizing thrusts of most of Johnson's efforts and some of Nixon's programs gained greater momentum (see the New Partnership Federalism column in Table 2.1), while the anticentripetal, pro–intergovernmental collaborative, and pro–better grants management efforts lost ground. In large measure, this was due to the elemental intergovernmental policy fact of the middle and late seventies that Congress and, to a lesser degree, the federal courts, except for *National League of Cities* v. *Usery,* 96 S. Ct. 2465 (1976), were the prime formal architects of a continually expanding federal role during these years. This meant Congress's distinctive approach to intergovernmental initiatives and to the federal domestic role generally prevailed. This approach entailed a combination of dramatic new legislative initiatives, especially in the environmental area and social regulation generally, as well as major expansions of the Great Society legacy, confrontational attitudes toward executive branch officials and increasingly toward state and local spokespersons, a continuing strong categorical orientation (for political, institutional, fiscal, and program accountability reasons), a hyperconsciousness of public opinion and of pressure-group concerns, and an unplanned centripetalism and managerial obtuseness in the cumulative impact of its proliferating policy actions.

The positive and many of the negative facets of the Nixon-Ford record helped generate more flexible and less confident

attitudes among federal grants managers. A 1975 Advisory
Commission on Intergovernmental Relations survey of these
managers (1977) found a less strident adherence to the "picket
fence" norms of program protectionism, stand-pattism, professionalism, and broader issue indifference than was the case a
decade before. Moreover, new themes were enunciated: a greater
willingness to face broad managerial and intergovernmental
issues, a certain skepticism about grant management reform efforts, and a sense of reduced influence and confused purposes.
These traits produced the "bamboo fence federalism" metaphor
as a substitute for Sanford's "picket fence" designation (Walker,
1977). But a fence that bends with any wind is a negative metaphor and a sign of slippage for career managers whose professionalism, strong position in the policy development process,
and overall strategic power in the previous decade had prompted
the tougher Sanford interpretation.

The Centripetal Dynamics of the New Activism
and Their Negative Impact on National Administrators

What explains this remarkable and prolonged transformation of the nation's policy agenda and its insidious impact
on career federal managers? This epochal expansion was caused
by the collapse of heretofore operational constraints in the political, judicial, fiscal, and administrative areas. In each, personalities, groups, events, and policy environmental conditioners
can be identified that singly, but more frequently in combination, explain the long centralizing chain of policy changes that
occurred from 1964 to 1980.

More specifically, a series of new nationalizing actors
emerged in the political field to end the formal ascendancy of
territorial forces and ultimately to undercut the bureaucratic
component of the functional iron triangles. The federal judiciary
throughout the period also was basically centralizing in all but
a handful of its decisions, and the fiscal policy of the national government's political branches was basically expansionist throughout. While federal career managers directly or indirectly were
negatively affected by most of these developments, the national

tendency to rely heavily on nonfederal implementation of nearly all federal domestic policies continued along with the concomitant habit of holding career federal officials responsible for their implementation. This nationalization of policy making and devolution of execution was yet another reason for the undercutting of these managers' heretofore authoritative role in the system. The continued multiplication of the number of domestic programs with divided responsibilities was a lethal development for top federal managers and for traditional public administration theories of control and accountability.

The New Era in American Politics and Party Changes. The country's traditional political system has changed drastically over the past two decades. The two-party component of the earlier, roughly 140-year-old system was comparatively noncentralized, nondisciplined, uncohesive, and nonideological in its national manifestations—at conventions, in Congress, and among political executives. What party cohesion, power, and discipline there was persisted within some state and local organizations and legislative bodies. Prior to 1964, with their near complete control over the nominating and electoral processes for their own as well as national elected officials and their prime function of organizing their respective electorate and financing their candidates, these subnational party instrumentalities and their leaders asserted an authoritative if not controlling role, both in national party conclaves and in national decision making.

Over the past two decades or so, the foundations of this noncentralized party system have eroded rapidly. Court decisions, state regulatory legislation, the increase in primaries, and the further spread of the merit system are some of the reasons for this. Another causal factor has been the newly strengthened national party organizations and their (especially the national Democratic Party's) ability to issue binding requirements on state/local participation in the presidential nominating process and other activities relating to the selection of national officeholders. This new relationship between the state/local and national party institutions was and is more federative, with few traces of the confederative format that dominated the previous party system. As Chapter One indicates, the emergence of a cluster of powerful political and other rivals at both national and state levels must not be ignored here (see also Advisory Commission on Intergovernmental Relations, 1986, pp. 162–233).

Totally apart from these recent interlevel developments within the parties, the parties' overall influence in politics has steadily declined over at least a quarter of a century. The broad underlying reasons are multiple: technological developments (notably in the communication and media fields), basic social and economic changes, shifting popular attitudes toward the parties, and the explosion in the number, types, and activities of pressure groups. The latter two deserve some explanation, since they are clearly in the realm of politics.

Citizen attitudes toward parties a generation ago reflected strong, continuing commitment to either one of the two parties, and this attachment was a primary factor conditioning their political behavior and their views on public issues (Advisory Commission on Intergovernmental Relations, 1986). Since the early sixties, an erosion in the proportion of partisans has set in. By 1980, independent and weak party identifiers dominated the electorate, accounting for 80 percent of the total. Paralleling this growing political fragmentation of the citizenry-at-large has been an even greater factionalization of the pressure group scene, as Chapter One clearly demonstrates.

Just as crucial as these external developments, however, was the growing, self-generating activism of the central government itself, much of it by top career administrators and their political executive chiefs in the sixties and by senators, representatives, and their staffs in the seventies. The national policy process thus became, especially from 1969 to 1980, the creator of new interest groups as well as the target of the riveted attention of existing ones. The growing hyperresponsiveness and aggressive entrepreneurialism of national legislators (thanks in part to the political party changes noted earlier and to the leveling congressional procedural reforms adopted in 1972 and 1974) and the resulting flood of enactments and disbursements served as a magnet, drawing to Washington a variegated mass of groups representing almost all single- and multi-interest elements of the country's demographic, social, economic, professional, technological, programmatic, government, and citizen components. In raw numbers, over 40 percent of the Washington-based organizations in 1980 had established their headquarters there after 1960 (Advisory Commission on Intergovernmental Relations, 1986). Moreover, a 1983 national survey found that 43 percent of the respondents preferred organized groups to best represent their political interests compared to 34 percent choosing either of the major parties (Advisory Commission on Intergovernmental Relations, 1986).

What do these political changes mean for federal career administrators? Above all, perhaps, they suggest that the centripetal forces that have given rise to a nationalization of many domestic policy decisions and a nonnational approach to their implementation are likely to be with us for some time.

From the Federal Judiciary: A Green Light. The political arena was not the only one in which earlier constraints on expanding national authority, actions, and programs collapsed. The federal judiciary was also very much caught up with some of the same proclivities.

Judicial activism characterized the Supreme Court record throughout this period and beyond (1964–1988). The trend was to aggressively expand those that began in the fifties. In the sixties, the Supreme Court not only upheld controversial congressional enactments but assumed the role of "a leader in the process of social change quite at odds with its traditional position as a defender of legalistic tradition and social continuity" (Kelly and Harbison, 1976, p. 856). Generally, its decisions enlarged federal power fundamentally by placing severe limits on the states, though in a few instances they reflected some sensitivity to the concept of state autonomy, and the Court's reapportionment and educational finance decisions actually strengthened the states.

While some expected a reversal or at least a reduction of the Warren Court's libertarian and egalitarian tendencies with the appointment of Warren E. Burger as Chief Justice and four other justices by Presidents Nixon and Ford, analysis of key cases in the civil rights and civil liberties areas during the Burger years indicates this Court had almost as much sensitivity to libertarian and racial justice values as its predecessor. Though the Burger Court engineered no judicial counterrevolution, it obviously was no carbon copy of the Warren-led body. In cases involving the rights of the accused or the imprisoned, sex discrimination, state environmental protection laws, and state legislative appropriation of federal grant funds, it exhibited some concern for state autonomy. Yet in constitutional areas of crucial significance to federalism—conditional spending power, regulation of interstate commerce, the supremacy of congressional enactments, and taxation—the Court generally played an assertive, usually nationalizing role (Walker, 1981).

Only in *National League of Cities* v. *Usery,* 96 S. Ct. 2465 (1976) did the Court enunciate a dramatic exception to this "trend." But later cases eroded *Usery*'s significance, until it finally was specifically overturned in *Garcia* v. *San Antonio Metropolitan Transit Authority,* 105 S. Ct. 1005 (1985). *National League of Cities* focused on the question of whether there are judicially enforceable constitutional constraints on Congress's power pursuant to the commerce clause to impose requirements on the states. By a 5 to 4 vote, the Court found that certain conditions must be satisfied before a state activity may be exempted from a particular federal regulation based on the commerce clause. More specifically, it held that the national Fair Labor Standards Act's minimum wage and overtime compensation provisions could not be extended to cover state and local employees performing "traditional governmental functions." This judgment was specifically overruled in *Garcia,* largely on grounds that there are procedural safeguards within the "structure of the federal government itself" that are adequate to protect the "role of the states in the federal system." Hence, the Court would not interfere with Congress's earlier decision to extend the FLSA to state and local employees and held that the states if threatened by this act could make their political voice heard in Congress.

Why this sustained judicial activism? Various factors combine to explain the Supreme Court's continuing interventionism and its predominant centripetalism since 1962 (the date of Felix Frankfurter's retirement). A passive adherence to precedents, as in the conditional spending and commerce powers areas, in effect amounted to handing over to expansionist (post-1963) political branches the authority to determine the reach and the usage of these powers, thus eliminating any judicial curb on questionable congressional intrusions into state and local affairs, which are based on these constitutional provisions.

"Responding to election returns" is also an explanation of Court behavior. The pickup in judicial centripetal assertiveness in the sixties in part mirrored the 1960 and especially the 1964 election returns. Of equal significance in the sixties were the personnel changes that came with Frankfurter's retirement and Byron White's and Thurgood Marshall's appointments. The five appointees of Presidents Nixon and Ford, however, failed to produce a predominantly conservative Court—even with the assistance of the increasingly more conservative Justice Byron White—since Justices Blackmun, Powell, and Stevens all proved capable of quite independent judgments that in various areas of constitutional law placed them alongside the two remaining liberals: Justices Brennan and Marshall.

Ostensibly conservative appointees with a predilection for narrow construction and judicial passivity confront a deep dilemma when they attempt to overturn liberal precedents. Overruling an earlier decision is, after all, a hallmark of judicial activism and can undermine the institutional integrity of the Court, usually an abiding concern of such judges. Finally, the very scope of national policy activism during 1964–1980 (and beyond) along with the ever increasing litigiousness of citizens, organized groups, and state-local governments guaranteed heavy federal judicial dockets and novel cases for which there were few if any precedents, and unclear indications of congressional intent almost guaranteed some form of judicial activism.

All this affected the administrative process in several ways. The broad scope of federal powers, sanctioned by the federal judges, has helped broaden the assignments given to federal administrators. Their intrusion into the administrative law arena has made federal administrative law judges much more conscious

of the procedures, the representativeness of participants, and
the substantive outcomes of their proceedings. Judicial handling
of the conditional spending power has helped convert federal
grants managers into regulators as well as administrators. The
Supreme Court's interpretation of the due process and equal
protection provisions has transformed personnel systems at all
levels, not the least of which is the national. Under Section 1983
of the U.S. Code, the federal courts have changed the administration of whole prison systems and of other state and local programs. These and dozens of other examples indicate the vastly
expanded role of the federal judiciary in federal (and state-local)
administration and especially in grants management—a role that
would have been rejected a generation ago. This judicial stance
adds yet another layer of constraints on an already overregulated
federal bureaucracy.

Financing Federal Activism, 1960–1980. The pace of growth
in federal domestic undertakings during these years was also
influenced by the condition of federal finances. In what ways
did the fiscal factor interact with other elements and strengthen
or reduce financial influence in the national policy arena?

The sixties in purely economic terms witnessed the largest
period of sustained economic expansion in this century (Bosworth,
1986). Worker productivity rose 3 percent annually and take-
home pay increased by 17 percent during the decade. Unemployment was low (3.5 percent in 1969), as was inflation, at least
through the mid sixties. These factors helped generate considerable optimism about future economic development and about
the central government's capacity to sustain growth without
recessions—primarily through its fiscal policies (an expansionist
expenditure strategy and the 1964 tax cut) and secondarily with
its monetary strategy.

In the seventies came double-digit inflation, lower worker
productivity, lower levels of real take-home pay, greater competition and adverse economic sanctions from abroad, and a
major recession (1975–1977), and the economic optimism of the
sixties collapsed. "Stagflation" became the economic challenge
of the decade, but there was no overall agreement as to its cure.

Congress took on the unemployment and slow-growth part of the problem, while the Federal Reserve addressed the inflation component.

Hence, an expansionist, largely congressionally crafted fiscal policy continued in the seventies, sometimes with and sometimes without presidential support. Three federal tax cuts were instituted (in 1971, 1975, and 1978); three large counter-cyclical programs were enacted to help mostly local jurisdictions cope with the second worst recession since the Depression; and outlays for ongoing domestic programs (direct and grant-in-aid) continued to rise to the point that in 1979 they accounted for 15 percent of the GNP, compared to 9.9 percent ten years earlier.

The Federal Reserve Board, on the other hand, gradually asserted a more aggressive anti-inflation stance—politics and unemployment levels permitting—through constraints on the money supply and higher discount rates. This trend reached a peak with President Carter's appointment of Paul Volcker as chairman.

In short, the success of expansionist fiscal policies of the 1961–1968 years, their encouragement of a greater national domestic program role, and their salutary impact on secular economic growth failed to provide all the answers to the complicated cluster of destabilizing challenges of the seventies. Monetary policy, especially under Volcker, pursued a restrictive course, while the political branches continued with an expansionist fiscal approach, even though it ran counter to the economic assumptions of the sixties and the monetary policy of the Federal Reserve in the seventies. The politician's chief worry was unemployment; the Federal Reserve's was double-digit inflation.

In practical administrative terms, the fiscal policies of the sixties and their positive results indirectly served as a sanguine factor in the budgeting, planning, and program calculations of key federal administrators for much of that decade. The ragged record of the seventies produced the opposite for most domestic program managers—despite the general climate favoring program growth. Fiscal and budget uncertainties, rising inflation, a major recession, and confused, if not conflicting, national economic/fiscal policies left many top federal managers in far less authoritative positions than their predecessors of the Great Society years had enjoyed. Then fiscal policy had been a matter of sound projected program and budgetary growth. By the late seventies, fiscal policy was either an unsound forecast of expansion or actually the beginnings of budget retrenchment.

Administering the New Activism. Implementation approaches and management personnel provided yet another dynamic that initially encouraged national program expansion. One crucial informal factor favorably influencing the extension of the federal domestic role in the sixties was the "can do" reputation and the professionalism of career federal domestic administrators of that era. Many of the senior managers had served during the late Roosevelt and the Truman years, and their image was one of management success, even in the area of intergovernmental programs. The size of the federal domestic civil service had grown only marginally during the fifties (by roughly 360,000), and most of this workforce was in the civilian component of defense or in the few agencies responsible for large direct-service operations. The Kennedy-Johnson years witnessed a continuation of these personnel trends, with some increase in the intergovernmental sector. These years also saw top professional managers assuming a major role in national policy development and administrative reform.

While the rate of civilian personnel growth stabilized during the seventies, the reputation of and degree of policy reliance on federal professional administrators, especially top management, declined appreciably. Their professionalism was undercut by the retirement of many senior executives and their replacement with less qualified and sometimes patently partisan appointees. Federal administrators' earlier reputation as successful managers was undermined by the early mixed-to-negative implementation records in various of the more novel Great Society and New Federalism initiatives. With grants administrators, their formerly influential role within their respective iron triangles was increasingly preempted by congressional and interest group entrepreneurs, even as their earlier resolute "picket fence federalism" vigor gave way to a much more malleable, less certain, though more broad-gauged behavioral pattern, as was noted earlier.

A major administrative factor prompting the acceleration of national domestic activism was the plethora of implementary methods available and the fact that nearly all of them involved an increasingly widening range of what Lester Salamon (1980) has dubbed "third party" implementors. Nearly all of these indirect methods—grants-in-aid, loan and loan guarantee commitments, regulations and grant conditions, tax deductions, and insurance underwriting—were in place by 1960. Their usage, however, had multiplied severalfold by 1980.

The sole exception to this trend was direct reliance on the federal workforce to directly implement Medicare, the SSI program, and some (but by no means all) of the new regulatory responsibilities of the Environmental Protection Agency and the Department of Labor. The preference of national policymakers for indirect methods has not been accidental. Although differing goals frequently dictate different techniques of execution, in numerous instances (notably in the regulatory and certain grant-aided areas), direct federal administration would be an implementary alternative, even a preferred one, if accountability alone were deemed of high importance. Yet, this has rarely been the option chosen.

Why? The basic reason for this phenomenon is the largely unrecognized continuing assumption among those of nearly all political persuasions that the federal bureaucracy must be kept relatively small, that its influence should be constrained, and that indirect implementation devices are less costly than direct ones. And these assumptions are not new to the system.

Yet this preference for third-party implementors and a division of responsibility in program after program produced in the seventies a massive policy centralization and equally massive implementary decentralization. The consequences in terms of administrative effectiveness, economic efficiency, and accountability were not positive, and federal managers, not the political policymakers, bore the brunt of the resulting criticisms.

Reform Approaches. Early attempts to correct this condition led to efforts at rationalizing the federal executive branch and improving intergovernmental administration through departmental reorganizations, headquarter-field and regional reforms, better lines of interlevel communication, block grants, and various government-wide management circulars. Most of these approaches were based on classical public administration principles, and they continued through the seventies with a special emphasis on curbing regulations by Presidents Ford and Carter, as well as a new budgeting approach and civil service reform with the latter.

State and local officials (and others) generally welcomed these undertakings. In the aggregate, these reforms appeared to support the claim that the new intergovernmentalized administrative system was indeed manageable; hence, national program expansion could continue. Yet, other developments in the seventies showed that many national policymakers and managers felt these applications of neoclassical public administration, organizational, and managerial precepts to be wholly inadequate. Many federal domestic program managers understood this better than anyone else, as many replies to the 1975 ACIR survey of such managers (cited earlier) indicated. They, after all, had to cope with legislation that often had such ambiguous goals (or such specific ones) as to be unadministerable, with mandates that involved both a regulatory and a grants disbursement role, and with frequent statutory changes in their respective programs. Many (administrators of the Safe Streets, CETA, and CDBG programs were prime examples) also had to contend with a proliferation of recipients and of client groups, frequently inadequate support staff, a steady stream of criticism in many instances, and, above all, little or no time to digest the lessons of the past and to comprehend the interest group, other political, and judicial reasons for their increasingly beleaguered status.

One indicator of disenchantment among policymakers was the mounting and largely successful drive to regulate federal civil servants themselves with a view toward making them more responsible and more accountable. A second was the sustained effort during the seventies to expand the political executive sector and, in some administrations (notably Nixon's), to politicize higher levels in the civil service, suggesting that in the minds of White House political operatives top federal personnel were the problem, not procedures, implementation approaches, or organization. Even the 1978 civil service reform legislation may be interpreted this way. Yet both the regulatory and politicizing efforts misdiagnosed the challenge. It was the heavy reliance by the political policymakers on third-party initiators and implementors as well as the sustained growth in national policy enactments that constituted the root problems, not federal personnel.

The good reputation of federal administrators and the wide range of indirect implementation approaches had served as factors favoring major national policy growth in the sixties. However, the former evaporated as an expansionist energizer in the seventies, even as new and counterproductive controls over top professional managers and the use of third-party providers increased.

To sum up, the underlying dynamics for the launching of the most expansive era in national domestic program development and enactments were political, judicial, economic/fiscal, and administrative. This activism persisted through most of the 1970s because of the continued centralizing energies in the political and judicial spheres and despite the implicit need for restraint and rethinking called for by developments in the fiscal and administrative areas.

The Reagan Reaction and Impact

The 1980 election of Ronald Reagan constituted a negative reaction to most of the national expansionist developments of the previous sixteen years and to their fostering dynamics. His campaign economic goals were framed in terms of bitter criticisms of high federal taxes, soaring domestic expenditures, rising levels of governmental borrowing, and increasing regulation. These, he argued, hindered business initiative, productivity and competitiveness, and private investment and as a result national economic growth.

The Reagan administration's approach to public management basically paralleled its supply-side economic strategy. This approach, as James D. Carroll, A. Lee Fritschler, and Bruce

L. R. Smith (1985) point out, involved both program and top personnel reductions, and it dominated most of the administration's basic decisions on financial and budgeting management, information policy, regulation, procurement, personnel, and program administration.

Reagan's New Federalism was as critical of the national government's past intergovernmental policies as his economic and management strategies were of past policies in their respective areas. Hence, he urged a surgical reduction in the federal government's intergovernmental role, a devolution of various program responsibilities on the states (sometimes with the needed funding resources), a strong effort to deregulate, a return to the traditional federal-state partnership principle, and a reduction in activism at the state and local levels as well as the national.

Fiscal Policy. The mix of wins and losses in achieving Reagan's secular economic growth goals in effect left the country and its public administrators with greater destabilizing difficulties in fiscal policy than had been confronted in the seventies. The president succeeded handsomely in getting tax and domestic expenditure cuts, with the Omnibus Budget Reconciliation Act (OBRA) and Economic Recovery Tax Act (ERTA) in 1981. Later tax hikes in 1982 and 1984, along with a gas tax increase (1982) and a mandated rise in Social Security revenues (1983), in no way seriously undercut the revenue reduction significance of ERTA. Presumably, the Tax Reform Act of 1986 was and is basically revenue neutral.

On the expenditure side, however, the OBRA scenario of steady and deeper domestic spending cuts in later years did not play out. In fact, outlays increased by nearly $213 billion between 1982 and 1986 (Advisory Commission on Intergovernmental Relations, 1987). Moreover, Reagan's drive to greatly accelerate Carter's last two-year effort to build up defense pushed DOD annual outlays from $168 billion in 1981 to $280 billion by 1986. These expenditure and revenue trends combined to produce the largest budgets and the largest deficits in our peacetime history. They also scuttled the Reagan campaign promise of a balanced budget by 1984.

Meanwhile, inflation was lowered significantly, thanks to the skillfully crafted monetary policies of the Federal Reserve and to the worst recession (1982–1983) since the Depression. The subsequent economic recovery, while exuberant in certain regions and certain areas of economic activity, left some areas and activities (notably those dependent on international trade) in bad shape. A 6—not 3—percent unemployment level was now accepted as a target goal. Much of the expansion had been financed by heavy foreign investment, which dampened the negative effects of large deficits on capital formation. The trade deficit began to mushroom, but the decline of the dollar, triggered by the massive domestic deficits, did not bring about any early turnaround. Serious efforts to reduce the deficit, ultimately including Gramm-Rudman, fell prey to a series of congressional-presidential standoffs, with each having very different budget priorities.

The cumulative impact of these economic, fiscal, and monetary developments has been to dampen the ardor of policy activists in Washington, to curb program growth, and to shackle the professional top managers.

A Supply-Side Management Strategy. The "supply-side" approach to public management at the national level in theory rests on two basic interrelated goals: slash the number of federal governmental managers (and personnel generally) and cut back on the number and funding levels of federally run or assisted domestic programs (Carroll, Fritschler, and Smith, 1985). A reduction in the managerial cadre's size would discourage detailed federal involvement in program operations, and with program eliminations and devolutions, the pressure to appoint more administrators would dwindle. Achieving both these goals, moreover, would tap into the managerial talent of state and local governments as well as the nonprofit and for-profit sectors.

In behavioral terms, supply-side managers are more interested in operational efforts than in staff activities, more concerned with ultimate program results than with system or agency preservation, more presidentially oriented than congressionally or clientele centered, and more believing in management by ob-

jectives and performance ratings than in improved administrative procedures, reorganizations, and program analyses (Carroll, Fritschler, and Smith, 1985).

As an administrative approach, this supply-side strategy
is not so very novel or consistent. After all, use of a range of
indirect techniques of program execution, many with weak
federal control features, has been a paramount aspect of the
system since the thirties. A reliance on other than federal managers and personnel to implement national program objectives
has also been a prime trait of federal domestic program implementation for over fifty years. A concern with keeping the
federal bureaucracy comparatively small has been an important implicit goal for even longer. Detailed federal managerial
interventions in the operational undertakings of aided subnational governments and others were attempted primarily with
the advent of the new "social regulation," but these congressionally mandated actions in reality were undercut by inadequate staffing, by the number of public, quasi-public, and private
bodies covered, and by the large number of these new regulations and conditions (see Table 2.1).

In terms of mutually complementary concepts, this ap-
parently simple administrative approach is riddled with conflict
and confusion. Program and administrative curbs or devolutions have been the primary means of carrying out this supply-
side managerial strategy, yet extraordinary centralizations of
policy formulation and administrative power are required to
achieve these goals. Moreover, the reduction in the number and
influence of professional federal managers, in both theory and
fact, involves an expansion of the size and roles of the political
executive sector.

In practice, these inconsistencies, along with the inherent
conflict between this managerial approach and other key planks
in the Reagan platform (notably a beefed-up Defense Department, nationally oriented business and "moral majority" concerns, and retrenchment itself), become more apparent. From
the outset, prime reliance was placed on strategic policy management, which involved establishing horizontal policy networks
at the very center of the executive branch (including officials

from the Office of Policy Development, cabinet councils, Office of Planning and Evaluation, OMB, and Council of Economic Advisers). The success of this strategy, at least during the first Reagan administration, was due largely to the strict ideological and political tests that were rigorously applied to the presidential appointments process, especially for Executive Office of the President personnel. Its collapse during the earlier years of the second administration was due to the departure of able key orchestrators of this strategy.

In the overall personnel area, vigorous efforts were mounted to reduce the supply of professional managers and of other federal workers in domestic agencies by a combination of appointments of noncareer managers, slow or no replacements for retirees, downgrading of middle- and senior-level positions, parsimonious pay and retirement policies, skillful manipulation of the Senior Executive Service, barring of professional managers from policy formulation activities, and agency eliminations. The size of the federal civilian workforce, however, is now larger than it has ever been in peacetime. Its total number rose by over 156,000 between 1981 and 1985, thanks largely to the DOD expansions.

The budget process initially was the focal point of implementing many of the administration's supply-side management objectives. It was used, chiefly in 1981, to achieve some program eliminations (hence some devolutions), some program mergers, rollbacks in the administrative costs of federal grants and other programs, limits on strict federal supervision of many third-party implementors of national policies, and a reduction in federal collection and dissemination of information. Yet, as is noted elsewhere, Congress from 1982 to 1987 did not accept many of the president's domestic cutback proposals. During these years, budgeting was a "top-down" process in the executive branch, but once the product reached Congress the pluralistic pressures of domestic program politics asserted themselves, though all within the confines of the deficit dilemma.

With procurement, the Reagan administration began early a drive against waste, fraud, and abuse in various domestic (notably social welfare) programs. Yet its own management of

the defense buildup produced the most extraordinary examples
of poor procurement practices (and of the resulting waste and
fraud) the nation has ever seen. With its campaign to reduce
the federal regulatory role, a mix of personnel, procedural, and
centralizing actions (OMB serving as the authoritative sifter of
proposed and amended regulations) succeeded in reducing the
number of issuances. Yet, as is detailed elsewhere, the administration's own support for tough retrenching grant conditions,
new pro-business constraints on certain state activities, and in-
trusive conservative social agenda–inspired regulations undercut much of this effort.

In short, Reagan management practices in the strategic
planning, personnel, budgetary, procurement, and regulatory
spheres, while initially successful in many instances, frequently
encountered opposition in the form of conflicting administration
policy objectives, congressional hostility, and pressure-group
politics. At the same time, they did succeed in rendering top
professional managers even more defensive, deflated, and de-
moralized than they had been in the seventies.

The Reagan Federalism Record. The Reagan intergovernmental
initiatives achieved more than what was deemed possible in 1980
but far less than what in 1981 seemed likely after OBRA. With
his drive to reduce the federal role in the federal system, an absolute reduction in grant outlays of over $8 billion (from the
proposed FY 1982 Carter figure) and in the number of grants
by more than 140 was achieved with OBRA. Proposed additional deeper cuts, more eliminations, and new consolidations,
however, were rejected by an increasingly assertive Congress.
Hence, federal aid totals rose gradually in both constant and
current dollars, from $88.2 billion in FY 1982 to $112.4 billion
in current dollars by FY 1986, or by nearly 7 billion constant
dollars. The number of federal grants also increased slightly,
from less than 400 in 1982 to 420 at the end of 1986.

The concomitant Reagan goal of devolving federal program responsibilities scored slightly better. In addition to OBRA's
program eliminations and block grants, greater management
responsibility in some of the environmental regulatory programs

was delegated to some of the states, categorical conditions in non–social welfare programs were loosened administratively, and the block grants were implemented in a highly permissive fashion. At the same time, no devolutions of total responsibility in any major grant area (multistate regionalism and certain housing programs excepted) occurred, and categoricals, not block grants or general revenue sharing (which was scrapped in 1986), dominated the grant scene throughout these years, accounting for more than 80 percent of total aid dollars.

The deregulation drive, as was noted previously, scored some successes and some real losses. The administration did not focus on actively eliminating intergovernment or other regulations as much as on softening the process—by its appointments, by personnel cuts, by permissive procedures, and by a centralized review of proposed or modified regulations (Lovell, 1984). Issuances were thus reduced, the impact of many regulations was lightened, and delegations of administrative authority in some programs, noted earlier, picked up. On the negative side, conditions in social welfare grants got tougher; congressional preemptions of state regulatory authority picked up, frequently with presidential support; and no frontal legislative assault was ever mounted by the administration on behalf of regulatory relief. For federal managers of social programs, this meant a much heavier administrative load. For those in the environmental, developmental, and block grant areas, it involved some lightening of their responsibilities.

The push to return to the old federal-state partnership was reflected in all of the new block grants wherein the states were the sole recipients, in the number of heretofore federal-local programs that were merged in these blocks, in the unsuccessful 1982 administration effort to achieve a "big swap" in program responsibilities, in the delegations of environmental administrative responsibilities (noted earlier), and in the decline in the proportion of grant monies that bypassed state governments (see Table 2.1). All of these, save for the ill-fated 1982 proposal, eased the job of affected federal grants managers. On the opposite side of the ledger, states and their administrators bore the brunt of the increased conditions and fiscal curbs in the social welfare area, they were most affected by the new pre-emptions and crossover sanctions (for example, tandem trailer truck regulation and teenage drinking bans), and they felt more than the other subnational governments the adverse effects of administration (and Congress's) unilateral intergovernmental initiatives.

Finally, the need to curb governmental activism at all levels proved to be a need that no level honored. In overall expenditure terms, federal outlays soared from $703 billion in 1981 to over $1,030 billion by 1986; state outlays from own revenue sources increased from $160 billion in 1981 to over $223.5 billion by 1985; and the local figures for the same years were $245 billion up to $328.6 billion (Advisory Commission on Intergovernmental Relations, 1987, pp. 12, 15). As a percentage of the GNP, total federal-state-local spending rose from 30.6 percent in 1979 to over 35 percent by 1986, a share that far exceeded that of the seventies (Advisory Commission on Intergovernmental Relations, 1987, p. xi).

To conclude, the administration (and Congress's) fiscal policies and the overarching shadow of the deficits slowed down but did not eliminate activist entrepreneurialism in Washington. The program scope and the jurisdictional depth of the federal grant sector was reduced, the latter more than the former. While the fiscal size of the domestic program budget had grown fairly steadily, its intergovernmental component had not. The net effect of the mixed regulatory record left the national role at the end of the Reagan years pretty much where it was in 1980. All this has produced a real attitudinal revolution in the minds of state and local officials and administrators: No longer will the federal government be able to play the paramount policy problem-solving role that it attempted to assume in the seventies. But this basic shift was caused more by the fallout from Reaganomics than from Reagan's intergovernmental efforts. For federal professional managers, these changes produced some lessening of implementary assignments, but this in no way compensated for the negative effects of the president's managerial strategy.

Epilogue

What basic findings emerge from this analysis and how do they relate to federal top managers?

1. Overall, national activism is still a prime trait of the national policy process, but the much slower rate of new domestic enactments and the marginal or static growth in outlays for most of the intergovernmental programs means that most federal professional managers outside the military now confront a more stabilized, a more predictable, and a bit less arduous mission assignment than they did in the previous two decades.

2. The constitutional position of the national government within the federal system is stronger than it has ever been, thanks to Supreme Court decisions—especially *Garcia* v. *San Antonio Metropolitan Transit Authority,* 105 S. Ct. 1005 (1985); and this indirectly fortifies the position of federal managers; at the same time, the specifics of carrying out broad congressional assignments, especially in the regulatory realm, have generated countless court cases and resultant headaches for the federal administrators involved.

3. The federal intergovernmental role programmatically is less broad, less big, and not as penetrating vertically as it was in 1980. This eases some of the operational problems confronting some grants managers.

4. The continuing national thrusts of the federal government's regulatory agenda, however, undercut these marginal program/recipient contractions and place top managers in a strategic and sometimes ambivalent position in a system that remains highly centralized.

5. The underlying centripetal dynamics of the earlier expansion have not changed in the political or judicial areas (as yet). Budget battles and the annual agonizing over the hike in the debt limit have generated some fiscally based constraints in the policy process; yet the failure of both the president and the Congress to rein in their differing expenditure priorities (defense for the president, few further domestic cuts for Congress, and Social Security and other entitlements largely sacred

cows for both) has only compounded the deficit dilemma. This, in turn, has placed some top financial managers in the position of attempting to honor the conflicting fiscal mandates of the administration and of Congress, while agency administrators frequently confront the dilemma of entirely differing executive and legislative branch views on the worth of their programs.

6. National reliance on indirect methods of implementing federal policies seems to be stronger than ever (although "Irangate" may prompt some rethinking on the issue), and this situation reinforces what Seidman and Gilmour (1985, p. 134) describe as the inevitable result of "administration through third parties," the transformation of many professional executives into "grant and contract administrators, paymasters, and regulation writers or enforcers."

7. Supply-side management, when applied, has achieved a greater overall concern with performance and end results of domestic programs, but the deficit crisis has been a far greater factor in generating these concerns. From the federal professional managers' perspective, this administrative strategy can only be described as a disaster. Its confrontational attitudinal, personnel, pay, and ministerial-role features combine to strike directly at the very professionalism such officials collectively embody. Above all, perhaps, it is founded on the perennial myth that career federal managers, not political policymakers, were the chief instigators of domestic program and agency expansionism.

8. In various ways, time has been helping managers. The passage of time has encouraged more dispassionate assessments of the Great Society and later federal domestic programs, assessments that have documented their positive social or economic impacts (Schwarz, 1983). The recent budget battles over domestic programs curiously seem to have generated a rough (in opposition to the White House) bipartisan congressional consensus on the continuance of various grants and implicit support for their professional managers. Another sign of how time helps to cure various ills comes from Paul Peterson and his colleagues (1986), who in their probe of grants found that even with the more redistributive types of grants a cycle of disburser-recipient

thrusts and counterthrusts ultimately produces a "cooperative federalism" synthesis.

9. In overall systemic terms, the strategic position, administrative power, and policy influence of federal professional managers today does not match that of their counterparts a generation ago, although they are less abused by Congress, the interest groups, and the press than they were in the seventies and early eighties. To chalk up a successful record in an administrative system that honors Hamilton's hierarchic principles in theory but Madison's pluralistic politics in practice is never easy. The recent period has been exceptionally onerous, but there are some signs that this phase is ending and a new, somewhat less repressive era for top administrators may be in the offing. None of the 1988 presidential aspirants, after all, made bashing the bureaucrats a basic theme of his campaign.

References

Advisory Commission on Intergovernmental Relations. *Summary and Concluding Observations (A-62)*. Washington, D.C.: Advisory Commission on Intergovernmental Relations, June 1976.

Advisory Commission on Intergovernmental Relations. *The Intergovernmental Grant System as Seen by Local, State, and Federal Officials (A-54)*. Washington, D.C.: Advisory Commission on Intergovernmental Relations, 1977.

Advisory Commission on Intergovernmental Relations. *Significant Features of Fiscal Federalism, 1981–82 Edition (M-135)*. Washington, D.C.: Advisory Commission on Intergovernmental Relations, April 1983.

Advisory Commission on Intergovernmental Relations. *Regulatory Federalism: Policy Process, Impact and Reform (A-95)*. Washington, D.C.: Advisory Commission on Intergovernmental Relations, February 1984.

Advisory Commission on Intergovernmental Relations. *Significant Features of Fiscal Federalism, 1984 Edition (M-141)*. Washington, D.C.: Advisory Commission on Intergovernmental Relations, March 1985.

Advisory Commission on Intergovernmental Relations. *The Transformation in American Politics: Implications for Federalism (A-106)*. Washington, D.C.: Advisory Commission on Intergovernmental Relations, August 1986.

Advisory Commission on Intergovernmental Relations. *Significant Features of Fiscal Federalism, 1987 Edition (M-115)*. Washington, D.C.: Advisory Commission on Intergovernmental Relations, June 1987.

Bosworth, B. "The Evolution of Economic Policy." In M. Kaplan and P. Cuciti (eds.), *The Great Society and Its Legacy.* Durham, N.C.: Duke University Press, 1986.

Carroll, J. D., Fritschler, A. L., and Smith, B.L.R. "Supply Side Management in the Reagan Administration." *Public Administration Review,* 1985, *45,* 805–814.

Kelly, A. H., and Harbison, W. A. *The American Constitution, Its Origins and Development.* New York: Norton, 1976.

Lovell, C. H. " 'Reregulation' of Intergovernmental Programs: Early Results of the Reagan Policies." *Public Affairs Report,* 1984, *25* (2).

McLean, J. E. *Politics Is What You Make It.* Public Affairs Pamphlet No. 181. Washington, D.C.: Public Affairs Press, April 1952.

Peterson, P. E., Rabe, B. G., and Wong, K. K. *When Federalism Works.* Washington, D.C.: Brookings Institution, 1986.

Salamon, L. *Rethinking Public Management.* Washington, D.C.: Urban Institute, 1980.

Sanford, T. *Storm over the States.* New York: McGraw-Hill, 1967.

Schwarz, J. E. *America's Hidden Success: A Reassessment of Twenty Years of Public Policy.* New York: Norton, 1983.

Seidman, H., and Gilmour, R. *Politics, Position and Power, From the Positive to the Regulatory State.* (4th ed.) New York: Oxford University Press, 1985.

U.S. Senate Subcommittee on Intergovernmental Relations. *The Federal System as Seen by Federal Aid Officials.* Washington, D.C.: 15 December, 1965.

Walker, D. B. "Federal Aid Administrators and the Federal System." *Intergovernmental Perspectives,* Fall 1977, *3,* 10–17.

Walker, D. B. *Toward a Functioning Federalism.* Boston: Little, Brown, 1981.

Walker, D. B. "The Nature and Systemic Impact of 'Creative Federalism.'" In M. Kaplan and P. Cuciti (eds.), *The Great Society and Its Legacy.* Durham, N.C.: Duke University Press, 1986.

White, L. D. *Introduction to the Study of Public Administration.* (4th ed.) New York: Macmillan, 1954.

Two

⊡⊡⊡⊡⊡⊡⊡⊡⊡⊡⊡⊡⊡⊡⊡⊡⊡⊡⊡⊡⊡⊡⊡⊡⊡⊡⊡⊡⊡⊡

The Effective
Public Program Manager

Effective public program management necessitates certain understandings and skills on the part of the public administrator. It demands an appreciation of the political and organizational context in which public administrators function, as noted in Part One of this book. But it also requires an understanding of such issues in the field of human resources management as the role of the professional in the public organization, the nature of those ethics and values by which public administrators ought to operate, and the basic personnel skills necessary to public management. Part Two is devoted to these matters, in an effort to isolate and then explore the fundamental human resource skills and understandings required for successful public program management.

In Chapter Three, Robert E. Cleary examines the role of the specialist in the public organization, noting that many specialists are professionals by education and training. Professionals often have a mandate to define "proper conduct" in their field of endeavor, a mandate that will on occasion run counter to political or organizational requirements. This reality leads to decisional problems, both substantive and procedural, for the professional in government, as well as to administrative problems for those who manage professionals in public organizations. Cleary argues that while some of the resultant dilemmas may prove incapable of resolution, most can be solved or significantly ameliorated by careful attention to personnel policy, the systematic application of professional ethical judgments, and an educa-

73

tional system that includes a full examination of the meaning of such concepts as civic duty and the public interest.

In Chapter Four, Ralph Clark Chandler explores the role of ethics and values in public administration. He examines the utility of ethical codes in public administration for the resolution of political and organizational dilemmas. He analyzes the ideas of trusteeship and social partnership as guides for the application of ethical principles derived from these codes. Chandler concludes that ethical considerations oblige public servants to utilize concepts such as social justice and accountability as standards in the performance of their official duties, arguing that time-honored internal norms that regularly guide individual behavior should also be used in public decision making.

In Chapter Five, N. Joseph Cayer declares that the development and nurturing of personnel in the organization is a prime task of management. He identifies various practical skills, people skills, political skills, and leadership skills as he focuses on the components of a successful personnel policy for the public organization. Cayer points out that effective public administration tends to depend on the development and maintenance of a favorable organizational climate, which in turn is dependent on the application of the skills outlined in his essay. He applies these principles to such aspects of human resource development and management as equal employment opportunity/affirmative action, the need to deal with employee organizations, and the increasing legalization of employer/employee relations, in an effort to assist public managers in the application of human resources principles as they carry out their program responsibilities.

3

𝍖𝍖𝍖𝍖𝍖𝍖𝍖𝍖𝍖𝍖𝍖𝍖𝍖𝍖𝍖𝍖𝍖𝍖𝍖𝍖𝍖𝍖𝍖𝍖𝍖𝍖

The Professionalization
of Program Management

Robert E. Cleary

United States government administrators work in a changing world. Here and elsewhere, there is an expanding need for professional managerial expertise that requires an understanding of politics and organizational processes, along with specific managerial tools such as budgeting and computing.

As the United States and the world grow more complicated, government decisions become more difficult to make and to carry out. America is a complex urban nation, attempting to cope with problems of inflation, unemployment, and pollution. Environmental issues, questions of energy and resource use, fluctuating cost-price relationships, and the impact of an increasingly interdependent international economy are complicating customary producer-consumer-government relations. In addition, during much of the time since the end of World War II, the American people have demanded expanded and improved services from their governments, thus altering the traditional relationship between the public sector and the private sector.

Moreover, social values are changing. Federal, state, and local governments are being asked to an unprecedented degree to mediate social problems, and even to resolve them, in cases of difference or disagreement. Government is an important regulator of personal conduct, subordinating certain individual rights in an attempt to preserve other important rights. Basic questions of public policy are continually being raised and answered by public officials. Which, for example, is more important: an employee's right to keep working until the age of seventy or beyond, or the need to open employment opportunities for younger people by requiring retirement at a specific age? Government is attempting to preserve individual rights in making choices on matters of this nature, but in doing so it is infringing on the rights of others.

The complex nature of modern government requires expertise to solve public problems. This expertise is typically found in executive agencies of government. As the people demand action on more and more problems, legislative bodies delegate responsibility to experts in executive agencies, often providing inadequate guidance on how to resolve key issues. Consequently, the administrative bureaucracy has become a major force in government decision making.

Max Weber once pointed out that bureaucracy has become commonplace in modern society because it permits maximum use of technical expertise:

> The decisive reason for the advance of bureaucratic organization has always been its purely technical superiority over any other form of organization. . . . Precision, speed, unambiguity, knowledge of the files, continuity, discretion, unity, strict subordination, reduction of friction and of material and personal costs—these are raised to the optimum point in the strictly bureaucratic administration. . . . As compared with all collegiate, honorific, and avocational forms of administration, trained bureaucracy is superior on all these points [Weber, 1946, p. 214].

Specialized professional education or training is often needed by the bureaucrat or the prospective bureaucrat to develop or enhance the skills necessary to deliver particular public programs and services. Thus, many civil servants are, in fact, professionals by training—scientists, engineers, accountants, attorneys, physicians, and those managers who by education and conduct are professional public administrators. Mosher (1982) has pointed out that the American governments are increasingly composed of professionals. Those civil servants who are specializing in a particular field or area of expertise tend to identify with the profession that has trained them, just as professionals outside government tend to so identify. What are the implications of this situation for the processes and actions of government?

The Conflicting Obligations of the Public Official

A profession is "a reasonably clear-cut occupational field, which ordinarily requires higher education at least through the bachelor's level, and which offers a lifetime career to its members" (Mosher, 1982, pp. 115–116). While there is some argument among students of the subject as to the criteria for a profession, there is also widespread agreement on the idea that specialized knowledge and training leads to an obligation on the part of the recipient to utilize it for the common good. Goode (1969) has noted, for example, that the two central qualities of a profession are a basic body of abstract knowledge and the ideal of service. Hughes (1958) has written of the license and the mandate of the professional—the license to carry out certain activities, and the mandate to define proper conduct in one's own field. He declares that professional training produces "a professional conscience. . . . The profession claims and aims to become a moral unit" (p. 33). As a result, the professional in government frequently feels personal responsibility for acting in a broader interest rooted in a concern about people. The overall feeling of many government professionals no matter what their field is that they are obliged as public servants to use their specialized knowledge in the best interests of society as they attempt to solve a problem or provide a particular service.

This attitude basically produces a collegial orientation that may not fit in a hierarchical organization. Such an orientation could well lead to disagreement with an organizational superior who sees the needs of a decision-making situation from a different perspective and thus in a different way. A doctor in the

National Institutes of Health, for example, may be willing to consult with his medical colleagues but may be unwilling to follow advice or instructions from an administrative superior. The result is likely to be a conflict between the professional and organizational authority and a basic resistance by the professional to administrative control.

A traditional response of a number of civil servants in such situations has been that the public official's responsibility is to the law as mandated by the legislature and thus the official's function is to follow the law. But the law is not always clear. Eligibility criteria for disability benefits are not self-applicable. The definition of income sheltered from taxation is not exact. The determination of which customs category to utilize to classify imported items is not always precisely mandated. Interpretations and understandings are often necessary to apply relevant laws and regulations to particular situations. It becomes the task of the civil servant, perhaps under the guidance of a supervisor, to supply these interpretations. This reality has led to the point of view that a public official's primary responsibility in a decision-making situation is to his or her superiors, all the way up to the agency chief and perhaps even to the elected chief executive, and to the mandates these officials set forth. Under this conception the individual bureaucrat may actively participate in debate over alternate policy options in a situation of value conflict, but the importance of loyalty to superiors requires obedience to policy decisions once they are laid down.

This formulation leads directly to another response to the conflict issue, however: the idea that the organization is doing such a good job in carrying out its responsibilities that it must be preserved and perhaps even strengthened. Consequently, according to this viewpoint, the bureaucrat's chief loyalty is to the future of the organization. The underlying implication is that the organization is serving the public interest and accomplishing meritorious work. The ultimate end is to serve the public. But whether or not this proves to be the case, the argument runs, organizational needs must be upheld in decisional situations.

Still another response regarding the proper locus of responsibility of the civil servant is that it is specifically to the public. Implicit in this idea is the importance of the public interest as a proper guideline for the public official. It is widely agreed that a *public servant* has a civic duty to serve the public interest. As former Comptroller General Elmer Staats (1988, p. 601) has written: "In its broadest sense, 'public service' is a concept, an attitude, a sense of duty—yes, even a sense of public morality." The public interest is generally defined in this context in terms of respect for the individual and the spirit of fairness, equality, and justice reflected in the ethical aspirations of American society as summarized in such fundamental documents as the Declaration of Independence, the Preamble to the Constitution, the Bill of Rights, and the Fourteenth and Nineteenth Amendments to the Constitution. In decisional situations of conflicting values, therefore, the common good broadly defined is often advanced as the standard that must be applied by the public servant to evolve a responsible course of action.

The differing attitudes outlined here overlap. Odegard (1954, p. 19) has written that a "truly responsible bureaucrat" is a person "of not one but many responsibilities." He declares that the public servant

> . . . owes a political responsibility to those who have final say as to policy and ultimately to the people who make and unmake them. He owes both a "political" and an "administrative" responsibility to his superior officers. He owes a legal responsibility to the courts (both administrative and judicial), lest he transgress the rights of citizens by abusing or exceeding his powers. He owes a . . . [functional] responsibility to his fellow bureaucrats to maintain high standards of integrity and competence, lest he bring dishonor or disgrace to the "guild" of which all are members. He owes a moral responsibility to the highest ethical and moral principles of the state and society in which he lives and to which he professes allegiance. And finally he owes a responsibility to his own soul—to the honor and integrity of his own person—for without self-respect he can scarcely be expected to have respect for others or to deserve their respect in turn.

Conscientious public servants attempting to reconcile these diverse responsibilities frequently base their actions on their political and social responsibilities to the larger public interest, in terms of moral, ethical, and professional standards, while recognizing a sense of accountability to their organizational superiors. Dilemmas may arise when a public servant feels that the organization of which he or she is a part is serving some special interest rather than the public interest. An analyst in the Food and Drug Administration who concludes that approval of a new drug is proceeding too quickly and without sufficient testing might well be a case in point. And history records the presence of a whistleblower like Gifford Pinchot, a professional forester and head of the federal Division of Forestry, in a far simpler period.

Special problems of reconciling conflicting obligations in decisional situations exist for those government officials who are professionals, with their own professional codes of ethics to guide their actions. As Gaus wrote after exploring the leading arguments concerning the proper locus of the public administrator's responsibility, "one important kind of responsibility . . . [is] that due to the standards and ideals of his profession" (Gaus, White, and Dimock, 1936, p. 40). But a professional's interests, competence, and values may well conflict with the organizational requirements of the agency in which he or she is employed, the needs of the program with which he or she is concerned, or the larger political situation.

Mosher (1982) points out that many professionals tend to concentrate on mastering and delivering the work substance of their field, rather than on becoming proficient in those systems and processes that must often be understood to assure programmatic success. The result is a heightened probability of value conflict for professionals in government as they attempt to implement the fruits of their expertise in the face of organizational and political constraints.

A scientist, for example, may be responsive to the norms and the reward structures of the scientific community. The greatest personal and professional job satisfactions for scientists are likely to come from contributing to the advancement of knowledge in the field, not from serving stated organizational or societal needs. Similarly, professionals in the engineering field lean toward making decisions on the basis of the technical standards of that field, not on political or even economic considerations. (A good example in recent years involved the support of engineers in the National Highway and Traffic Safety Administration for an air bag requirement in all new automobiles.) Accountants who practice their profession in government must operate in terms of the standards of the profession, regardless of political requirements, to fulfill their legal and fiduciary responsibilities. Lawyers who represent a client must emphasize the interests of that client, regardless of so-called larger needs. Even social scientists, who because of their specialization in the area of public affairs are often more politically or organizationally oriented, rely heavily on professional judgment in assessing social problems. This generalization might have particular application to economists, given the nature of the field and the problems economists study, but it also pertains to other social sciences. Political scientists, sociologists, social psychologists and other social scientists employed in a variety of government agencies—federal, state, and local—have on occasion run into difficulty by following beliefs and processes developed in their disciplines, despite organizational instructions and directives.

The Dilemma of the Professional Public Manager

Do public *managers* face a fundamental problem in reconciling conflicting responsibilities in their roles as public administrators? In beginning the response to this question, let us pose another: Are public managers *professionals* in their administrative role? To answer this query, let us apply the criteria for a profession to public administration and management.

First, a specialized body of knowledge exists in the field of public administration, at least some of which deals with the abstract. While we may not have unanimous agreement on the specifics of this knowledge or its scope and boundaries, most students of the subject can identify broadly with the "common curriculum components" listed by the National Association of

Schools of Public Affairs and Administration (1981):

- Political and legal institutions and processes
- Economic and social institutions and processes
- Organization and management concepts, including human resource administration
- Concepts and techniques of financial administration
- Techniques of analysis, including quantitative, economic, and statistical methods

Second, a reasonably clear-cut occupational field exists, which much more often than not offers lifetime careers to its members. The federal government identifies a substantial number of positions as managerial, supervisory, or administrative. So do state and local governments and not-for-profit organizations. And in practice, a number of other positions not so identified supplement these lists.

Third, the practice of public administration finds formal education and training exceedingly helpful for credentialing purposes and even more important for genuine assistance in learning how to perform on the job. As Lewis (1987) has recently found, formal education in public administration is more likely than education in other fields to lead to managerial or supervisory positions and to "positions of authority" in federal employment.

Finally, one has only to refer to the meaning of the concept of the *public service* to note the obligation of public managers to work for the common good. When we reduce the basic role of government in a democracy to its essentials, we focus on the civic duty of public servants to advance the public interest in a spirit of humaneness and a context of fairness, integrity, and justice.

By these standards, public administration is a profession. There is a body of knowledge, an occupational field, a system of formal education and training, and a sense of responsibility for the public interest. Consequently, public managers attempting to apply the learning of their field to their programmatic responsibilities can well face decisional dilemmas similar to those confronting professionals in the public service who possess other specializations. A supervisor in the Department of Health and Human Services who is attempting to reconcile a professional staff report that summarizes the human costs of establishing a lower hospital reimbursement rate for the use of dialysis machines with an organizational directive to contain medical costs would certainly be a leading case in point.

One way of reconciling diverse responsibilities in a conflict situation of this kind is by reference to and utilization of a professional code of ethics. A mark of a profession that has been noted by a number of students of the subject is the existence of a code of ethics that attempts to summarize the ethical values and standards of the field clearly and succinctly (see Chapter Four). There is a code of ethics for physicians, a code of ethics for educators, a code of ethics for engineers, a code of ethics for the bar, and the like.

Given its somewhat fragmented nature, the public management field is characterized by a variety of ethical codes. A code of ethics for the International City Management Association was adopted in 1924. A federal employee code of ethics was promulgated by Congress in 1958. The first state code of ethics was set forth in 1967, with a number of others following shortly thereafter. The American Society for Public Administration (ASPA) adopted a code of ethics for its members in 1984. The ASPA code is reproduced in this book in Chapter Four.

The federal employee code of ethics focuses on the responsibilities of public servants. Later statements of federal ethical standards—for example, the Ethics in Government Act of 1978—strengthen this emphasis. The tenth and last point of the federal code observes that "public office is a public trust." Points one and two emphasize loyalty to moral principles, country, the Constitution, and the law. Points three and four stress hard work and efficiency. Points five through eight prohibit conflicts of interest. Point nine requires the exposure of "corruption wherever discovered."

The ASPA code focuses more directly than does the federal code on the need to serve the public and to promote the public interest. Point one declares that ASPA members should "demonstrate the highest standards of personal integrity, truthfulness, honesty and fortitude in all our public activities in order to inspire public confidence and trust in public institutions" (American Society for Public Administration, 1985). Points two and three, as well as nine and ten, deal with conflicts of interest. Points four and five treat affirmative action and discrimination. Point six then declares that members of ASPA should "serve the public with respect, concern, courtesy, and responsiveness, recognizing that service to the public is beyond service to oneself." Point seven comes close to a statement of *professional* responsibility when it urges members to "strive for personal professional excellence and encourage the professional development of our associates and those seeking to enter the field of public administration." Point eight emphasizes the importance of "open communication, creativity, dedication, and compassion." Point eleven urges "*professional* competence, fairness, impartiality, efficiency, and effectiveness" in the performace of the public's business. Point twelve urges "respect, support, study, and when necessary, work to improve federal and state constitutions and other laws which define the relationships among public agencies, employees, clients and all citizens."

The ASPA code is broader than the federal code. The latter focuses on the need to advance the law, to emphasize productivity, and to avoid corruption because "public office is a public trust." Except for an implication in point one of the federal code ("Put loyalty *to the highest moral principles* and to country above loyalty to persons, party, or Government department"), there is no mention of *professional* responsibility, of the contribution of *professional* training to the development of administrative competence, of the need of *professionals* to fulfill a mandate to define their own proper conduct in their field.

The ASPA code goes beyond the federal code in two basic respects. First, it urges "the highest standards of personal integrity" and the serving of "the public with . . . responsiveness." The essential point here may well be covered in the federal code by the need to emphasize "loyalty to the highest moral principles," or perhaps by the statement in point three on the need of the public servant to give "the performance of his duties his earnest effort and best thought." The ASPA code is clearly more specific, however, on the matter of a *personal* responsibility to the public. Two of the strongest points of the ASPA code, one and seven, are simply not found in the federal code. As a result, the tone of the two documents is different, with the ASPA code more likely to leave stronger feeling concerning the public trust involved in holding public office. This seems evident even though the federal code ends with the statement that "public office is a public trust."

Second, the ASPA code specifically includes the concept of professional responsibility, while the federal code does not. "Personal professional excellence," "professional development of our associates," and "professional competence, fairness, impartiality, efficiency, and effectiveness" add up to a recognition of professional responsibilities in the ASPA code. This recognition contributes a different dimension to the responsibility of the public servant, making it even more clear that multiple obligations influence and contribute to the public administrator's decision making and that this decision making must emphasize striving "for personal professional excellence."

It might be worth mentioning at this point that neither the federal code nor the ASPA code goes as far in this last respect as the code of ethics of the International City Management Association (ICMA), which declares that its members should "Resist any encroachment on professional responsibilities, believing the member should be free to carry out official policies without interference, and handle each problem without discrimination on the basis of principle and justice." The ICMA code carries the autonomy of the profession considerably further than either the federal code or the ASPA code.

All three codes, however, basically provide general guidance only, and not specific guidance for public servants involved in a decisional conflict situation. Moreover, by introducing a source of legitimacy that differs from the authority of the state, the ASPA and ICMA codes heighten certain value conflicts for public administrators. The effect may well be an increased requirement for the professional public manager to compromise between his or her sense of responsibility as a professional and the perceived public needs of the larger society.

Balancing Professional Obligations
with Governmental Needs

The public servant who is a professional, when faced with conflicting purposes or responsibilities, may well try to respond in terms of the moral and ethical implications of Odegard's last point: responsibility "to the honor and integrity of his own person" as the public official has learned to assess it in the perspective of professional training. The civil servant must recognize, though, that the requirements of democracy demand a subordination to administrative superiors, to legislative mandates, or to political requirements, even when this subordination conflicts with professional ethics or an inner sense of responsibility. Therefore, an economist may temper professional advice to administrative superiors, a military officer may resign, or a physician may write a prescription under a fictitious name to preserve the anonymity of a co-worker. But this last example illustrates the utility of a feeling of professional responsibility, for it refers to a situation in which a doctor's professional ethics should not be ignored. In the particular case at reference, the doctor felt a personal and political obligation to protect the privacy of a colleague working in an important, high-pressure job. On the other hand, his medical code of ethics would seem to require a recorded identification of the name of the patient as well as of his own as the physician.

In the final analysis, the individual civil servant who is a member of a profession must accept personal responsibility for his or her actions and must make a decision on the application of ethical standards to a particular situation in the context of political, legal, and administrative responsibilities. The public official must take his or her code of ethics and sense of morality, along with the law and the requirements of administrative responsibility to superiors, into account in the decision. If he or she is unable to do so, the consequences of the decision may well involve resignation. This would be particularly true for the public servant who feels strongly about his or her professional responsibilities and who has a sense of integrity regarding what he or she believes is right and necessary. A case in point is found in the resignation of Attorney General Elliot L. Richardson in 1973, after he was instructed by President Richard Nixon to terminate the appointment of Watergate Special Prosecutor Archibald Cox. Richardson declared that he had no choice but to resign after he received this order, given his deeply felt belief about the nature of proper actions for a public servant.

The higher one's level in government, the more probable it will be that one's professional tenets will eventually conflict with organizational needs. This is particularly likely to be true as the professional accepts managerial responsibility. Simpler issues are usually settled at lower levels or by individual specialists; more complex issues tend to face higher-level experts or managers. Lambright and Teich (1978) give the example of the professional scientist serving as a bureau chief who is faced with the requirement of amalgamating scientific pressures from below with political pressures from above and even from outside the organization.

Often the tendency is such cases is to decide in terms of political or organizational needs. Thus, those medical doctors in the old federal Department of Health, Education, and Welfare who in the mid 1970s opposed their colleagues' proposal to carry out a massive nationwide immunization program against swine flu because of possible serious side effects were overwhelmed. They were in effect buried by the organization's felt need to close ranks and by the reluctance of political superiors—up to and including the president of the United States—to appear weak in protecting the public health (Neustadt and Fineberg, 1978). The fact that the side effects proved to be as severe as death in more cases than anticipated did not make the dissidents feel any better about their judgment after the fact.

In addition to being poor public policy, situations like this result in a loss of public confidence in both professionals in government and the politicians to whom they report. Professionals—and for that matter politicians—tend not to be perceived as having any special cachet to act in the public interest, despite the tenets of their profession. The ultimate result may well be a diminution of the acceptance of, and therefore the application of, professional skills in government. If a professional simply becomes another voice in the political process, with no special credence, the fruits of expertise will be diminished and perhaps even negated.

The Watergate scandal during Richard Nixon's presidency provides a classic case for examining the obligations of career public servants in addition to those of political appointees. The latter group received far more attention in the early 1970s. But Mosher (1982) points out that Watergate also brought forward the question of whether a public servant appointed to office under the authority of an elected official must be responsive to that official or his associates when the directives set forth run counter to the appointed civil servant's principles. As Mosher then goes on to observe:

> Watergate generated doubts in the nation as a whole, not only about the President and his immediate entourage but about the public service as a whole, both career and noncareer. It kindled new concern about ethics in government, about loyalty and responsibility, and about the proper roles and relationships of political and career officials. Perhaps most serious of all was the further loss of repute and confidence of the general public in the public services; the level of such repute and confidence had not been very high since the days of Andrew Jackson and . . . could ill afford further degradation [p. 105].

It is essential that those who manage professionals in government understand that these managers have an additional task beyond their other responsibilities. In the interests of improved public policy, supervisors must recognize the expertise of professionals and the problems the latter have in the organizational context. They should accept a special obligation to work with these professionals to resolve such problems in the larger public interest that all represent. Public organizations must operate in terms of hierarchical needs and political realities. Individual employees of government, no matter how "expert" in their fields, cannot be permitted to operate on their own in a vacuum. They must accept supervision if the value of expertise is to be maximized. As Mosher declares, however, the Watergate experience raised "frightening questions" about our governmental system, including whether "the political and hierarchical ethic" should take precedence over *all* other norms, even those engendered by conscience or by a professional ethic. This query leads us to the key question of how the American system melds professional expertise and obligation with hierarchical and organizational needs. How do we enhance the probabilities of achieving what are fundamentally competing realities? The answer to this question is a multiple one, involving matters of governmental career entry, personnel policy, a sense of responsibility, and education. Let us examine these matters.

The Role of Personnel Policy in Improving Professionalism in Government

A prime method of expanding professional expertise in the public service is through the direct recruitment of new college graduates who have an academic specialization in public administration or in a particular field needed in government. The task of recruiting talented people to government begins with entry-level positions. For many years, the federal government used a formal examination process to recruit young professionals to its ranks. In its last manifestation, the federal professional recruitment exam was known as the Professional and Administrative Career Examination (PACE). The PACE examination was phased out in the early 1980s on the grounds that it was culturally biased and therefore discriminatory. At the time of this writing, the federal government was using various other methods to develop and attract new professionals.

A number of states have also developed formal processes to recruit management professionals. There has been more flexibility in the development of testing procedures on the state level than on the federal level in recent years. Michigan, for example, requires candidates for selected civil service managerial positions to complete a series of in-basket exercises that measure ability in decision making, analyzing problems, communicating, delegating, managing conflict, and conducting meetings. Some state agencies in Pennsylvania do this, too. In addition, along with certain agencies in North Carolina and other states, Pennsylvania assesses management skills in as many as fourteen areas through a structured series of test exercises and activities.

In the category of professional development, the federal government emphasizes the identification of promising employees already in service and helps train them for management and, in some cases, for other professional jobs. Well over half the states do the same thing, according to a 1986 survey sponsored by the Council of State Governments, the National Governors Association, and the National Association of State Training and Development Directors. A substantial amount of this training, federal and state, is done in house. A significant portion of the federal government's education and training efforts are coordinated—and in some cases directly delivered—by the Office of Training and Development of the U.S. Office of Personnel Management. These efforts include executive development programs, interagency training programs, and courses and programs in such areas as financial management, information resources management, personnel management, and supervision and management. These programs are offered on site in Washington, D.C.; at the Federal Executive Institute at Charlottesville, Virginia; at executive seminar centers in Denver, New York, and Oak Ridge, Tennessee; and elsewhere. Certain states provide similar—but usually not so extensive—training opportunities for upper- and middle-level managers through the state civil service commission or the department of personnel administration. California, for instance, has developed an executive institute, operates executive seminars, and organizes interagency management training programs in planning and management, performance appraisal, budgeting, accounting, contract management, labor relations, program evaluation, and other areas. It also offers a career opportunities development program for economically disadvantaged persons.

Additional training may be carried out under contract with colleges and universities. A number of universities have created professional master's programs built around carefully organized curricula to serve the needs of key executives and other government managers. The federal government and some states send promising employees to these executive training programs designed to maximize career development.

Professional development programs may be as short as a day or two or as long as two years. The more carefully structured programs are organized to meet particular needs of selected agencies, job levels, or categories. More than 200,000 federal civil servants participated in one or more of the various federal training programs in the 1985 fiscal year.

In the category of recruitment, a number of programs have been designed to attract outstanding students to government positions. These programs have included cooperative education and internship assignments, which are being used more and more extensively for promising young people to "try out" for government service—federal, state, and local. The most important federal government management recruitment tool is the Presidential Management Internship program, under which some 200 of the most able young people completing master's degrees in public policy analysis or management enter the federal service at the GS-9 level each year after an extremely competitive selection process. Certain states have similar programs. The Pennsylvania management internship program, for example, selects up to twenty-five new graduates each year for a one-year training experience in state agencies.

The federal Presidential Management Internship program evaluates applicants on the basis of academic achievements; school recommendations; interpersonal and communications skills; assessment of problem-solving, planning, and decision-making abilities; perceived leadership capacity; and commitment to the public service. Each intern constructs an individual development plan and works with a mentor as well as supervisors in his or her agency to put this plan into effect. Typically, the intern rotates to different job assignments in the agency over a two-year period. The great majority of interns receive career appointments in the federal service at the GS-12 level after the internship. The program has been extremely successful since its creation in 1977, bringing over 2,000 well-trained, highly motivated, and qualified young professionals into the federal service since then.

State and local recruiting efforts often center in a department of personnel or are divided between hiring agencies and a central personnel office, with vacancies being announced regularly in a periodic bulletin. The great majority of the federal government's overall recruiting activity is carried out by individual agencies rather than centrally. Although this system permits agency supervisors to define and implement agency-specific job description and hiring rules, many prospective federal employees have substantial difficulty in identifying job vacancies and in qualifying for them.

As of 1988, a number of personnel specialists in the Office of Personnel Management (OPM), at the National Academy of Public Administration, and elsewhere were exploring ways of creating a comprehensive federal recruiting program. This program would enable OPM to better disseminate timely information to possible job applicants regarding current or forthcoming professional vacancies and would help agencies to find highly qualified applicants representative of the diversity of the American population. It was in this spirit that the Panel on Public Service of the National Academy of Public Administration issued a report in 1987 in which it urged OPM to coordinate the development of new competitive entry examinations for agencies to use for identifying prospective managers and other professionals. The panel further urged the OPM to stress that the government seeks and rewards excellence, that it selects and advances people on the basis of merit, and that it offers challenging and rewarding work in the public service. At bottom, most experts agree, the "bureaucrat bashing" that became so common in the 1970s and continued in the 1980s at the federal level must be reversed if the national government is to attract sufficient numbers of the nation's best young people to federal service.

For a variety of reasons, the U.S. civil service came under strong attack in the 1970s. It became fashionable to talk about "pointy-headed bureaucrats" on the banks of the Potomac (to use the words of former Alabama governor and presidential candidate George Wallace). Presidents Jimmy Carter and Ronald Reagan were so critical of the federal bureaucracy during their successful election campaigns that they were accused of running for office on the backs of the members of the civil service. Reagan's associate and confidant, Attorney General Edwin Meese, by comparison with many other Reagan cabinet members a friend of the bureaucracy, more than once told the story of the "bureaucratic doll," the doll "which would just sit there when placed at a desk."

Yes, it is true that some public servants do a poor job. Yes, members of the public get irritated and angry about actions or lack of action, or perhaps about perceived actions, by the bureaucracy. This anger is often justified. Consequently, there is political gain for political candidates in disparaging the work of the public service. But such comments are not in the national interest, especially when we look at the detrimental results for the morale of current civil servants and its implications for recruiting quality young people to the civil service.

As the Report of the Twentieth Century Fund Task Force on the Senior Executive Service declared in 1987, "At one time, many of the most gifted young people flocked to [federal] government jobs, which promised to reward them with important work." Observing that this situation no longer prevails, the authors of the Report went on to state: "For our best graduates, service in the federal government languishes near the bottom of the list. The Task Force believes that young people will willingly forgo the temptation of higher private sector salaries—in fact, will turn to government service in numbers—if they can be assured that they will be doing challenging work in an atmosphere that acknowledges their efforts. To this end, our political leaders must make every effort to reawaken the sense of pride in government that can alone tap the latent patriotism and enthusiasm of the young. They must support efforts . . . that expose outstanding individuals . . . to the satisfactions of public service" (pp. 9–10).

The National Academy Panel on Public Service emphasized the importance of recognizing and rewarding professionalism in government. Professional public administrators and other experts in government are most likely to maximize their contributions to public service if they are allowed, even encouraged, to apply their professional expertise in the context of their organization to the upholding of the public interest. This must be done in cooperation and conjunction with others in the agency and elsewhere in government, but the organizational constraint should work in a way that enhances and encourages professionalism and dedication and not in a way that inhibits it.

It was in this context that Congress, at the urging of the Carter administration, reorganized the higher levels of the federal civil service in 1978 to create the Senior Executive Service (SES).

In the late 1960s and through the 1970s presidents and a number of their major department heads and associates argued that the federal civil service had grown too autonomous; that it had gained too many protections in the area of job security, which led to a significant reluctance by bureaucrats to accept and follow instructions from political superiors. As new administrations came into office, they argued that career civil servants— particularly those in policy-making or semi-policy positions— were committed to the programs of the previous administration and therefore were resisting new policies. At the same time, a number of students of public administration as well as practicing public administrators concluded that the traditional civil service system did accentuate job security at the expense of the application of responsible judgment, which in effect emphasized a *lack* of professionalism. When President Carter appointed Alan K. Campbell, former dean of the Maxwell School of Citizenship and Public Affairs at Syracuse University, as the chair of the U.S. Civil Service Commission, Campbell (1978) took the lead in proposing a series of changes in the law to reverse this situation.

The Senior Executive Service was created as part of the Civil Service Reform Act of 1978. The SES is an elite cadre of federal executives, encompassing some 7,000 of those managers who have reached the top rungs of the federal career ladder. The SES was planned as a general civilian officer corps, staffed by highly trained and broadly experienced administrators who could be shifted from one assignment to another to provide political leaders with expert assistance as governmental needs dictate. SES members would receive higher pay, performance bonuses, better career opportunities, and enhanced recognition. In return, they would give up some of the traditional job guarantees of the civil service system and be held to higher standards of accountability and performance.

Unfortunately, this system was not implemented as planned. Congress and the administration imposed severe reductions on the promised merit bonuses and pay raises. The changes included a decrease in the percentage of employees eligible for bonuses from 50 percent to 20 percent even before the Carter administration left office. As a result, subsequent salary increases in the SES lagged far behind promises. In addition, the federal government has struggled in its efforts to create a fair and widely acceptable system of performance evaluation on which to base judgments about employee merit. Perhaps just as important, the promise of career mobility has proven illusory. And finally, efforts to improve the public standing of federal careerists have been relatively weak and fragmentary.

Thus, while the concept of the Senior Executive Service was aimed at improving professionalism in the federal career service, the system was implemented in a way that did not encourage or even permit maximum utilization by the government of the expertise of our most competent and experienced federal public servants. This fact contributed to a significant exodus from the SES, with more than 40 percent of its members leaving government between 1979 and 1983. Efforts by OPM, the National Academy, and other organizations to more fully implement the original Senior Executive Service idea are worthy of applause and support. This action would constitute a key step in strengthening the development of a management career concept in the federal government.

The Central Role of Education and Training

Conscious efforts to strengthen linkages between practitioners of public administration and university scholars specializing in the field of public administration will be of substantial benefit to both groups and to the institutions they represent. The value of academic ideas about public management is confirmed only when the ideas test out in practice. Academics who develop public management concepts or constructs and refine them in the laboratory of practice are engaged in the construction and expansion of the basic corpus of public administration knowledge and understanding. The practitioner is essential to the testing of these ideas. At the same time, the practitioner must depend on the academic to build a knowledge base that goes beyond personal or agency-related experience in the resolution of public problems. An expansion of university management education programs for in-service civil servants, as well as for preservice students, will help broaden the network of interrelationships between theory and practice in a way that is bound to benefit both academics and practitioners. In addition, the recruitment of promising professionals to government will certainly be enhanced by the construction of stronger working relationships with the educational institutions that train them.

Mosher (1982) points out that a number of European nations have traditionally had an approach to the professionalization of the civil service that involves a conscious linkage with higher education. Developed first in Austria and Germany, this system rests on the proposition that certain knowledge and skills are requisite for public officials and it is appropriate for colleges and universities to provide these skills. Post–World War II reforms moved France into the forefront of countries utilizing this approach. The Ecole Nationale d'Administration, with a curriculum that includes a strong emphasis on administration and management, became the sole recruiting and selecting agency for all higher civil servants other than technicians.

Mosher strongly advocates an increased reliance on higher education to improve competence and performance in the American civil service. He writes:

> The higher officials in the public service are products of the colleges and universities, and principally their professional departments and schools. This

will be increasingly, even mayhap exclusively, true in the future. These persons will have a growing influence in the determination of public policy. Ultimately the possibilities of a truly democratic public service will depend upon (1) the mobility whereby intelligent individuals from all walks of life may progress to higher education and (2) the kind of orientation and education they receive in the universities. . . .

Truly meritorious performance in public administration will depend . . . [in part] upon the values, the objectives, and the moral standards which the administrator brings to his decisions, and upon his ability to weigh the relevant premises judiciously in his approach to the problems at hand. His code can hardly be as simple as the Ten Commandments, the Boy Scout Code, or the code of ethics of any of the professions; his decisions usually will require some kind of interpretation of public and public interest—explicit, implicit, even unconscious.

Such decisions are difficult, complex, and soul-testing, for the qualities they demand search the depths of both mind and spirit. As Bailey (1965, p. 285) wrote, "Virtue without understanding can be quite as disastrous as understanding without virtue." Understanding entails a degree of knowledge, a sense of relationships among phenomena, an appreciation of both social and private values. Most of the ingredients of understanding can be learned and many of them can be taught. . . . Understanding in this sense must become a major ingredient of public service merit in the future. This will require a degree of modesty and even humility on the part of individual professionals (and professors) about their fields; a curiosity about, and accommodation toward, other fields of study and vocation; a sense of the society and the polity, and of

the relationships between them and the field of occupational concentration.

Governmental agencies have for the most
part . . . minimized the broader understanding discussed in the preceding paragraph as an element
in appointment or advancement. . . .

As in our culture in the past and in a good
many other civilizations, the nature and quality of
the public service depend principally upon the system of education. Almost all of our future public
administrators will be college graduates, and within
two or three decades a majority of them will have
graduate degrees. Rising proportions of public administrators are returning to graduate schools for
refresher courses, mid-career training, and higher
degrees. These trends suggest that University facul-
ties will have growing responsibility for preparing and for developing public servants both in
their technical specialties and in the broader social
fields with which their professions interact'' [pp.
217-219].

I have found no other statement that makes the essential
point better. The nurturing of a public administration professional ethic is likely to contribute significantly to a proper understanding of the role, responsibilities, and limits of government and
the consequent role of the civil servant in advancing the public
enterprise. College and university faculty in public administration—*professionals* in their own right—have a special obligation
to assist their students to develop their own understandings of
the calculus involved in the reconciliation of professional and
hierarchical and organizational obligations and responsibilities
in the public interest. At the same time, *professional* managers
and supervisors in government have a requirement to understand this same calculus and to work with the *professional* experts in their organizations (and, if necessary, outside the organization), to advance the general interest. Emphasis on the

development and recruitment of thoughtful professionals, who are aided by their education to deal with problems and issues in the context of conflicting pressures and ramifications, imbued with the specialized knowledge of their field and dedicated to the public good, will substantially strengthen the quality of the public service. Improved career-entry procedures, more self-conscious education (including preservice education, as well as special seminars for managers and professionals already in service), and a reemphasis on the meaning and implications of public service, integrity, ethics, and civic duty will maximize the possibilities of attracting a larger number of competent professionals to government and of utilizing their professional expertise in the broader context of government's diverse and conflicting needs and requirements.

References

Abrahamson, M. (ed.). *The Professional in the Organization.* Chicago: Rand McNally, 1967.

American Society for Public Administration. *Code of Ethics and Implementation Guidelines.* Washington, D.C.: American Society for Public Administration, 1985.

Bailey, S. K. "Ethics and the Public Service." In R. C. Martin (ed.), *Public Administration and Democracy.* Syracuse, N.Y.: Syracuse University Press, 1965.

Campbell, A. K. "Civil Service Reform: A New Commitment." *Public Administration Review,* 1978, *38* (2), 99–104.

Council of State Governments, National Governors Association, and National Association of State Training and Development Directors. *Achieving Management Excellence in State Government.* Lexington, Ky.: Council of State Governments, 1986.

Gaus, J. M., White, L. D., and Dimock, M. E. (eds.). *The Frontiers of Public Administration.* Chicago: University of Chicago Press, 1936.

Goode, W. J. "The Theoretical Limit of Professionalism." In A. Etzioni (ed.), *The Semi-Professions and Their Organization.* New York: Free Press, 1969.

Heller, W. W. *New Dimensions of Political Economy.* Cambridge, Mass.: Harvard University Press, 1966.

Hughes, E. C. *Men and Their Work.* New York: Free Press, 1958.

International City Management Association. *Code of Ethics.* Washington, D.C.: International City Management Association, 1976. (Originally published 1924.)

Lambright, W. H., and Teich, A. H. "Scientists and Government: A Case of Professional Ambivalence." *Public Administration Review,* 1978, *38* (2), 133–139.

Levine, C. H. "The Federal Government in the Year 2000: Administrative Legacies of the Reagan Years." *Public Administration Review,* 1986, *46* (3), 195–206.

Lewis, G. B. "How Much Is an MPA Worth?: Public Administration Education and Federal Career Success." *International Journal of Public Administration,* 1987, *9,* 397–415.

Mosher, F. C. *Democracy and the Public Service.* (2nd ed.) New York: Oxford University Press, 1982.

National Academy of Public Administration Panel on Public Service. "A Statement Concerning Professional Career Entry into the Federal Service." Washington, D.C.: National Academy of Public Administration, 1987. (Mimeographed.)

National Association of Schools of Public Affairs and Administration. "Standards for Professional Master's Degree Programs in Public Affairs and Administration." Washington, D.C.: National Association of Schools of Public Affairs and Administration, 1981. (Mimeographed.)

Neustadt, R. E., and Fineberg, H. E. *The Swine Flu Affair.* Washington, D.C.: U.S. Government Printing Office, 1978.

Odegard, P. H. "Toward a Responsible Bureaucracy." *Annals of the American Academy of Political and Social Science,* March 1954, *292,* 18–29.

Rainey, H. G., and Backoff, R. W. "Professionals in Public Organizations: Organizational Environments and Incentives." *American Review of Public Administration,* 1982, *16,* 319–336.

Rosen, B. *Holding Government Bureaucracies Accountable.* New York: Praeger, 1982.

Staats, E. B. "Public Service and the Public Interest." *Public Administration Review,* 1988, *48* (2), 601–605.

Twentieth Century Fund Task Force on the Senior Executive Service. *The Government's Managers.* New York: Priority Press Publications, 1987.

U.S. Congress. *Code of Ethics for Government Service.* Concurrent Resolution. 85th Congress, 2nd session, July 11, 1958.

Weber, M. *From Max Weber: Essays in Sociology.* (H. H. Gerth and C. W. Mills, eds.) New York: Oxford University Press, 1946.

4

口口口口口口口口口口口口口口口口口口口口口口口口口口口

Dealing with Ethical Issues and Value Conflicts

Ralph Clark Chandler

For thousands of years bureaucratic man has adapted human values to the organizational requirements of technocratic society. The values, organizations, and technologies have changed, but humankind generally has been able to perceive not only meaning and purpose in social institutions but personal fulfillment as well.

The question is now open as to whether this adaptation process has stalled. Internal goods fall victim to the monolithic technical world frequently enough in the closing years of the twentieth century so that modern men and women are rather out of practice in defining what they are. Moral discourse is reserved for the presumed elite, because the atmosphere in which public administrators manage their programs assumes that the organizational good is the new internal good for anyone who manages with care. The organizational man or woman in fact has no internal good except as it is translated into organizational prosperity. Such a manager is unaware of transgressions against the art of public administration, for example, because he or she does not know that quantitative analysis does not necessarily involve enough moral choice to qualify for virtuous behavior in Aristotle's system of thought.

Aristotle who? A 1987 survey of the nation's seventeen-year-olds by the National Endowment for the Humanities

(NEH) revealed that over two-thirds of them identified Socrates as an American Indian chief and the Great Gatsby as a magician. The same two-thirds did not know what the Magna Carta or the Reformation was, or who Dante, Dostoevsky, Hawthorne, and Melville were. Yet they knew a lot about computers and the processing of information. They just did not have much information to process (Cheney, 1987). When I discussed the NEH report with a friend who is a successful program manager in the Michigan Department of Natural Resources, he asked curiously, "Now just what is the Magna Carta?"

Is there a body of knowledge that one must possess to be a moral man or woman and act competently and ethically at the workplace? Is there a way of thinking that equips the public administrator, for example, to deal with the moral ambiguities and uncertainties that accompany discretionary choice? Should there be a code of ethics to guide those who manage public services? These are the kinds of questions that have precipitated the current debate about professionalism.

Professionalism

Professional ethics for public managers has been connected traditionally to classical ideas about civic virtue and transcendent moral reason. Greek and Roman political theorists, many of whom were practicing public administrators, were concerned with cultivating practical prudence, providing moral education *(paideia),* and forming good character. The highest form of practical knowledge for them was political and moral knowledge. In such a tradition one does not speak of "implementing ethics." Ethics reflects a disposition. It is well-ingrained practice, a pattern of conduct, and a state of conscience. It is not a technique or an instrumental tool.

But instrumentally defined rationales of modernization and bureaucratization have loosened professional ethics from these traditional moorings. Although the recent writings of Jurgen Habermas (1979) and Alasdair MacIntyre (1984) have tried to draw political authority and law back into their former context of virtuous public service, the force of the ideas of the

Progressive Era have kept their writings at arm's length in the minds of most contemporary practitioners.

The self-conscious public administration that emerged in the United States in the late nineteenth century was full of faith in organization, technology, and science, especially the science of management. Urban-minded and collectivist, competitive and voluntaristic, it looked to the development of techniques of public management, indicative planning, and a reliable, positivistic social science. Ironically, the Progressive reforms did not enhance the control and participation of the citizenry, however. Instead, they enhanced the image and power of an emerging new class of technically oriented administrators who saw themselves as state managers giving effect to the tenets of positive science. With this trend came also a scientization of politics, the characteristics of which were:

1. An increasing tendency to divorce legality and administration from concepts of moral obligation
2. A means-end orientation toward efficient implementation of policy
3. A focus on instrumental leadership skills and the science of decision making in order to cut through the routinizing and ritualizing practices of bureaucracies and the consequences of these practices for a disaffected public

Thus, the classical understanding of the practical was subsumed under the requirements of the technical. The practical problem of how to live virtuously in the *polis* was transformed into the technical problem of regulating social interaction and enforcing compliance with an organizationally referenced and defined public good.

Yet morality is about principled conduct, not automated efficiency. It involves choices of action based on communally held values about what is right and wrong. It endures where it is able to test, justify, and redeem the claims of its legitimating principles in rational discourse. It cannot exist apart from a communal consensus about what we are commonly obliged to do or refrain from doing. The ethical activity of a public administrator has a *habitus,* a culturally situated internalized reality that holds under continuing review who we are, who we have been, who we will be, and who we could be. The moral career of each of us is a logbook about how we have dealt with value conflicts and how we have resolved the question of how much of our personal center of value we will give up to the external world. When we have given up all of it and no longer have a personal center of value, we have been dehumanized.

The critical question for the public manager is not *whether* he or she shares a mutuality of norms *(Sittlichkeit)* with anyone else, but *who* that anyone else is. The idealized role of the civil servant is not merely a reflection of the functional needs of a complex and differentiated society. It also represents a critique of the claims of civil society to complete power. Our speech acts anticipate shared moral identity because they reach out for positive consensus in the *telos* of human understanding (Habermas, 1979). It is in speakingness that one's moral identity emerges as both commitment and obligation. Ethics is the commitment and obligation fulfilled.

There are many improvisations in ethical behavior. It cannot be a preformed code of conduct, and it is not based in a stock of knowledge. It is not a technique or a tool. It is not instrumental. It is the voice of reason *(ratio)* rather than the sanction of force *(voluntas)*. Ultimately, all models of morality are communicative. We know what is moral in dialogue with each other. Insofar as these models are displaced by functional organizations whose managerial logic reflects only the whims of the market or the authority of the state, they cannot command the affective loyalty of the individual moral actor or the public. A proceduralist approach to ethics and public administration might suit the functionalist-oriented budget director and the systems theorist concerned with steering the organization, but it will not engage adherents of democracy about what we value as a community. We must talk about these values or give up our freedom to do so.

The historical role of professionalism is to seal a social bargain between the members of a profession and the society in which the members of the profession work. In return for

special prerogatives and privileges ranging from the granting
of social status to restrictions on entry and competition, not to
mention direct monetary returns, the profession agrees to a certain measure of self-policing. This bargain is made entirely
within the existing structures of society, it supports those structures, and it makes them more effective.

In negotiating a social contract that gives them delegated
public authority, American public administrationists attempt
to carry on the style of the medieval guilds. This is especially
true for such professions as city manager, civil engineer, and
certified public accountant, which have strong and enforceable
codes of ethics. The American Society for Public Administration has been reaching for guild status since it adopted a code
of ethics in 1984. It remains to be seen whether such a large
and diverse organization can indeed police its members, or
whether it ought to do so, but there is no doubt that many
specialized public service occupations have succeeded in establishing exclusive associations.

The guilds are responsible for honor and ethics among
their members, and they have the authority to chastise, discipline, and punish wayward brethren. Furthermore, professional
associations provide guidelines for enforcing an agreed-upon image and specified character traits within a division of labor.
Cynics argue that professional codes of ethics are not true guidelines for behavior at all but are really public relations devices
adopted to protect classes of people intelligent enough to know
how to use them.

There are many ways to understand professionalism. It
is an ideology, a justification system, and a set of principles by
which a group rationalizes or accounts for its conduct. Professionalism can also be seen as a symbolic smokescreen through
which a new class of public managers bids for prestige and status,
installing itself as the paradigm of virtuous and dedicated concern for the society at large (Gouldner, 1979).

French sociologist Emile Durkheim saw the professions
and the standards and practices they engender as the source of
modern morality. They provide the ethics and rules needed both
to regulate a complex social system and to rescue humanity from
a normlessness rooted in an economy controlled by the runaway

locomotive of capitalist determinism. The professions provide a shared identity, common values, unequivocal role definitions, reasonably clear limits, and cognitive unification.

Professional codes of ethics are geared toward the spelling out of specific injunctions for behavior. They point to an ethics of character rather than an ethics of action even if they are couched in actional language such as "do this" and "avoid that." Their meaning emerges only when we look beyond their prescriptions to a comprehension of the overall picture of the type of person who is to embody their actional language.

Professional codes indicate something of the kinds of ethical dilemmas that professionals encounter or expect to encounter, the loyalties they are expected to have, the tasks they must perform, and the nature of the conflicts they experience among role expectations. Understood this way, codes of ethics are not codes for action but guideposts to understand where stresses and tensions have been felt within the profession and what image is properly held up to assist professionals through these stressful periods. Professional codes are geared primarily toward establishing expectations of character. They incorporate an image of the person the professional is supposed to be (see Chapter Three).

Dealing with Personal Value Conflicts

The 1980s provide three illustrative artifacts of the communicative ethics model I've been discussing. Together they provide a state-of-the-art description of how public administrators might deal with personal value conflicts within the current definitions of professionalism. These artifacts are:

1. A workbook and study guide published by the Professional Standards and Ethics Committee of the American Society for Public Administration titled *Applying Professional Standards and Ethics in the Eighties* (Mertins and Hennigan, 1982)
2. The Code of Ethics of the American Society for Public Administration (ASPA) and its Implementation Guidelines
3. Workshop materials on ethical dilemmas developed by teachers and practitioners

The workbook and study guide postulates that administrators in the public sector are confronted with two competing imperatives: satisfying their individual standards of professional performance and ethics on the one hand, and adhering to the standards imposed on them by their agencies and public policies on the other. Meeting these dual expectations requires a reconciliation process that often makes the abdication of individual responsibility a safe haven. Yet the real world of public administration admits few safe havens, especially since administrative decisions frequently revolve around making interpretations of the law, tiptoeing on the margins of the law, and taking personnel and budgetary actions too complex to be guided by rules of thumb.

Given the limitations of rules, the workbook suggests that the most effective way to address personal value conflicts is through self-evaluation (Mertins and Hennigan, 1982). That process is developed from two perspectives: consideration of the ethical dimensions of individual behavior, and examination of the ethical issues inherent in the administration of particular public policies. The topic areas covered in the workbook, in the order of their presentation, are:

Relationship to law
Responsibility and accountability
Commitment
Responsiveness
Professional development and achievement of potential
Citizenship and the political process
Conflicts of interest
Whistleblowing
Public disclosure and confidentiality
Professional ethics

For each of these topic areas, the book provides a background discussion as well as a list of self-diagnostic questions for personal reflection and group discussion. The diagnostic questions for the chapter on whistleblowing, for example, are

1.   Do I know about violations of law, abuse of funds, or gross mismanagement in my organization?

2. What routes are open to me to express my concerns about such problems?
3. What is the most appropriate way to express my views on such issues? In writing or verbally? And to whom?
4. How far am I willing to go in calling attention to violations or abuses? In the extreme, am I willing to risk my position and future?
5. Under what circumstances would I consider ''going public'' outside the organization?
6. How effective are the mechanisms protecting whistleblowers in my organization?
7. Under what conditions do I view whistleblowing as a legitimate activity?
8. Are there situations in which whistleblowing would do more harm than good?

Following the chapters are a list of related case materials from the Inter-University Case Program (ICP) and Harvard Business School (HBS) Case Services, and a bibliography of texts and casebooks where other case studies can be found. This little workbook, only forty pages long, has significantly influenced a generation of public administrators since the first edition was published in 1977.

Another artifact of the ethics discussion of the 1980s is the Code of Ethics and Implementation Guidelines of the American Society for Public Administration. The code was approved by the National Council of ASPA on April 8, 1984, after years of wrangling about whether such a dispersed organization as ASPA should have a code at all, and then about what the wording should be.

The tenets of the code are important in themselves, but equally important for the professional dealing with personal value conflicts are the code's guidelines. Here is the code in its entirety, followed by the first paragraph of the guidelines for tenet one, presented as an example of all the guidelines:

The American Society for Public Administration (ASPA) exists to advance the science, processes, and art of public administration. ASPA encourages professionalism and improved quality of service at all levels of government, education, and the not-for-profit private sector. ASPA contributes to the analysis, understanding, and resolution of public issues by providing programs, services, policy studies, conferences, and publications. ASPA members share with their neighbors all of the responsibilities and rights of citizenship in a democratic society. However, the mission and goals of ASPA call every member to additional dedication and commitment. Certain principles and moral standards must guide the conduct of ASPA members not only in preventing wrong, but in pursuing right through the timely and energetic execution of their responsibilities.

To this end, we, the members of the Society, recognizing the critical role of conscience in choosing among courses of action and taking into account the moral ambiguities of life, commit ourselves to:

1. demonstrate the highest standards of personal integrity, truthfulness, honesty, and fortitude in all our public activities in order to inspire public confidence and trust in public institutions;
2. serve in such a way that we do not realize undue personal gain from the performance of our official duties;
3. avoid any interest or activity which is in conflict with the conduct of our official duties;
4. support, implement, and promote merit employment and programs of affirmative action to assure equal opportunity by our recruitment, selection, and advancement of qualified persons from all elements of society;
5. eliminate all forms of illegal discrimination, fraud, and mismanagement of public funds, and support colleagues if they are in difficulty because of responsible efforts to correct such discrimination, fraud, mismanagement, or abuse;

6. serve the public with respect, concern, courtesy, and responsiveness, recognizing that service to the public is beyond service to oneself;

7. strive for personal professional excellence and encourage the professional development of our associates and those seeking to enter the field of public administration;

8. approach our organization and operational duties with a positive attitude and constructively support open communication, creativity, dedication, and compassion;

9. respect and protect the privileged information to which we have access in the course of discharging our official duties;

10. exercise whatever discretionary authority we have under law to promote the public interest;

11. accept as a personal duty the responsibility to keep up to date on emerging issues and to administer the public's business with professional competence, fairness, impartiality, efficiency, and effectiveness; and

12. respect, support, study, and, when necessary, work to improve federal and state constitutions and the laws which define the relationships among public agencies, employees, clients, and all citizens. [See Chapter Three for a commentary on and a discussion of the ASPA Code of Ethics.]

Then the first paragraph of the guidelines for tenet one reads:

Perceptions of others are critical to the reputation of an individual or a public agency. Nothing is more important to public administrators than the public's opinion about their honesty, truthfulness, and personal integrity. It overshadows competence as the premier value sought by citizens in their public officials and employees. Any individual or collective compromise with respect to these character traits can damage the ability of an agency to perform its tasks or accomplish its mission. The reputation of the administrator may be tarnished. Effectiveness may be impaired. A career or careers may be destroyed. The best insurance against loss of public confidence is adherence to the highest standards of honesty, truthfulness and fortitude.

Proceeding alongside the development of the workbook and the code of ethics was the third major artifact of the 1980s: large amounts of workshop materials invented by academics and practitioners alike to increase ethical awareness in the classroom and on the job.

My analysis of twenty sets of these materials reveals the following common characteristics:

1. Discussions of the ethical complexities of public management performance when career managers are bombarded daily by wide-ranging and often conflicting signals for appropriate behavior.
2. Descriptions of frequently employed coping mechanisms such as humorous discussion of unethical conduct and indirect personal attacks and rumor milling, which in turn produce undesirable organizational norms.
3. Efforts to expand the range of personally credible options for action.
4. Presession evaluations asking such questions as:
   a. Have you ever experienced a conflict between your personal conception of ethical behavior and what your organization or your superior expects of you?
   b. What personal ethical conflict or situation would you most like to work on or get some answers to during this workshop?
5. Invitations to make lists of such things as:
   a. Specific ways in which public managers behave unethically.
   b. Things you do in your professional life about which you feel guilty or uncomfortable.

    c.   What you believe could be done in public organizations to achieve a higher level of ethical performance.

6.   Ethical dilemmas questionnaires asking for responses to such situations as:

    a.   The police officer is justified in carrying out the chief's order to release without arrest the mayor's drunk-driving daughter.

    b.   A manager acts appropriately in writing a selectively worded but positive recommendation in order to transfer a troublesome employee to another department.

    c.   It is appropriate for an examiner to rate a minority candidate higher than otherwise justified in order to compensate for another examiner's bias against that minority person.

7.   Analyses of personal cases such as those presented in Joseph Fletcher's *Situation Ethics: The New Morality* (1966), with two columns available for written comment: one for listing as many alternative actions as the workshop participant can think of, the other for listing the possible consequence of each alternative.

    The dialogue precipitated by such workshop materials advanced the relevance and popularity of the ethics discussion in the 1980s, although it did not necessarily deepen it in terms of the intellectual foundations of moral choice. Toward the end of the decade a vanguard of administrative theorists was still searching for explanatory idioms to translate ancient categories of moral obligation and bridge the gap between ethical theory and practice.

Trustee Versus Social Partner

    There are two competing views about how the modern public administrator should view himself or herself as an ethical actor. One point of view describes the professional civil servant as a trustee and a representative citizen who has the task of renewing communal values and taking the lead in making public institutions more reflective of the ideals of justice and equity. Civil servants are fiduciaries, citizens in lieu of the rest of us.

They partake in the reserve functions of the state. They embody the ultimate values that bind conflicting and contending groups, and they secure the common ground where groups representing the public can communicate and where particularistic interests can be mediated by a higher public interest. The management of scarcity forces the civil servant more and more to play the role of entrepreneur and broker.

The trusteeship position maintains a strong democratic-elitist bias. Public administrators are carriers of the creed. They retain a broad slope of moral discretion. They are not bound by the narrow legalist rationale of administrative action or the positivist model of the public administrator as technician. They are not limited by the due process egalitarianism of pluralism because they do more than promote adjustments among the conflicting particularistic interactions of civil society. They act as guardians.

The ultimate values that a trustee serves are based on different levels of professional obligation. They include:

1. *Allegiance*—confidentiality, avoidance of conflict of interest, and shunning personal involvement with clients, contractors, and interest group representatives
2. *Autonomy*—giving sound and independent advice, regardless of offense given or taken
3. *Knowledge and competence*—a command of a specialized body of knowledge and mastery of a set of utilizable techniques in a defined jurisdiction
4. *Guild loyalty*—conducting oneself with integrity, honor, and fidelity with reference to one's fellow professionals and to the corporate body of the guild

The trustee also has a responsibility to the social science in which he or she may be trained and to which he or she must add additional professional knowledge. But in the face of admitted nondiscretionary statutory responsibility, the trustee must also from time to time charismatically cut through the red tape and delay of bureaucracy, as well as do battle with legislative and interest group politics.

What motivates the trustee is public obligation. His or her obligation goes beyond disciplinary codes of ethics, administrative procedures, and legal stipulations. There is in this creature of the moral imperative a sense of calling to public service and an awareness of a collective sensitivity to the public interest. This calling and awareness is often translated into a commitment to ultimate moral values such as patriotism and dissent. The trustee is a Roman Republican and a Puritan combined into one. He or she has read not only Plato but Cicero and John Winthrop as well. The professional role of the trustee is anchored in a religious view of the social world.

The other view of administrative ethics, that of social partnership, is rooted in Hegel's vision of the civil servant as mediator. Hegel warned that the professional's concern with status prevents alliances between civil servants and citizens. Only such alliances can stand in the way of the modern state's ability to manufacture its own publics. Habermas follows Hegel's argumentation with his doctrine of communicative ethics.

The social partner charges the trustee with professional arrogance. The social partner says the thrust of the ideology of professionalism is to secularize the feudal notion of noblesse oblige. As early as 1952 Emmette Redford cautioned American public administrators about the dangers inherent in an uncritical admiration of the British and French administrative classes. He warned of the pride of those administrative classes, and he argued for the need of a publicly conditioned expertness.

Insofar as the trustee may unconsciously wish to emulate the British and French administrative classes, he or she must defend the charge of absolutism constantly hurled at these role models. The recent socialist and right-wing populist uprisings in both Britain (Benn and Thatcher) and France (Rocard and Chirac) reflect demands for a more publicly conditioned accord with community values and a greater reliance on the initiatives of civil authority.

The social partner follows Habermas in maintaining that the public was intended as a sort of overseer of the state apparata, and its institutionalization coincided with such claims as the right to representation and freedom of speech and assembly. The public sphere based its legitimacy on the justice of the claims constituting it. These were claims for (1) consensus formation, that is, rational self-enlightenment on issues concerning collective interests, and (2) the unbiased opportunity for all classes to utilize the state's services and benefit from its regulatory interventions.

Mary Parker Follett (1940) once described a communications model of ethics and public administration as seeking power *with* the citizenry rather than power *over* the citizenry. In this way, she reasoned, the profession of public administration can mediate the nonreflective and particularistic interests of the civil society, increase the ability of citizens to comprehend the total picture, and encourage them to act unselfishly in the making of public policy.

Today public managers recognize that the outcomes of administrative action are in many ways not the outcomes of the authoritative implementation of preestablished norms of prestructured programs but rather the result of the coproduction of public managers and affected social groups. Public administrators are increasingly dependent on securing a willingness to cooperate from those who must be their social partners. Rather than act as either autonomous agents of the state or pluralist-oriented brokers of competitive interests, public managers are forced to act as consensus builders. In so doing they endeavor to minimize conflict among the competing interest groups whose assistance public managers must rely on in assessing capital growth and development. Indeed, the theme of growth management looms larger and larger on the agenda of modern public administration. Of critical concern, therefore, is the fostering of a culture of reciprocity, obligation, and responsibility.

The ethics of social partnership in the United States today is focused in the coproduction movement, in which public administrators share responsibility for service delivery with citizen groups. Civil servants, as Hegel said they should be, are mediators tailoring service delivery to particular community needs. It is the job of professionals to train citizen coproducers to be partners rather than clients or supplicants. Out of this partnership evolves shared commitments and bonds of communication and association that first undermine and then transcend the moral limitations of administrative organizations served only for their own sake. The truly moral public administrator is a mediating social partner.

These are the contending points of view in the ethics debate of the late 1980s. We may expect that a larger social ethics will emerge from this dialogue. Ideally, a synthesis will be built to include the character prescriptions of professionalism, the public calling that the office of the civil servant represents, and the more enveloping normative thought within which the public administrator's personal identity will continue to be defined.

Conclusion

The interfaces of the practical and the theoretical are constantly being reevaluated in modern public administration. What does talk about trusteeship and social partnership have to do with the real world of program managers?

All parties agree about the tendency of hierarchical organizations to demand absolute loyalty to the purposes of the organization and the fact that such loyalty often displaces other values. Is it possible for individuals to realize a moral identity grounded well enough in respectable thought that functional alternatives to blind and dehumanizing obedience can be developed?

Somehow it helps to know that this is an old problem. What contemporary theorists are trying to do much of the time is translate old solutions for modern applications. Alasdair MacIntyre (1984), for example, tries to deliver public administration from the suffocating professionalism discussion by developing the concept of *practice* and the virtues attendant on practice. MacIntyre says that professionalism does indeed connote images of elitism and self-protection that in turn engender notions of paternalism, which are inappropriate to a democratic society. The idea of practice, on the other hand, is a larger framework suggesting that the work of the public administrator needs to be understood in terms that transcend employment in a particular public organization. Practices are forms of activity that possess the following characteristics (Cooper, 1987, p. 321):

1. They exhibit coherence and complexity.
2. They are socially established.
3. They are carried out through human cooperation.

4. They involve technical skills which are exercised within evolving traditions of value and principles.
5. They are organized to achieve certain standards of excellence.
6. Certain internal goods are produced in the pursuit of excellence.
7. Engaging in the activity increases human power to achieve the standards of excellence and internal goods.
8. Engaging in the activity systematically extends human conceptions of its internal goods.

In this understanding of human activity, the skillful throwing of a football is not a practice but the game of football is, and so is the game of chess. Bricklaying is not a practice, but architecture is. Planting turnips is not a practice, but farming is. The inquiries of physics, chemistry, and biology are all practices, as is the work of the historian and the painting of the artist. The making and sustaining of family life is a practice. Practices include many human activities other than professions. The persons who engage in these practices are engaged in ministries that involve traditions of thought and standards of excellence.

Organizations are only the setting for administrative practice. The practices of the administrator have norms of their own quite apart from what is defined external to him or her as the organizational good. These norms are the goods that are internal to the public administrator and that have to do with such concepts as the public interest, social justice, popular sovereignty, accountability, and efficiency.

The internal goods of public administration can be defined only by those who practice them and submit to collegially determined standards of excellence growing out of consensus about what constitutes virtue. Until and unless public administrators self-consciously explore the internal goods unique to their role in society, they will remain vulnerable to organizational definitions of what is good and be at the mercy of arbitrary organizational authority.

Is professionalism the preferred model, or trusteeship, or social partnership? The program manager may take his or her pick or choose elements of all three. The one thing certain is that the question of how we deal with personal value conflicts cannot be disconnected from the core of administrative practice and the sure knowledge that the personal and the public good are a seamless robe.

So what? Is there any practical relevance for such philosophic talk? The title of this volume implies that we manage public programs and services by integrating politics and administration. Every program manager in the real world knows that political leaders of both parties have tried very hard in recent years to reassert the dichotomy in which politics and administration are *separated,* not integrated. Public administrators have responded in various ways to the well-documented efforts to bring them to heel. One strategy has been to reestablish the old claims to technical competence, efficiency, and administrative rationality. Another has been to retreat into the time-honored techniques of organizational guerrilla warfare. A third alternative, the one recommended and explored here, is to advance the theoretical basis for the idea that civil servants are sworn to uphold the same Constitution as other officers of government and are in fact competent to define and meet public needs on their own authority. Such a position is an adequate defense against those who habitually denigrate the public service for political ends. In the end professionalism rooted in moral reasoning is the most practical management consideration of all.

References

American Society for Public Administration. *Code of Ethics and Implementation Guidelines.* Washington, D.C.: American Society for Public Administration, 1985.

Cheney, L. V. *American Memory: A Report on the Humanities in the Nation's Public Schools.* Washington, D.C.: U.S. Government Printing Office, Document Number 036-000-00050-3, 1987.

Cooper, T. L. "Hierarchy, Virtue, and the Practice of Public Administration: A Perspective for Normative Ethics." *Public Administration Review,* 1987, *47* (4), 320–328.

Fletcher, J. *Situation Ethics: The New Morality.* Philadelphia: Westminster Press, 1966.

Follett, M. P. *Dynamic Administration: The Collected Papers of Mary Parker Follett.* (H. C. Metcalf and L. Urwick, eds.) New York: Harper & Row, 1940.

Gouldner, A. W. *The Future of Intellectuals and the Rise of the New Class.* New York: Seabury, 1979.

Habermas, J. *Communication and the Evolution of Society.* Boston: Beacon Press, 1979.

MacIntyre, A. *After Virtue.* (2nd ed.) Notre Dame, Ind.: University of Notre Dame Press, 1984.

Mertins, H., Jr., and Hennigan, P. J. *Applying Professional Standards and Ethics in the Eighties: A Workbook and Study Guide for Public Administrators.* Washington, D.C.: American Society for Public Administration, 1982.

Redford, E. *Administration of National Economic Control.* New York: Macmillan, 1952.

5

⌐⌐⌐⌐⌐⌐⌐⌐⌐⌐⌐⌐⌐⌐⌐⌐⌐⌐⌐⌐⌐⌐⌐⌐⌐⌐

Qualities of Successful
Program Managers

N. Joseph Cayer

Public managers are expected to develop and maintain productive personnel and agencies. In attempting to live up to these
expectations, they are faced with demands from outside forces
such as political leaders, clientele, interest groups, and citizens.
Additionally, they have to contend with internal pressures from
their own superiors and subordinates. Successful managers must
have many varied skills, must be able to turn challenges into
positive strategies, and must integrate positive people management into development of their subordinates.

Managers in the public and private sectors have much
in common. For example, the techniques of managing and processes for maintaining records or evaluating performance may
be the same. Despite these similarities, public managers differ
from their private sector counterparts in several important ways.
Public managers are subject to more legal restrictions, and their
lines of authority are much less clear. Public managers answer
to many different authorities, including formal superiors, political executives, the public, and the legislature, among others.
While formal lines of authority to all these elements do not exist, public managers must be responsive to each of these participants in government.

Public managers operate in the public spotlight to a greater
extent than private sector managers. The media and public are

likely to be more concerned because public managers are doing the public's business. Similarly, ethical behavior is defined differently in the two sectors. Public managers who come from business are often surprised to learn that practices prevalent in the private sector are considered conflicts of interest or unethical in the public sector. Lavish entertainment of prospective clients is an accepted way of doing business and getting a contract in the private sector, whereas public managers who allow such courting by contractors find themselves in trouble.

Among measures of managerial success are the level of productivity and the quality of work performed. Contemporary evaluation requires a look at other factors as well, such as absenteeism and turnover rates. Another indicator of how good a manager is, is the organizational climate. Organizational climate refers to such things as how members of the agency feel about one another, about other agencies, and about management. The climate has an effect on how well work continues in the absence of managers or supervisors. It is also characterized by the number of grievances filed or number of disciplinary actions necessary. As these factors suggest, the successful manager has to work hard at managing.

Identifying Successful Managers

The skills required of a successful manager may be characterized as practical skills, people skills, political skills, and leadership skills. Each type of skill overlaps with other types, and they all interact to foster managerial success. Obviously, managers vary in how well developed any one of these skills is, but it is difficult to imagine anyone being successful without some level of each.

Practical Skills. Practical skills are those that relate to the specific tasks or actions required in organizing and accomplishing the work of the agency. They include such things as conducting successful meetings, making decisions, handling conflict, and establishing work flow. If managers are to carry out the work of the organization, they must develop these skills.

Michael Doyle and David Straus (1976) estimate that top-level managers spend more than half of their work time in meetings, while those lower in the organization spend slightly less. Although managers spend much of their work life in meetings, most have little or no training in conducting meetings. It is usually assumed that anyone can conduct a meeting, but it actually takes skill to do so.

What goes wrong with meetings is that much time is often wasted. Additionally, people often leave meetings with little sense of what action is to be taken or how issues are to be resolved. Good managers are able to steer the meeting in such a way as to accomplish intended goals. They establish a climate in which decision making is facilitated. To do so, it is necessary to know and communicate beforehand what the meeting is supposed to accomplish. Thus, for example, it must be understood by all involved that a meeting is going to provide a recommendation for action or that it is going to result in a decision about how to proceed. The difference between these two outcomes is extremely important. If the intent is to get a recommendation that the manager may or may not accept, those participating in the meeting should know. If they are under the impression that the meeting is to actually make the decision and the manager then acts contrary to the group, participants in the meeting are likely to be upset, and justifiably so. Thus, a major component of a successful meeting is a clear understanding of what is actually going to be accomplished.

Once people understand the purpose of the meeting, it takes skill to follow through and get the appropriate action taken. For most meetings, a well-planned agenda is a crucial part of the climate. The agenda ought to identify the issues and what type of outcome or action is expected. In that way, before leaving an agenda item, participants can determine whether the expected action has been taken. For example, an agenda item may be just for presenting information or it may be for deciding how to proceed on a particular project or how to spend a new budget allotment. Whether the indicated action is accomplished provides a test of the success of the meeting.

Perhaps the most difficult part of meetings is keeping people on target. Much irrelevant information is likely to be brought up, and people may want to discuss past history relative to the issue rather than what to do about it now. Some amount of undirected discussion is the cost of including everyone in the decision-making process. However, once the relevant information has been covered and the discussion becomes repetitive, the skilled manager can use techniques to move the discussion along to resolution of the issue.

The manager, or someone designated by the manager, can direct the discussion by simple techniques that summarize what has taken place and the options that are available. By recapitulating the discussion in terms of clarification of the problem, of who or what agency can act to address the problem, and of the alternatives available for dealing with it, the meeting leader can direct discussion to some desired action. An effective manager is able to conduct meetings without making participants feel manipulated or pressured. Each has an opportunity to participate, but discussion is steered toward the original objective or expectation.

The elements of a successful meeting can be summarized as follows:

Purpose of meeting:
  Recommendation
  Actual decision
Agenda identifies:
  Issues
  Action required
    Presentation of information
    Reaching a decision
Process:
  Targeting discussion
  Separating relevant from nonrelevant information
  Recapitulation
    Clarification of problem
    Who has responsibility or can address the problem
    Identification of alternatives
    Selection of appropriate action

Making decisions is another major activity of managers. As with conducting meetings, many managers are not skilled in decision making. The decision-making process requires identification of the problem and analysis of the situation. The next step is to examine the alternatives for resolving the problem. Alternatives should be evaluated in terms of costs and benefits. Costs and benefits reflect not only monetary factors but such things as likelihood of success, political reality, reaction of the public, and effect on working relationships with other agencies. Once the evaluation is completed, an alternative may be chosen and then implemented. These steps represent a simplified version of what is known as rational decision making (Pfiffner, 1960).

Although the steps in the decision-making process seem straightforward, there are many difficulties with them (Downs, 1967). The manager is usually faced with making a decision in a limited amount of time, thus making it impossible to get complete information. Even if complete information is available, managers would probably not be able to integrate all of it into the considerations. It is also impossible to predict the future; thus, calculations may be based on erroneous expectations. Managers also have to contend with sunk costs arising from what has already been done. It is difficult to abandon a project that has already utilized a lot of resources, for example.

Because managers are not able to overcome the obstacles to completely rational decision making, they are forced to make decisions on partial information and normally act according to the immediate needs to get something done. Herbert A. Simon (1976) refers to this type of decision making as "satisficing." Clearly, managers have to work within constraints, and the best managers attempt to consider as much information and as many alternatives as possible while still performing the activities of the organization in a timely and responsive fashion. Having a clear vision of the goals of the organization makes it easier to choose alternatives and proceed.

Effective managers also involve employees in decisions that affect them. Participation of employees in the decision-making process gives them a sense of ownership in the decision; thus, they are likely to have a strong commitment to seeing that the decision is implemented. Gaining that commitment is an important part of effective management. Not restricting participation to those who have an actual stake in the decision may result in costly effects, however, such as great inefficiency and much uninformed input. Too much participation can be just as dysfunctional as too little.

Conflict in organizations is pervasive and results from, among other things, poor communication, differing views and values, incompatible objectives, changes in the organization, and personality clashes. Whereas traditional management theory assumed that conflict was bad and should be eliminated, more contemporary approaches recognize that it is inevitable and can be constructive. The emphasis now appears to be on how to manage conflict in the interest of the organization.

Conflict can certainly be dysfunctional by dissipating energies that should be directed at accomplishing the work of the organization. Excessive conflict may also lead to subversion of the goals of the organization, create unnecessary tension, screen out or distort useful information, and lead to disintegration of the cohesion of the unit.

Complete suppression of conflict is impossible and not necessarily desirable. Some conflict is helpful to the agency to the extent that it allows differing perspectives and ideas to come forth. It may help to debunk false assumptions or challenge old ways of doing things. Conflict may also energize people to get involved in the activities of the organization.

The challenge for managers is to handle conflict (Brown, 1983). Poorly managed conflict may lead to major difficulties in getting the work of the organization done. The common temptation is to attempt to avoid conflict because most people do not deal with it easily. However, avoiding or ignoring conflict is likely to result in increasing conflict and more problems for the organization. By openly dealing with the conflict and focusing on the needs and concerns of all those involved, it is possible to resolve the issues and get employees to work together toward the common goals of the organization.

Dealing with conflict requires patience and sensitivity. Moving too quickly or too forcefully can lead to resistance by parties to the conflict. It is important to avoid personalizing the issue in working with those involved. By focusing on the work and what can be done to facilitate it, efforts at cooperation can develop. Flexibility in considering alternatives and approaches enhances the chance of resolving the issue.

Managers must also establish and maintain the flow of work in the organization. Developing and implementing the management skills associated with successful managers will lead to good work flow. Beyond these skills, it is necessary to develop procedures and reporting systems to ensure that necessary activities get done.

People Skills. People skills refer to those abilities of the manager to inspire confidence and trust in others so that they are willing to perform assigned tasks. Just telling or asking someone to do something usually is not the most effective way of getting it done. Subordinates must be willing to accept the direction of the manager first (Barnard, 1938; McGregor, 1960). To gain the cooperation of subordinates, the manager needs to develop a good working relationship with subordinates.

Each employee is unique; thus, the manager must be able to understand each as an individual. To do so requires the ability to listen, empathize, and develop interest in others. In essence, managers need to be counselors to some degree, although they cannot solve all problems of employees. Being understanding and considerate of subordinates' concerns, however, may lead to development of mutual trust. Empathetic listening goes a long way toward earning the confidence of employees. Trust and confidence in the leader are important to subordinates' acceptance of the leader as authoritative.

Skills in dealing with people also rely on ability to communicate. Good managers facilitate communication among individuals in the organization. Effective communication produces understanding among individuals and helps build the bond on which organizational activity depends.

Political Skills. Public managers must deal with internal as well as external political considerations. While the internal political factors are usually handled through good people skills, the external forces require a different set of skills. In particular, public managers must be concerned with survival of the agency and thus must work on maintaining support for their activities. At the same time, they need to keep the organization insulated from undue political pressure.

In dealing with political forces, the manager has to balance pressures from differing ideological perspectives, from legislative versus executive branch interests, from the media, from interest groups, and from the general public. To do so requires great diplomacy and the ability to engender trust and confidence among people. It is important for the manager to be able to evaluate situations and issues without appearing to be biased, except in support of the mission of the organization.

Managers can gain support through being forthright and forthcoming in dealing with the various interests. Providing complete and accurate information on issues is a good way for managers to earn the respect of all involved. Efforts to mislead or misinform are fraught with problems. Honest and open explanations are usually accepted by those involved, even if the information is not what they want to hear. If a manager has been found to mislead or misinform, he or she will find it difficult to ever establish the trust and confidence needed to work with those who feel deceived.

Leadership Skills. Debates concerning leadership in organizations have not resulted in any clear agreement on what constitutes leadership, whether leadership skills can be learned or are inborn, what style of leadership is best, or how to identify prospective leaders (Barnard, 1938; Follett, 1924; Selznick, 1957; Stogdill, 1974; Thompson, 1967). What has been learned is that leadership is a complex process and requires understanding of people and what motivates them.

Leadership relates to two major functions or roles in organizations: task roles and maintenance roles (Benne and Sheats, 1948). *Task roles* have to do with accomplishing the work of the organization through identification of goals and selection of methods for their accomplishment. Task roles also include the actual work activity of the organization. For example, the individual who focuses on adapting software to estimating costs of serving welfare clients is task oriented. *Maintenance roles* are human-centered activities, including the nurturing of workers, fostering of positive interpersonal relations, and resolving of conflict. The manager's maintenance role helps keep the organization together. All leaders combine some elements of the task and maintenance roles, but each individual tends to emphasize one over the other. Good leaders are able to balance the roles and emphasize which is best for the given situation.

Leaders in the organization are not always managers. People anywhere in the hierarchy may be leaders, but managers need to be able to lead if they are to be effective. As manager/leaders, they are the formal leaders and have responsibilities to direct the activities of the organization and to motivate their subordinates to perform those activities. Much of leadership is intangible; it depends on a convergence of values and on acceptance between the leader and the led (Barnard, 1938). What causes individuals to suspend their judgment in favor of accepting someone else's lead is difficult to determine. Clearly the cause is different for each individual. Many individuals who are not in positions of formal authority become informal leaders because others respect their judgment, expertise, or the like.

Traditional research focused on leader traits or characteristics, and efforts were made to develop a complete list of such traits. The main finding was that not all effective leaders had the same characteristics. Then research began to focus on the subordinates and their traits, with similar results. The situation or context of activity was also recognized as contributing to leadership. Debates in the literature have led to the conclusion that leadership is dependent both on the situation and on the traits and needs of leaders and subordinates alike. Thus, it is almost impossible to predict leadership success.

Leadership style, ranging from a highly directed to a highly nondirected approach, also affects organizational activity. Directed leadership is usually termed authoritarian, while nondirected leadership is usually referred to as laissez-faire. Between the two extremes is the democratic or participative style. Much research has been done on the effectiveness of each style, with the conclusion that the democratic style tends to be most effective over the long term. However, each situation may require a different approach; thus, there may be instances in which a more directed approach is called for (Dubin, 1959; Kaplan and Tausky, 1977). However, changes from one style to another may be disruptive and dysfunctional.

In contemporary society, participative (democratic) approaches to leadership seem to be gaining in acceptance. In the United States, societal values reinforce democratic approaches. Because the experience of people in their government and other social institutions is usually based on democratic participation, it is not surprising that they expect participation to be a part of the decision-making process at work. Thus, managers find it difficult to avoid some form of participation.

Additionally, the increasingly better educated workforce is not likely to be patient with managers who do not allow participation. Contemporary training of managers probably contributes to their comfort by allowing more participation by subordinates. The rise of collective bargaining in the public sector has also expanded the issues in which employees have had an opportunity to exert influence. Governmental policy has reinforced such approaches through rules and regulations affecting employee input into decisions.

Leadership is also dependent on such things as formal authority, the personal respect and trust with which subordinates hold managers, and the knowledge and expertise of the manager. Formal authority provides the basis for being able to lead a particular organization. However, if the manager does not hold the respect and trust of employees, they are not likely to be good followers. Managers who gain respect and trust communicate effectively with employees and act with integrity in dealing with the organization and its employees.

Effective managers should spend time getting to know their employees and should attempt to fit the work situation to the employee. By acting according to the situation and the individual, the manager is likely to gain the confidence of the employees. The successful leader understands that his or her approach must be flexible, so as to adjust to the needs of any given situation. The manager who demonstrates too much concern for the employee is likely to be much more successful as a leader than the one who shows too little concern.

Employees also tend to react positively to managers with a vision of what the organization can be. Thus, effective leaders tend to be those who can create a sense of commitment to a goal and to the future.

There is no one way to be a good leader. However, honing of people skills and demonstration of sincere concern for the welfare of employees will go a long way in creating the basis for effective leadership.

Dealing with Challenges

Challenges and conflicts arise unexpectedly from many situations. Some areas tend to be the source of difficulty more than others. For example, managers often run into difficulty regarding equal employment opportunity/affirmative action, employee organizations, and legal rights of employees. The problems may arise out of neglect of issues rather than any intent on the part of managers. Nonetheless, managers need to be aware of these potential problems and attempt to minimize their development.

Equal Employment Opportunity/Affirmative Action. Equal employment opportunity arose out of the 1964 Civil Rights Act, although the policy was not officially extended to the public sector until passage of the Equal Employment Opportunity Act of 1972 (actually an amendment to the original act). The 1972 amendment added state and local government employers to those covered by the act. The purpose of the act was to outlaw discrimination on the basis of sex, race, creed, or national origin. Other factors, such as disability and age, were added to the list of nondiscrimination items through later legislation and regulations.

Although most managers believe that they do not discriminate on the basis of these factors, practices may have discriminatory impact or an employee may believe that illegal discrimination is taking place. For example, promotion may be based strictly on seniority in the organization, resulting in only white males being in high-level management or supervisory positions. While the seniority rule seems nondiscriminatory on its face, it may have discriminatory impact because females and minorities have not been employed in the organization until relatively recently; thus, they have not developed seniority. It is possible that the rule could be in violation of equal employment opportunity policy and that the organization would be held liable for corrective action.

Affirmative action requires positive steps to overcome potentially discriminatory actions. Many organizations have affirmative action plans that spell out the process for encouraging minority and female representation in the workforce. Some have affirmative action plans imposed upon them after being found discriminatory in their personnel practices.

Basically, managers need to examine all their policies and procedures that could have discriminatory impact. Review of such policies with sensitivity to whether and how they might affect different groups is important. Although managers may not have authority over personnel policy, they can alert those who do have such authority. It is particularly important for managers to examine their own decisions and actions to ferret out those that are discriminatory. Careful consideration of such issues can help avoid problems. How are females and minorities distributed among positions, pay scales, and office functions? Are females accorded the same input into decision making as males? Is the same true for minorities and nonminorities? Answers to these questions help identify potential problem areas.

Sexual harassment has been held to be a form of discrimination in a 1986 U.S. Supreme Court decision (*Meritor Savings Bank* v. *Vinson*). The case affirmed the concept that employers can be held liable for work environments in which individuals feel sexually harassed. Sexual harassment can include off-color comments, personal questions and comments, or physical touching that leads to discomfort for individuals. Of course, the less subtle forms of harassment include sexual advances and requests for sexual favors. As a result of the Supreme Court case and other litigation, employers and managers have the responsibility to make it clear that these offensive forms of behavior are not acceptable.

Employee Organizations. Employee associations and unions also pose a challenge to managers. By the time employees get to organizing, managers have probably lost their effectiveness with them. Many times, however, employees organize because of factors beyond the control of the manager, such as legislative policy or new personnel rules. By standing up for the employees' interests in the first place, managers can avoid much of the difficulty associated with unionization and bargaining.

If, however, the organization engages in bargaining with its employees, the managers and supervisors have specific rules to follow. The most important thing for managers to remember is that they must know what is in the collective bargaining agreement and follow it closely. Otherwise, grievances will be filed, consuming much time and energy. Managers who recognize the proper place of the employee organization usually develop good working relationships and get along smoothly. Those who spend their time fighting the employee organization reap the rewards of continuing dysfunctional conflict.

Although most managers are not necessarily representatives at the negotiating table in the collective bargaining process, they are constantly involved in negotiating. Any situation in which people attempt to resolve a difference in perspective or position requires some form of negotiation. Negotiation skills that focus on mutual gain and benefit are usually more successful than those that focus on one side winning and the other losing.

Fisher and Ury (1981) suggest a method called *principled negotiation*. In their method, negotiation focuses on the merits of the issue rather than on haggling. Specifically, they suggest four points to successful negotiation:

1. Separate the people from the problem.
2. Focus on interests, not positions.
3. Generate a variety of possibilities before deciding what to do.
4. Insist that the result be based on some objective standard [p. 11].

Use of these suggestions facilitates compromise and decision making. It minimizes the tendency to harden one's attachment to a position. When positions are not solidified, people find compromise easier.

Increasing Legalization of Employer-Employee Relations. Public employees, like other groups, use litigation in the courts to secure and protect their rights. Managers, or their organizations, find themselves the subject of lawsuits at an ever increasing rate. The result is often disruption of the work of the organization and much lost time to prepare defenses.

While it is impossible to avoid all legal actions, it is certainly possible to minimize them. By understanding the rights of employees in such things as performance evaluations, discipline, termination, and other personnel actions, managers should be able to act in concert with them. Due process procedural rights are especially important to observe and easy to follow once understood. Managers who do not acquaint themselves with such issues often live to regret it. Even more important, however, is the development of a caring relationship with employees. If managers are perceived as caring, they are usually able to resolve problems before they get to the point of litigation. Employees who have caring managers with whom to work share their frustrations and do not allow problems to build up.

Human Resource Development and Management

It is a cliché but true that the productivity of the organization depends on the efforts of the employees. Human resource development and management should foster an environment in which employees feel a commitment and desire to contribute to the work of the organization. Successful managers pay close attention to their human resources. In addition to the traditional personnel management practices that every supervisor is expected to understand and practice, contemporary managers must pay attention to training and development of employees, performance measures and productivity improvement, counseling, and employee assistance efforts.

Training and Development. Training and development are ongoing activities of any organization. Traditionally, many public sector organizations did not pay much attention to training and development. However, during the 1970s, training and development became a major concern of public agencies (Hyde and Shafritz, 1979). Although personnel departments or other separate units were often created to provide the training and development function, the everyday training and development on the job frequently got lost in the process. With fiscal constraints and cutback management, training and development are often the first items to go; therefore, the role of operating managers is critical in assuring the best in human resources potential and contribution.

The terms *training* and *development* are often used interchangeably, but there is a difference between the two concepts. Whereas training is designed to improve or develop specific skills, development refers to broader, long-term organizational goals. Training has a specific goal that is usually relatively short term. Development refers to growth and improvement of members of the organization. In addition to dealing with individual employee growth, development also often includes creating or changing the atmosphere in the organization to facilitate greater cooperative effort.

The first responsibility of effective managers in training and development is in determining the need for them in the organization. To adapt to constantly changing conditions, it is necessary for the organization to be flexible. Once needs have been identified, the manager can develop the appropriate strategies for change. The organization that ignores changing needs and conditions risks becoming stagnant and unresponsive to the public it serves.

Determining training needs sets the stage for development of appropriate strategies for meeting them. Training and development needs are best met by programs developed through training or personnel offices. However, the operating manager is better able to deal with on-the-job training of people so they can learn exactly what needs to be done in the specific job. Additionally, orientation to the specific unit is best handled by the manager and employees of the unit. Orientation and on-the-job training are critical in how well employees become socialized to the working of the unit.

One effective strategy is developing appropriate patterns of work activities and interpersonal relationships. These factors will determine, to a great extent, how effective the employee will be in the organization. Effective managers train by leadership and by example so that employees have appropriate behavior reinforced by management.

Performance/Productivity Improvement. Employee performance depends on a combination of ability and motivation. Because the employee selection process should ensure that employees have the ability to do their jobs, it becomes the manager's responsibility to see that employees perform. Some students of motivation believe that it is possible for one person to motivate another (Barnard, 1938; Blau, 1963; Brown, 1962; Whyte and others, 1955). Others believe that motivation comes from within the person and that all management can do is provide the situation in which the individual can reach full potential (Ford, 1969; Herzberg, 1966). Regardless of one's views on motivation, managers must deal with it, and the successful manager must find ways to ensure the highest level of performance possible.

The manager needs to recognize that the employee's commitment to the goals of the organization is the basic element in motivation to help attain those goals. It is important to understand that each person may do the same thing for a different reason. Each employee is affected by past experiences, expectations, and feelings and values. Managers who attempt to understand each employee are likely to be able to develop strategies for getting the most out of each.

Motivation is often related to satisfying the needs of the individual. The hierarchy of human needs developed by Maslow (1954) has been viewed as helping to understand human motivation (Herzberg, 1966; McGregor, 1960). In Maslow's hierarchy, the needs in order from lowest to highest are physiological, safety, social, ego, and self-actualization. Each need has to be met at a minimum level before the next higher one becomes a motivating factor. Because individuals differ in their needs, the manager must try to determine the need level of each employee to find ways of motivating that individual. Obviously, managers do not have time to learn every detail about the life of each employee; nonetheless, it is possible to develop a general understanding of what is important to each individual and be sensitive to it.

Along with influencing performance, managers have to evaluate it. Performance evaluation is one of the most difficult tasks for managers because of the anxiety of both evaluator and evaluatee (Nalbandian, 1981). One of the basic elements of any evaluation process is a clear understanding of the performance standards that are to be met. If employees do not know what is expected of them, it is difficult to hold them accountable. Thus, it is incumbent upon managers to counsel with employees on what their jobs are and what performance standards will be used in evaluation.

The most effective evaluation system is a continuous one, in which employees receive constant feedback. Once-a-year feedback does nothing to improve performance or motivate employees to be productive. In fact, this approach is usually characterized by anxiety and defensiveness. If continual feedback is given, however, the annual evaluation report and counseling session usually go smoothly. Good managers also realize that positive feedback is usually much more effective than criticism and increases commitment of the employee to doing a good job. Much evaluation is informal, in the form of a compliment or a question about how some process might be improved.

Generally, a problem-solving approach to inadequate performance will be more effective than telling the employee how to improve. Problem solving allows employees to be part of the solution through suggestions of how the situation can be corrected. Using a problem-solving approach also focuses attention on the performance issue rather than on personal failings of the employee, thus reducing defensiveness. If performance evaluation is effective, employee productivity is not a problem.

Counseling and Employee Assistance. Contemporary approaches to management include efforts to provide a supportive environment for employees. Employees are affected in their work by factors outside as well as inside the organization; the problems they encounter in their daily lives can affect both performance and productivity. Realizing that good employees are costly to replace, and taking cues from humanistic organization theories, managers have begun to seriously consider the emotional well-being of employees.

The most elementary aspect of assisting employees is to be a good listener and to be sensitive to employees' concerns. Taking an interest in the employee and being willing to listen and take problems seriously often is enough. The manager who has empathy goes a long way in gaining the confidence of employees.

Some problems are resolvable through actions of the manager, but many are not. Managers need to develop an understanding of what they can help with and what is beyond their capabilities. Often, professional assistance is necessary. Ordinarily, the manager should not be referring employees to professional help unless asked to do so by the employee. However, in recent years many organizations have developed employee assistance plans (EAPs). Use of these services is usually voluntary, but in some cases the employee may be referred mandatorily by the manager. Mandatory referrals usually take place only after the manager has discussed performance inadequacies with the employee and has given the employee an opportunity to improve. Referral is a last resort to save the employee; failure to go through with the assistance program can result in dismissal.

Many EAPs grew out of programs for dealing with alcoholism and other substance abuse. In recent years, controversy has surrounded methods for identifying these problems. In particular, drug testing is advocated by many employers but opposed by many employees and their associations or unions. What use managers can make of test results beyond referring individuals to EAPs is the subject of litigation and conflicting court decisions.

Employee assistance plans have become common because they are thought to save employees and to increase the productivity of the organization. They also represent good people management values, which are popular in contemporary society. Modern EAPs cover virtually any type of personal problems that can interfere with job performance. Actually, many plans permit employees to use the program without reference to the effects of the problem on job performance. Employees tend to be suspicious of EAPs. Preventing such negative reactions requires strong efforts to foster confidentiality and to assure that employees will not be negatively affected by using them.

The Contemporary Public Manager

The issues raised and suggestions made in this chapter are many, and some may seem contradictory. Nonetheless, the contemporary public manager is faced with myriad challenges that are not susceptible to easy solution. The public manager must be a master politician (while avoiding politics), a technical expert, decisive, personable, a counselor, a leader, and a problem solver among many other things. Every participant in public affairs expects something from the public manager, and most times the expectations are conflicting. Therefore, the public manager must be able to reconcile conflicting demands and still get work done.

Securing effective public management requires the ability to get people to do things in a coordinated fashion with attention to the goals of the organization as perceived by numerous participants in the process. Securing the cooperative effort of employees is the key to success and depends on some basic understandings of people. This chapter concludes with several suggestions for how managers might integrate some of the approaches that have been outlined.

A major issue for most employees is how they are treated. Most desire to be treated fairly and with dignity. Fairness of treatment is often a matter of perception; however, the manager who strives to be equitable and does not show favoritism goes a long way in establishing a sense of fairness. Fairness also requires that employees know what is expected of them and that evaluation be relevant to that expectation. Thus, it is necessary to establish standards of performance and criteria based on performance. Employees understand such standards and criteria and are usually willing to be judged by them as long as they are reasonable.

Successful managers also provide feedback to employees on a regular basis. They give credit and recognition to employees and criticize constructively when necessary. They get employees involved in solving the problems of the organization and foster independence and participation in decision making as appropriate. At the same time, they make every effort to ensure that the work is interesting and challenging. Providing independence to the employee can help in this endeavor. Overmanaging, or supervising too closely, must be avoided, because it shows distrust of the employee's judgment.

Good communication is also a hallmark of the effective manager. Communication flows many ways, and the healthy productive organization is one in which employees feel free to communicate with as well as hear from management. Channels must exist for airing complaints and grievances before they become so large that they cannot be resolved. Management must recognize that it is not infallible and must be open to criticism and respond honestly but not defensively. Explanation of the situation is often enough to defuse concerns.

When a problem develops, effective managers realize that trying to place blame does little to solve it. Instead, they focus on the problem and look for ways to address it. Employees are counseled when they are the problem, but good managers avoid personalizing the issue. Progressive counseling with efforts at improving performance should be used before formal discipline comes into play. Even then, discipline should be directed at improving performance and not at punishing people.

The successful manager is also one who can be trusted. Promises are kept or else they are not made. Nothing is so demoralizing to employees as expecting something on the basis of conversations with managers and then not having those expectations fulfilled. The morale of the whole organization suffers.

Basically, managers who treat their employees as adults and have high expectations for them are successful managers. Obviously, there are always some employees who do not respond to positive management and must be dealt with in other ways. However, the vast majority of people just want to be treated as worthy human beings. Managers who understand that are usually the most successful.

References

Barnard, C. *The Functions of the Executive.* Cambridge, Mass.: Harvard University Press, 1938.

Benne, K., and Sheats, P. "Functional Roles of Group Members." *Journal of Social Issues,* 1948, *4,* 41–49.

Blau, P. *The Dynamics of Bureaucracy: A Study of Interpersonal Relationships in Two Government Agencies.* (2nd ed.) Chicago: University of Chicago Press, 1963.

Brown, J.A.C. *The Social Psychology of Industry.* Baltimore, Md.: Penguin, 1962.

Brown, L. D. *Managing Conflict at Organizational Interfaces.* Reading, Mass.: Addison-Wesley, 1983.

Downs, A. *Inside Bureaucracy.* Boston: Little, Brown, 1967.

Doyle, M., and Straus, D. *How to Make Meetings Work.* New York: Jove Publications, 1976.

Dubin, R. "Persons and Organizations." *Proceedings of the 11th Annual Meeting of the Industrial Relations Research Association,* 1959, *11,* 160–163.

Fisher, R., and Ury, W. *Getting to Yes: Negotiating Agreement Without Giving In.* New York: Penguin Books, 1981.

Follett, M. P. *Creative Experience.* London: Longmans, Green, 1924.

Ford, R. N. *Motivation Through the Work Itself.* New York: American Management Association, 1969.

Herzberg, F. *Work and the Nature of Man.* Cleveland, Ohio: World Publishing, 1966.

Hyde, A., and Shafritz, J. M. "Training and Development and Personnel Management." *Public Personnel Management,* 1979, *8,* 344–349.

Kaplan, H. R., and Tausky, C. "Humanism in Organizations: A Critical Appraisal." *Public Administration Review,* 1977, *37,* 171–180.

McGregor, D. *The Human Side of Enterprise.* New York: McGraw-Hill, 1960.

Maslow, A. *Motivation and Personality.* New York: Harper & Row, 1954.

Nalbandian, J. "Performance Appraisal: If Only People Were Not Involved." *Public Administration Review,* 1981, *41,* 392–396.

Pfiffner, J. M. "Administrative Rationality." *Public Administration Review*, 1960, *20*, 125–132.

Selznick, P. *Leadership in Administration.* New York: Harper & Row, 1957.

Simon, H. A. *Administrative Behavior: A Study of Decision-Making Processes in Administrative Organization.* (3rd ed.) New York: Free Press, 1976.

Stogdill, R. M. *Handbook of Leadership: A Survey of Theory and Research.* New York: Free Press, 1974.

Thompson, J. D. *Organizations in Action.* New York: McGraw-Hill, 1967.

Whyte, W. F., and others. *Money and Motivation.* New York: Harper & Row, 1955.

Three

◨◨◨◨◨◨◨◨◨◨◨◨◨◨◨◨◨◨◨◨◨◨◨◨◨◨◨◨◨

Tools and Strategies for Managing Public Programs

Public managers need understandings in a variety of skill areas if they are to be in a position to fulfill their official responsibilities. Part Three focuses on the key functional areas, along with personnel management, in which basic skills and understandings are essential to effective management. Public administrators need not be experts in these areas, but they must develop certain fundamental understandings in the fields of financial management, computers and data processing, strategic management and planning, contracting out, and program evaluation.

In Chapter Six, Frank Sackton presents the major tools for the financing of public programs. He summarizes their utility for supporting programs while controlling costs in a period of fiscal constraint. Sackton points out that during the last generation government has grown faster than the population, which has led to demands for program cutbacks and controls. It is in this framework that he discusses the usefulness of such techniques as performance budgeting, cost-benefit analysis, productivity management, cutback management, forecasting, and performance auditing for the maintenance of program effectiveness, equity, and organizational cohesion.

In Chapter Seven, Alana Northrop, Kenneth L. Kraemer, and John Leslie King examine the utilization of computers in program management. They argue that managers should understand not only the basic terms, concepts, and processes of computers but also their possibilities and limitations. Northrop, Kraemer, and King's overriding theme is that public administrators who understand the role of the computer as a management tool, particularly with regard to such matters as the retrieval of information, the projection of data, and the analysis of data, are more likely to be successful in fulfilling their programmatic tasks. It is not so much the technical skills necessary to process data themselves that are important for managers but rather an appreciation and realization of the uses of the data that can be produced.

In Chapter Eight, Jerry L. Mc Caffery analyzes the utility of strategic management and strategic planning in public organizations. In his view, strategic management is a more inclusive term than strategic planning, one that utilizes the systematic processes of planning in relation to the organizational mission, management goals, and environmental opportunities and constraints to formulate policy proposals and develop courses of action calculated to advance the public enterprise. Mc Caffery concludes that the use of systematic techniques drawn from strategic planning in conjunction with the "creative power, analytic thinking, and interpersonal negotiation skills" that the public sector possesses will lead to more effective program management.

In Chapter Nine, John Rehfuss explores the impact of today's contracting-out movement on the skills necessary for program management. He points out that, while privatization has long been with us, it is occurring at a faster pace, in new areas, and at all levels of government. Rehfuss presents criteria by which a decision to contract out a program or service can be evaluated. Even when careful judgments on contracting out are made, however, problems of quality and accountability may ensue. These problems are certainly not new, but their nature is often different when a program is contracted out. Do public officials need different administrative skills as a consequence? Probably not, for in the final analysis, management skills for contracting out tend to be the same skills required for direct public program management.

In Chapter Ten, Sharon L. Caudle examines the utility of the tools of program evaluation for public program management. She notes that evaluation is a systematic process that involves analytic judgments that should be and often are made in the public setting. These judgments include the declaration of program goals, a statement of the purpose(s) of the evaluation, a declaration of the standards to be used for evaluating program performance, a list of priorities to be emphasized in the evaluation, and the establishment of a time line for the evaluation. The public manager must understand above all else, however, that public program evaluation is a political process. The technical components of evaluation must be examined not only in terms of their analytic properties and capabilities but in light of their potential political impact as well. Caudle concludes that this is no reason to fear or to avoid evaluations, as they remain a valuable tool for program managers.

To summarize, each chapter in this section argues that the techniques and skills presented are just as important, or perhaps even more important, for their political and organizational implications as they are for the particular skills themselves. This, of course, is the basic message of the book: Public managers must understand their political and organizational environment and be able to act within it if they are to be effective in fulfilling their programmatic responsibilities.

6

𓏺𓏺𓏺𓏺𓏺𓏺𓏺𓏺𓏺𓏺𓏺𓏺𓏺𓏺𓏺𓏺𓏺𓏺𓏺𓏺𓏺𓏺𓏺𓏺𓏺

Financing Public Programs
Under Fiscal Constraint

Frank Sackton

Over the years, federal, state, and local fiscal problems have been addressed largely in terms of procedure, budgeting concepts, and the mechanics of collecting revenues and making expenditures. Much progress has been made in the area of budgeting as we have moved from the haphazard governmental piecemeal budgets at the turn of the century to line-item budgeting with the emphasis on strong accounting practices. Fiscal managers scored a breakthrough when they added output measures so that the results of budget expenditures could be evaluated. Thus, *performance budgeting* was born, ushering in a new era in better management of government resources. Innovations of the past ten years influencing improvement in governmental financial operations have included a host of practices and techniques grouped into what we call *program budgeting*. With the emphasis on planning, we have sharpened our tools of analysis as we have moved forward with the more modish ideas of cost-benefit and systems analysis, management by objectives, planning-program-ming-budgeting systems, zero-base budgeting, and the so-called sunset laws.

Those engaged in the craft of governmental budgeting may take a measure of comfort in the knowledge that they have been able to apply the advanced technology of mathematical tools, the art of models, and the electronic data processor. But before resting on past laurels, financial managers must appreciate that they are confronted by a new environment today. The answers to the problems that confront public program managers in a time of fiscal constraint will not be found in the improvement of procedures.

The problems are basic but difficult. Simply stated, the citizens are not happy with the manner in which governmental managers are conducting public business. It is abundantly clear that citizens everywhere are disturbed about their tax bills and about governmental deficit financing. They have a more than passing interest in government finance matters. The people are not seeking economy through the elimination of essential services, but they are seeking, and have a right to demand, the elimination of waste and extravagance along with improvements in governmental effectiveness.

Before we undertake a discussion of possible actions that may be taken to improve the handling of financial operations at the federal, state, and local levels, a review of some aspects of the problem confronting governmental finance managers may be useful. In recent years, the people have become increasingly aware of the growth of government and of the additional services provided by governmental jurisdictions. As the tax bills to individual citizens become larger and government deficits mount, citizenry are beginning to ask: Is this growth desirable? Is it consistent with the needs of the people? Are the essential programs being managed effectively and economically?

The Essence of the Problem

It has been a popular practice to criticize the federal government for growth of its programs. The fact is that government at the state and local levels has grown as well. During the twenty-year period 1965–1985, the population of our country grew by 23 percent (U.S. Bureau of the Census, 1986). Federal expenditures grew by 700 percent, and state and local expenditures were right up there with a growth of 500 percent. After we adjust for inflation, the expenditure growth at all levels was about 113 percent, almost five times higher than the population growth (U.S. Office of Management and Budget, 1987a).

Another way to measure the growth of government is to trace the number of people it employs. Between 1965 and 1985, government employment in the United States grew much faster than employment in the private sector. While government employment grew by 65 percent, private nonagricultural employment increased only 49 percent (U.S. Office of Management and Budget, 1987b). In 1965 there was one government employee for every nineteen people in the country; by 1985, the ratio was one to fourteen.

Similar comparison can be made with economic growth. While the gross national product (GNP) was growing 73 percent during the twenty-year period, government expenditures grew by 113 percent. All these data have been adjusted for inflation (U.S. Office of Management and Budget, 1987a).

By whatever measure or comparison we wish to make, it is clear that government, taken as a whole, is growing faster than the population, the economy, inflation, and the private sector. This is the essence of the problem that appears to be continuing. What can public administrators do about it?

One way in which all government workers can help reduce government spending is to perform government tasks more effectively through productivity improvement techniques. Everyone should strive to improve operations in some productive way, and to be more effective. Here we must differentiate between "efficiency" and "effectiveness." To illustrate, take the example of the man who was out canoeing when he hit a submerged rock and began to take on water rather rapidly. With great presence of mind he removed his sun helmet and began to bail out the water. His actions were a model of efficiency: strong arms, quick strokes, swift removal of the water. But he was not effective—the canoe sank. Similarly, work may be carried out seemingly efficiently in a government agency, but if it does not accomplish the objective, it is not effective. Productivity improvement is today's practical approach to the classic concerns of government effectiveness and economy. This concept focuses on whether the right things are being done right, without wasting valuable resources. Unfortunately, too many of our citizens still think that productivity improvement is simply getting lazy bureaucrats to work harder. They are terribly wrong, of course—they confuse activity with effectiveness.

Performance Budgeting and Productivity Measures

Perhaps the most important step in productivity improvement is to establish goals and objectives for government agencies and then to measure accomplishment based on the effective delivery of services or the least-cost method of performing
the assigned mission (Harrill, 1972; Sackton, 1979).

This form of budgeting is particularly useful in organizations that provide services and wish to anticipate the cost of
those services. The performance budget emphasizes the effectiveness of operation in achieving the funded goals. It retains
the good features of line-item budgeting, such as effective accounting controls, while focusing on the actual results to be obtained as justification for the monies requested. The heart of
performance budgeting is the use of measurement data that allow
a quantitative comparison of anticipated and actual results, thus
providing a performance "track record." These data then provide the justification for budget requests for the following year
and become a basis for further improvement.

Although managers don't like to be measured, good management demands a process that measures what is done and how
well it is done. It bases new proposals on experience and evaluations of past actions. Some would argue that while street maintenance and pothole repairs can be measured, the same cannot
be said for the delivery of social services. But the fact is that
productivity measures do exist to measure their effectiveness.

Some of the more difficult areas for productivity measurement are in vocational rehabilitation, general training, employment and job services, medical and hospital functions, mental
health care, and treatment of drug and alcohol abusers. To be
effective, productivity measurement for these activities starts with
the development of a "system model" for the specific operation to be measured. The model is no more than a comprehensive framework or checklist describing all the functions to be
performed in each of the social services activities. The starting
point for such a model is usually a "needs assessment" for that
particular service. It answers the questions: Who needs it? How
many need it? Where? and What is the magnitude of the prob-

lem? In short, what we are seeking is measurable *demand*. Indicators of demand should measure the need for the program or the service. Specifically, measurements can be requests or applications for the service, deficient conditions in need of the service, or specific populations that need to be served. Most demand indicators show either the total demand or the difference between the total demand and existing efforts to meet that demand.

The quantifiable response to demand is given as *workload*. Workload indicators quantify the services or activities actually being conducted. The workload includes clients or patients processed or populations served. Occasionally, workload indicators will measure total hours spent per given period—month or year—in providing a service.

The manner in which the workload is handled results in a measure of *productivity*. Indicators of productivity measure the average time or cost of providing one unit of service. Indicators quantify the efficiency of the program, that is, cost per item or hours per item. Productivity indicators are computed by dividing total input (money or time) by total output (workload). In the delivery of medical or health services, useful measures at each point of client treatment in the system model could be any of the following:

1. Number of completed treatments as a proportion of total number of individual clients
2. Proportion of treatments carried out at each step within the system model
3. Professional costs per hour of service
4. Total costs per hour of service
5. Total cost per patient at each level of treatment or of handling within the system model

All of these measurements can lead not only to improvement in the condition of the clients being treated but also to improvement in the condition of people outside the system. This latter element may not be completely quantifiable, but it is important as an additional favorable outcome.

Finally, we seek a measure of the quality of performance in handling the workload. This is the *effectiveness* with which the service has been delivered. Effectiveness indicators quantify the proportion of need that is met and the extent to which services are satisfactory. Effectiveness measures frequently indicate the percentage of demand that has been met or the percentage increase or decrease in the demand.

Productivity Measurement in Local Government

Although we have been addressing the problem of productivity measurement at the federal and state levels, the same general rationale applies to local government. The following four applications of productivity measurement appear to be the most useful (Hatry, 1973):

1. *Cost reduction.* This encourages work accomplishment measures in such tasks as picking up trash, repairing streets, and repairing and maintaining mechanical equipment. Unfortunately, some governments do not go beyond this simple first type of productivity measure.
2. *Managerial control of operations.* Productivity measurements such as comparisons of the various service districts or neighborhoods will help agency managers determine what resources are required and where. In trash pickup, for example, manpower can be more effectively allocated if waste collection efficiency data are available for each neighborhood and for each collection route.
3. *Program and policy planning.* Such planning is accomplished more effectively with productivity measurement. Government officials are able to identify major problem areas and apply manpower and financial resources to changing demands for services. As comparable data are collected over time, they will also reveal trends and indicate whether progress is being made.
4. *Development of employee incentives.* The role of productivity measurement is to help governments and their employees develop a fair system of rewards based on observed improvements in productivity. Such incentives should apply

to supervisory personnel also. At the managerial level in government departments, existing incentives are often perverse. The manager tends to gain prestige and earnings by increasing the size of his or her budget and workforce. If the manager reduces his or her budget and staff in the interests of efficiency and economy, his or her own responsibility and salary may decline in the long run. It may be possible to avoid this dilemma by using performance incentives, such as bonuses, that are related to measurable improvements in effectiveness.

Cutback Management

When budget or revenue resource problems begin to surface, governments can cope by the exercise of three actions:

1. Buying time to assess the situation, and planning for future actions
2. Increasing revenues to cover the funding shortfall
3. Reducing expenditures so that revenues and outlays will be in balance

Additionally, the budget managers should determine whether the cutbacks to be made will be short term, mid-term, or long term. Identifying the duration of the cutbacks is essential in determining how deep the reductions should be made and how the cuts are to be implemented (Wolman, 1980).

Buying Time. When fiscal problems become evident, managers and budget directors must have enough time to plan, to study, and to arrive at sound decisions on the future course of events. Some of the options to buy time and conserve revenue include hiring freezes, across-the-board percentage cuts, layoffs of temporary employees, elimination of overtime, early retirement, deferring of routine maintenance, and deferring of equipment purchases.

A hiring freeze hurts no one already employed, as it relies on natural attrition. However, it does have some ill effects on the organization. It takes away from the manager the decision of whom and where to cut. Also, it is more likely to hurt minorities and women, who are more likely to be next in line for hire. A predictable result will be an uneven distribution of remaining skills, thus injuring normal production schedules. Hiring freezes affect some units of government more than others. Units with a large number of personnel departing by retirement, resignation, death, or other reason can be crippled during hiring freezes. Units that are more affected by the hiring freeze can have serious problems providing services, while remaining employees might suffer a loss of morale. A partial remedy to some of these problems is to permit the unit manager to hire one person for every three lost by attrition until an established target level is reached. Another useful strategy is to employ flextime in order to distribute fewer employees over a longer period of time.

Cutting the budget by a certain percentage across the board is a "quick fix" that is frequently used because it relieves the senior manager of a good deal of stress. But this approach is insensitive to the varying needs for service delivery by different units. The same percentage cut may have only a mild effect on units that provide a routine service that can be simply slowed down a bit, yet could cripple a unit of highly skilled individuals providing a sophisticated service or product.

A reduction in temporary employees combined with a reduction in (or elimination of) overtime can affect productivity of the remaining career employees. Although there is a positive effect in that no regular employee is being terminated, the remaining workforce may feel that more work will be required of them while the necessary time to do the work is being curtailed.

Deferring routine maintenance and putting off the purchase of equipment are easy fixes used by managers on a regular basis in times of fiscal shortage. Therein lies the problem with this course of action. Routine maintenance and equipment purchases may already be behind schedule when the next budget crunch comes along. Managers must be alert to the sensitivity of this option. The action could result in more breakdowns of facilities and vital equipment. Also, this strategy can increase the frustration of employees trying to get more work done with fewer resources.

Increasing Revenues. Several years ago a form of cutback management was created in California by a citizen rebellion against high property taxes; the voters overwhelmingly approved a ballot initiative, Proposition 13, that set ceilings on property tax levies. This tax rebellion movement then swept across the country. Thus, a tax increase of any kind to solve a fiscal problem may well meet with resistance. Notwithstanding this prevailing political climate, instead of increasing taxes outright governments can increase user fees. This option has been tested in many communities, where it has been more favorably accepted than a general tax increase. It is important to ensure that such user fees fit the government task being performed. In addition to the more obvious user-fee prospects such as trash pickup and sewer and water services, there are a host of areas where user fees are applicable. For example, special requirements for police security and street cleanup resulting from a private organization function can appropriately be charged. In areas of new construction, fees for hookups, building inspections, street pavements, and land needs for school, library, and recreational facilities are legitimate charges to developers. Currently, in most jurisdictions, only nominal fees and license charges are levied, with the bulk of the funding coming from the general fund. As a matter of fact, all services being delivered by governments to individuals and organizations that have an ability to pay should be explored and considered a prospective revenue source.

Two other areas should be explored for increased revenue: federal and state aid. A study should be made to sort out responsibilities and mandates and to connect them to the appropriate revenue sources. However, with cuts being made in federal programs, this option is becoming less viable.

Reducing Expenditures. Of all the options available to public managers in a time of fiscal constraint, the most acceptable to the citizens is a cutback in expenditures. Attention to this option is critical, particularly if the fiscal shortage is expected to be long term. In this situation, drastic steps must be taken, and sometimes substantial cutbacks or reductions have to be made in programs and jobs. An appropriate method to deal with this

problem is to use a priority-setting process to come to terms
with the impending decision (see Chapter Eight).

While there are many ways to set priorities and to choose
appropriate actions in cutback management, one method is to
consider both preliminary and implementation steps for setting
cutback priorities before taking action. Preliminary steps give
the manager a systematic method in which to study the situation and to develop options. First, the manager must review
and be aware of statutory mandates. Cutbacks in certain activities may be precluded if they are required by law. The manager must be clear on the agency's role and mandated duties.
Next, the manager must be completely familiar with personnel
rules and regulations, affirmative action practices and requirements, and any organized labor agreements. This knowledge
will give the manager insight into what personnel actions can
or cannot be taken to achieve necessary cutbacks. The manager
must also assemble necessary cost and budget information to
identify the cost of each option under consideration. This will
assist the manager in determining the cost saving of any decision. Finally, the manager should generate a preliminary list
of possible cutbacks. Generally, they can come from two areas.
One would be to reduce expenditures through alternative delivery systems; the other would be to save money through direct
cost savings and service reduction methods.

Alternative Delivery Systems. There are at least four ways to provide the public with the same level of service at a reduced cost:

1. Contracting with volunteer community groups to provide
    services free of charge
2. Privatizing services
3. Eliminating duplication through interagency agreements
    with other governments
4. Utilizing part-time and lower-cost personnel

Reducing costs through volunteerism is an area worth exploring because of the success it has achieved at the state and
local levels. Essentially, the volunteer community group or or-

ganization enters into a contract with the government to provide certain services at no charge or for minimal operating expenses. Examples of successful use of this system are citizen groups providing park maintenance services, neighborhood security watch, traffic control, clerical assistance in public offices, and citizen study and planning groups to solve public problems.

Another avenue for expenditure reduction is privatization of services (see Chapter Nine). This is a relatively new term for a fairly old practice. It refers to the contracting out of services to private companies and consultants instead of using public employees to perform the tasks. Implicit in this practice is the belief that private contractors can do the job more effectively, more cheaply, or both. The concept is receiving renewed interest because of mounting government personnel costs. Areas that have been subject to privatization include janitorial and custodial services, printing and reproduction, street cleaning and repair, tree planting and landscaping, and garbage and trash collection.

In recent years, the concept has branched out to include new areas and forms of contractual services. Some government agencies have learned that public-operated automatic data processing is not cost-effective, because its utilization rate is much lower than that of private computer organizations. Yet whether utilization is high or low, the costs of skilled computer personnel and the investment, maintenance, and operating costs of computer centers are uniformly high. Similarly, firefighting and fire departments do not have to be government agencies operated by public employees. Since 1948, various communities in Arizona have contracted with a private company to handle firefighting. The communities have found this to be a cost-effective way to provide the service.

Other traditional government functions that have been contracted out to private operators include medical, sanitation, nursing, engineering, inspection, licensing, prison, and social work operations. Of course, each activity requires special study to determine whether privatization is feasible and cost-effective. In this respect, important experiments have been undertaken by several of our large cities with their own trash collection services. In a demonstration of good privatization planning, they contracted with private companies to take over a small portion of the service. Over the period of about two years, city officials were able to compare the effectiveness and quality of their own operation with that of the private contractor. Short-term and long-term investment and personnel costs were computed, and a determination was made as to the best way the public could be served at the lowest possible cost. However, in some cases reliable service levels were not maintained after the task was taken over by the private company. This situation can be alleviated by retaining both the public and private trash collection services in order to maintain a spirit of quality competition between them.

Another area of privatization has been the temporary employment of specialists. The hiring of consultants has been particularly rewarding. Although the hourly salary of a professional consultant appears high at first, it must be remembered that the consultant is on the payroll for a specific period of time to produce an identifiable product. There are none of the continuing lifelong costs and extra benefits with consultants that employers incur with permanent public employees. Also, if the consultant doesn't perform, termination is easy. Consultants have been particularly useful in planning, conducting studies of personnel operations, developing administrative and management procedures and systems, performing program evaluations through the use of systems analysis techniques, and conducting survey research.

Direct Cost Savings. Many services provided by government agencies are also provided by other agencies in the same general area. A promising field of cost reduction may be in the reorganization of local services to eliminate some of this duplication. For instance, land use planning staffs and commissions may be combined for several adjacent communities or on a city/county level. Other areas that may benefit from reorganization or sharing of services include building inspection, court administration, purchasing, safety and training, and animal control services. Savings may result from fewer staff, price reductions for supplies in quantity orders, and the need for less office space or fewer support facilities (Novak, 1983).

Finally, low-cost personnel may be substituted for or used as a supplement to full-time staff positions. Students, interns, and temporary service personnel may be used in certain areas that do not require specialized skills or full-time coverage. Substantial savings can result from the nonpayment of full-time salaries and benefits. Many prospective workers seek part-time jobs because of homemaking or other responsibilities. This is particularly true of two-wage-earner families and retired personnel seeking part-time work to augment other income or to remain busy and productive.

Priority Setting. After the manager has assembled the list of options for cutbacks, a series of steps can be taken to inform and involve interested parties in the priority setting and implementing functions:

1. Inform interested parties of the need for cutbacks and hold appropriate forums to solicit their input.
2. Determine criteria for priority setting.
3. Using the established criteria, set preliminary priority list.
4. Build consensus through workshops and hearings to finalize the priority list.
5. Obtain approval of priority list from elected officials and other decision makers.

While there will never be complete agreement in this difficult situation, the priority-setting process will help the community and government employees understand why the actions need to be taken.

During the entire process, managers must remain calm and professional. If they suffer from stress, they must be careful not to transmit or convey it to their employees. Above all, managers must be perceived by employees as being honest and open (Pederson, 1979).

Accurate Forecasting

Closely related to cutback management techniques is the need to focus on the importance of forecasting in periods of economic recession. Regardless of the type or form of budgeting used in a time of fiscal constraint, that process will not produce the required results without an accurate forecast of the revenue to become available.

Among the 82,341 governments in the United States (U.S. Bureau of Census, 1986), the federal government employs sophisticated and effective forecasting systems. The same is generally true of the fifty states and the largest cities and counties. However, forecasting techniques are spotty to nonexistent in over 82,000 units of government. In a time of fiscal constraint, this level of government will desperately need some forecasting tool to avoid a chaotic budgetary situation. Thus, it becomes important that simple and usable forecasting methods be developed at this level if none exist.

Forecasting is concerned with those revenues and other resources that will become available to support a budget. In short, forecasting attempts to profile the future economic condition and how it will affect taxes, fees, receipts, and all other forms of revenue. Forecasting is not planning. Whereas forecasting is concerned with what the future *will* look like, planning is concerned with what the future should look like (Armstrong, 1978).

The advances made in recent years in computer technology, including the advent of the personal computer, have greatly increased the use of many types of statistical analysis and modeling in the forecasting process. Among techniques that can be performed using a personal computer are regression analysis, time series, and simulation models (Seitz, 1984).

Regression analysis is a widely used statistical technique for analyzing the relationship between an item to be forecast and other factors that are believed to affect it. It is used primarily for forecasts involving a few months to a few years. The input is historical data related to the variables involved in the forecast.

The output is a line or a graph that approximates the relationship between the variables.

Regression analysis allows the budget analyst to forecast or estimate particular revenues or expenditures for future budget cycles. For example, general administration expenditures for education deal with administrative costs for the operation of the entire institution. Most state formulas and guidelines relate the level of costs for this activity to the size of the instructional budget. Based on the theory that more students and more faculty require more administration, as a school increases its enrollment and increases the size of its instructional budget, the size of the general administration budget will also increase.

A *time series* analysis forecasts the value of an item by studying past movements within the same time frame. The methods include trend analysis (regression analysis using time as the explanatory variable), moving average analysis, and exponential smoothing. This system uses historical data and is generally used for short forecasting periods.

One of the simpler approaches in time-series analysis is to compute moving averages. These averages can be used to estimate a variable value for a short-term forecast of one to three time periods (months, years). The concept of the moving average is based on the assumption that the past data observations reflect an underlying trend that can be determined and that the averaging of these values will eliminate the randomness and seasonality in the data. The process requires a series of historic values that can be averaged by totaling and then dividing by the number of observations.

As with regression analysis, *simulation models* are used when the forecast item is affected by other variables. A simulation model describes a situation through a series of equations, which then provide a basis for testing the impacts of various factors that might affect the item to be forecast. Simulation models, often referred to as econometric models, can be used for longer forecasting periods than the other techniques mentioned.

This process is useful in budget analysis and forecasting when the analyst must incorporate large amounts of complicated information into an estimation of expenditures. For example, at the state level, social service expenditures are directly related to the state economy, while education and criminal justice expenditures are related to state demographics and economic factors. Models can be used that not only predict likely expenditures but also help policymakers understand the most sensitive factors that influence each functional activity.

One such example is the Massachusetts Welfare Model developed by Data Resources, Inc. The model is used for short-term forecasts and sensitivity analyses of eligibles, caseload, and expenditures in various welfare assistance categories. The model contains:

1. Earnings distribution of the state and individuals
2. An estimation routine for calculating Aid to Families with Dependent Children (AFDC) and General Relief (GR) eligibles from a combination of welfare policy standards and state demographic parameters applied to the earnings distributions for families and unrelated individuals
3. Econometric equations explaining eligibles' rate of participation in AFDC and GR, by sex and family status
4. Econometric equations explaining average expenditures per case in AFDC and GR
5. Identities deriving AFDC and GR caseloads by a combination of items 2 and 3
6. Identities deriving AFDC and GR total expenditures by a combination of items 4 and 5

The model uses seventy-seven variables, including economic, welfare policy, and endogenous variables, as well as eligibles definitions, rates of participation, miscellaneous inputs, and numerous simultaneous econometric equations.

In forecasting, the model works in several steps. First, U.S. and state economic data are used to derive family earnings distributions and to determine persons eligible for welfare. Next, welfare participation rates are calculated, using such factors as work availability and wage opportunities. (Normally, if the economy has worsened, welfare benefits and participation are higher.) Welfare caseload and total project welfare expenditures are then calculated. Finally, administrative costs are determined.

While all these forecasting methods are widely used at the state level and the more sophisticated local levels of government, the size and complexity of the budgetary process, as well as the availability of a greater variety of forecasting resources, dictate the use of more advanced forecasting techniques at the federal and some state levels. Here, econometric models are by far the most important forecasting tool used in the budgetary process. These models are nothing more than complex simulation models made possible by modern computer technology. A vast array of variables can be plugged into these models and be changed and manipulated to provide various forecasting scenarios. Most of the forecasting done by these models is of the short-term variety—from one to two years, usually expressed in three-month increments. However, the models are updated constantly and are sometimes used for much longer forecasting periods (see Chapter Seven).

A host of ''leading economic indicators,'' compiled and provided by the federal government on a regular basis, can also be incorporated into the forecasting methodology. Here again, computer technology provides the capability to make use of these models and economic indicators and to constantly alter and change the forecast as the variables change.

Using the easily operated personal computer, smaller units of government can employ the more simple models of forecasting to predict revenues. With regression and time-series techniques, revenue sources can be shown statistically to be correlated with either the passage of time or another explanatory variable. For example, the property tax levy is strongly related to the passage of time and to the effects of inflation. Even if the actual data do not become available until the end of the budget process (which is normally the situation), a regression model on a personal computer can be used to provide the preliminary estimate each year.

There are other revenue sources that can be estimated using regression analysis as a forecasting method. An example found in local government is the sales tax. It can be shown statistically that this tax is correlated quite strongly with personal income, an indicator that is available in most communities.

Other tools available to small governments are simulation forecasting and modeling using the personal computer. One such model can be programmed to project revenue based on several variables in the community such as population, personal income, salaries and wages, bank deposits, and even airport activity and post office receipts.

Another model, more recently available, is called REVEX. It was developed for use by municipalities and other local entities by the Government Finance Research Center in conjunction with Data Resources, Inc. It consists of a model to be installed on a personal computer, and it will project both revenues and expenditures based on about thirty-five economic indicators. These indicators are updated quarterly by Data Resources and are tailored to each regional location.

The smaller units of government should explore the prospect of "piggybacking" onto computer mainframes and economic indicator models of local banks, universities, and financial institutions. Frequently, a shared enterprise can be established at relatively low cost to the government unit.

Not to be overlooked is the value of judgmental forecasting. Its major components are common sense and the experience of the forecaster. Even with the use of analysis, simulation, and modeling, judgmental forecasting is a valuable adjunct to all of the models. Frequently, there is no substitute for the "feel" that an experienced economist or forecaster can bring to bear on a specific situation.

Performance Auditing

No budget process or productivity measurement program will work without executive or legislative oversight. Performance or program auditing can be described as an analysis of operations to determine whether an agency's actual operations are adhering to policies established by the government body having jurisdiction. Performance auditing also relates program accomplishments to performance standards where they exist. The audit may also review operations to determine their effectiveness.

Financial audits or fiscal audits perform two functions. First, they verify that all receipts that should have been received have in fact been accounted for, that all expenditures have been properly made, and that services or materials paid for have actually been received. Second, the audit examines and certifies the financial statements of the organization being audited.

In actual practice, performance audits include an analysis of the agency's financial operations to determine program effectiveness through productivity measurement and the costs of achieving performance standards. It is this more enlarged concept of "auditing" that explains the current trend away from requiring government auditors to be certified public accountants. Intertwined with that trend is the movement toward performance auditing, creating a need for an interdisciplinary staff made up of professionals from business and public administration and from law and accounting. Auditing is more effective when performed by independent agencies.

Conclusion

Government managers must be prepared for the possibility that they will be confronted with a cutback situation in a time of fiscal constraint. Logical priority-setting systems have worked in the past. From those experiences, managers can go about the trimming process in their agencies. They will be faced with the dilemma of maintaining effectiveness, equity, and agency cohesion while smoothing or resisting organization decline. Some organizations will have the foresight to plan ahead for the lean periods by contemplating the use of zero-base budgeting (or the ability to turn to it), by ongoing compilation of program performance data, and by developing a plan that will inform all interested parties and the public of what to expect during the cutback operations. All these are important considerations to avoid uncertainty and conflict during retrenchment. It should be noted also that these are sound management principles in periods of expansion.

References

Armstrong, J. S. *Long-Range Forecasting, from Crystal Ball to Computer.* New York: Wiley, 1978.

Harrill, E. R., "A Multi-Purpose Budgeting and Accounting System for Governments." *Governmental Finance,* November 1972, pp. 19–20.

Hatry, H. P. "Applications of Productivity Measurement in Local Government." *Governmental Finance,* November 1973, pp. 6–8.

Novak, T. L. "Piecemeal Reorganization: City-County Cooperation in Spokane." In G. W. Wynn (ed.), *Learning from Abroad—Cutback Management: A Trinational Perspective.* New Brunswick: Transaction Books, 1983.

Pederson, R. R. "Thanks, Howard." In E. K. Kellar (ed.), *Managing with Less.* Washington, D.C.: International City Management Association, 1979.

Sackton, F. J. "Budgetary Reform in Arizona State and Local Governments." In N. Henry (ed.), *Toward Tax Reform.* Phoenix: Arizona Academy of Public Affairs, 1979.

Schick, A. (ed.). *Perspectives on Budgeting.* Washington, D.C.: American Society for Public Administration, 1987.

Seitz, N. *Business Forecasting on Your Personal Computer.* Reston, Va.: Reston Publishing Company, 1984.

Society, Sept.-Oct. 1986, pp. 48–74.

U.S. Bureau of the Census. *Consolidated Federal Fund Report,* 1986, p. 2.

U.S. Office of Management and Budget. *Historical Tables.* Washington, D.C.: U.S. Government Printing Office, 1987a.

U.S. Office of Management and Budget. *Special Analysis, Budget of the U.S. Government.* Washington, D.C.: U.S. Government Printing Office, 1987b.

Wolman, H. "Local Government Strategies to Cope with Fiscal Stress." In C. H. Levine and I. Rubin (eds.), *Fiscal Stress and Public Policy.* Beverly Hills, Calif.: Sage, 1980.

7

🁢🁢🁢🁢🁢🁢🁢🁢🁢🁢🁢🁢🁢🁢🁢🁢🁢🁢🁢🁢🁢🁢🁢🁢🁢

What Every Public Manager Should Know About Computing

Alana Northrop
Kenneth L. Kraemer
John Leslie King

Computers were first introduced into public organizations well over thirty years ago. Today the federal government, all fifty state governments, and virtually all city and county governments utilize computers. And they use computers for some 300 information-processing tasks (Kraemer, Dutton, and Northrop, 1981), such as paying employees, sending utility bills, analyzing demographic data, routing vehicles, and allocating manpower. In fact, computers are used to maintain hundreds of different types of records. For example, the American citizenry appears on some 240 federal computer files. Furthermore, governmental use of computers is only accelerating with the proliferation of microcomputers—consider the National Aeronautics and Space Administration, which intends for every one of its white-collar workers to have a PC by the early 1990s.

   It is safe to say, therefore, that computers have permeated government. It is also safe to say that public managers are not well prepared for working in the information age. The current guidelines of the National Association of Schools of Public Affairs and Administration (NASPAA) require, for example, only that master's students learn how to run statistical packages such as SPSS and SAS. And it appears that most schools are not attempting to exceed this requirement (Kraemer and Northrop, 1984), although there has been some improvement recently. As a consequence, one of the biggest impacts of computers in the public sector is the insecurity being felt by administrators. They feel insecure because they lack experience with computers and because computers are supposed to dramatically change their work world.

While fear seems to be a natural accompaniment to lack of experience, computers inspire a particularly deep level of fear (Gardner and others, 1985). Those who are familiar with computers are thought to form an inner sanctum of the initiated, while those who are not familiar with computers appear to lack any basis from which to communicate with those who are. This sharp distinction between the two groups is at the root of the insecurity felt by public managers, or for that matter, by the public at large.

This sense of insecurity has been compounded by the many assertions that have been made about the impact of computers on the work world. For example, many people predicted that computers would have a substantial effect on the bureaucratic structure of organizations. In addition, it was predicted that computers would affect the number of people employed as well as employee satisfaction and performance. Furthermore, computers and their information were seen as forces that would alter the decision-making process and political power in organizations.

If computers have had these effects, then the art of public administration should have been revolutionized by the computer age. But the art of public administration has not been revolutionized by the profusion of computers, nor need it be. In this chapter we will first review the empirical literature on the impacts of computers. Our continuing thesis will be that computing impacts are conditioned by the organizational and social context. Computing does not appear to be an independent factor that significantly influences the nature of public administration. But lack of knowledge of computing does hinder program managers. It is our contention that managers need only a low level of literacy in terms of computing *practice* but a high level of literacy in terms of computing *impacts*.

Computing Impacts

Most of the debate about computing and bureaucratic structure focuses on whether computing would result in centralizing or decentralizing the organization. *Centralization* refers to the distance between where a problem emerges and where in the organization's hierarchy decisions about that problem are made. Generally, a centralized organization is one in which most decisions are made at the top by a single individual or small group—in other words, the classic Weberian bureaucratic structure.

Those who claim a centralizing influence from computing cite one of two factors as relevant in this process. Leavitt and Whisler (1958) predicted that computing systems would execute routine decisions and pass the remainder to top management. Thus, computing would centralize most organizational decision making (or at least human decision making) by replacing human decision makers with machines. An alternative view of the centralizing influence of computing is based on the traditional tendency of organizations to centralize computing operations due to the economies of scale inherent in consolidated operations (King, 1983). Centralizing the processing of important information that could be used for decision making would make centralized decision making easier. Centralization of decision making would only occur, of course, when some individual or group exploited this potential.

Those who claim a decentralizing influence from computing have been less numerous than those proclaiming centralization. The former claim that through decentralized access to central information (provided through time-sharing systems, distributed computers such as PC's or departmental minicomputers, and distribution of reports), many decisions formerly handled by top management would be handled by middle management, either because the decision authority would be delegated downward as information became available to middle managers or because middle managers would expoit the opportunity available.

The empirical research suggests that computing per se is neither a centralizing nor a decentralizing influence. Some early studies (Argyris, 1971; Mumford and Banks, 1967; Myers, 1967) as well as a few later studies (Leduc, 1979; Lippitt, Miller, and Lalamaj, 1980) suggest that computing has had a centralizing effect on organizational decision making. Yet other studies suggest that computing has led to decentralization (Blau and Schoenherr, 1971; Pfeffer, 1981; Withington, 1969). Still others suggest that computing has been followed by centralization of some decisions and decentralization of others (Kraemer, Dutton, and Northrop, 1981).

When one carefully examines the details of these studies, it becomes clear that a simple characterization of computing as centralizing or decentralizing is meaningless. The context in which computing is used appears to be a much stronger influence than technology on whether organizations centralize or decentralize. The technology supports either arrangement, but the history and traditions of the organization determine which arrangement will be followed. Bjorn-Anderson and Pederson (1977), Kling (1980), and Kraemer and Danziger (1984) all found that predictions about computing's centralizing or decentralizing influence did not stand up to careful investigation. Rather, computing tends to reinforce the prevailing tendencies in organizations. Those that are inclined to centralize can utilize computing to do so, and vice versa.

These findings reveal a critical fact about computing and organizational structure, which is that computing is much too weak a force in and of itself to affect structure in significant ways. An organization will not centralize or decentralize just because tasks are automated. This does not mean, however, that computing plays no role in the structure of organizations. Computing can be a powerful tool for enabling structural reforms determined for other reasons (Kraemer and Dutton, 1979). For example, centralization of fiscal authority is facilitated by centralized financial accounting, which in turn is greatly facilitated by use of a computerized central accounting system. Access to financial information can still be provided to departments through terminals, but transaction control can be retained at the center. Alternatively, use of local computers can permit effective departmental accounting under a decentralized fiscal authority structure (Kraemer, Dutton, and Northrop, 1981). The important point is that computing can be used as an instrument to reinforce structural reforms or to reinforce existing structures, but it cannot bring them about in the first place.

Overall, there remains the question of whether, after computing is in place across organizations, the resulting structures are more centralized or decentralized. Robey's (1981) research suggests that centralization more commonly follows computing implementation than decentralization does. But since computing can be used for either structural approach, it is not clear whether Robey's finding is due to greater facilitation of centralization by computing or simply a result of a current (or maybe usual) tendency of many organizations to centralize when they can.

The basic lesson thus far is that computing does not necessarily yield any changes in organizational structure and in most cases does not result in much structural change at all. Where structural change does occur, it is primarily related to the computing function itself. For example, in most organizations computing was originally a subunit of the finance or controller's department. Subsequently, it has been moved into an independent department. It is now, in some cases, being decentralized back to operating departments for some things while being retained in the central department for others (King, 1983).

In summary, managers are still in control of their organizational units. Computing is a tool that one can choose to use to alter or support the existing organizational structure.

Work: Employment, Job Satisfaction, and Performance. The issue of computing's effect on employment was hotly contested for many years but has since been bypassed by increased concern regarding impacts on other work-related issues. Still, the first empirical studies of computing impacts in organizations were conducted by the Department of Labor to determine whether administrative computing would result in massive displacement of clerical workers. The concern about employment arose naturally because a central "benefit" of computing was the computer's ability to perform certain tasks much more rapidly and accurately than people. Computing was seen by some critics as the ultimate capitalist dream, allowing wholesale replacement of people by machines. This view was reinforced by an often explicit, and always implicit, feature of the ads for computing systems, which was the claim that such systems would save money and reduce costs by allowing organizations to cut personnel. The response in defense of computing has been that even if computing did result in reduction of need for people in some jobs, it also created new jobs. The argument, in short, has centered on the net effect: Are there more jobs or fewer jobs after the arrival of computers?

The answer to this question is not clear. It is possible to find cases where automation has clearly resulted in the elimination of jobs. The number of dispatchers has declined as fire and police emergency systems have been automated. But such clear-cut cases are uncommon. Clerical workers, for example, do a wide variety of tasks, some of which can be automated and some of which cannot. It is therefore difficult to determine the effect of automation on employment for individual job categories. Moreover, the statistical measures used to determine employment conditions simply are not precise enough to answer the question of what effect computing has had on employment.

The primary thing we know about computing and employment, therefore, is that we do not know enough to decide what is happening. It should be borne in mind that most applications of computing thus far have been for administrative purposes. Thus, the impacts would be felt mainly in white-collar work. Overall, the number of people employed in white-collar work has been expanding over the last two decades, as for that matter has the number of clerical workers.

Perhaps, the more important question to ask about the impact of computing on the work life of employees is whether jobs become "worse" or "better" as a result of automation. On the down side, some have predicted that computing will result in the "de-skilling" of jobs by stripping skilled jobs of their conceptual content (Braverman, 1974; Driscoll, 1982). On the up side, others have predicted that computing will upgrade the jobs of workers by taking over mundane tasks and freeing workers to perform the interesting and creative tasks (Bell, 1973; Giuliano, 1982).

Unlike the situation with employment and computing, there is empirical evidence about computing's effect on work life. Computing is generally seen by employees as having positive effects on their quality of work life (Dubnoff, 1978; Jaffe and Froomkin, 1966; Kraemer, Dutton, and Northrop, 1981; Rumberger, 1981). For example, in our 1976 study of computer utilization in forty-two U.S. cities, we found that employees who used computers felt that computing raised their senses of accomplishment and improved their job performances without affecting the degree to which their work was supervised (Kraemer, Dutton, and Northrop, 1981). These positive assessments were made by a wide variety of employees, including clerical staff, detectives, patrol officers, budget analysts, and planners as well as top city officials. Moreover, our respondents overwhelmingly wanted to use computers more in their jobs and felt that computers would greatly improve the operations of their governments. Using independent measures of job performance, we also found that computing improved operational performance. Here again, improved performance due to computerization was found to be conditioned by the organizational and social context.

In sum, the empirical evidence strongly suggests that computing has improved the quality of work life. Employees fear computers until they use them. Once familiar with computers, employees feel better about themselves as workers and also perform better. While positive, the extent of these effects is still conditioned by the organizational and social context. Improved performance has been found to be as dependent, or even more dependent, on professional management practices, financial resources, bureaucratic structure, and even population size and growth as on number of computerized applications (Northrop, Dutton, and Kraemer, 1982). Thus, we again conclude that the rules have not changed. Managers are in as much control of their organizational units as they were before computing. Service demands and budgets are still key constraints. Computers can aid in improving performance, but they are not a solution in and of themselves.

Decision Making. Computing has long been heralded as a boon to decision making. Computing's contribution is said to come from two things. First is the enhancement of one's ability to organize and maintain the base of factual information that must be used to understand the situation. This function includes collection and storage of information. But more important, it also includes the ability to retrieve the right information at the right time. Second is the provision of greater power to analyze information, particularly quantitative information. This power is derived from the modeling capabilities of computing, in which large amounts of information can be reduced to key indicators that are comprehensible to decision makers. Most characterizations of the decision-making assistance offered by computers have focused on these two capabilities. The vision of a decision support system (DSS) in which the decision maker has on-line access to powerful models and all the data necessary to run the models under different assumptions is idealistic and has no parallel in practice.

The impact of computing on decision making has not been at the level of decision making envisioned by DSS proponents. For example, even decisions about whether to buy PC's so departmental analysts can run spreadsheet programs are typically resolved through analysis of information that is not on any local computer system. Issues such as "Shouldn't we really wait for new, more powerful PC's?" and "Maybe the department head should get one before the analysts do" are the ones that need answers and involve managerial judgments. Computing has, though, made it possible to answer "enabling" questions, such as whether there will be sufficient funds to afford any computing equipment. Thus, computer-based information is used to set the stage for decisions, which is an important but often overlooked contribution to decision making.

Similarly, computing contributes to the process of determining whether decisions need to be made. An excellent example is provided by the exceptions-reporting capabilities in most financial systems. A decision about what to do with a department that is overspending its budget is only worth considering when a department is overspending. Computing has made it possible to build such routine exceptions reporting into most financial and personnel management systems, and these capabilities have become critical to effective organizational control. Computing makes it easier to monitor for situations in which decisions need to be made. Thus, computing has made a major contribution to decision making through helping decision makers determine when they need to decide certain matters, and at times computers may alert decision makers that a decision needs to be made earlier than they would have been alerted without computing.

But these contributions to decision making do not carry the excitement that surrounds the DSS vision. They also pale in comparison to potential developments in expert systems and other emerging fields of computer science. Still, they are important in practical terms because they reflect the realities of organizational decision making.

Admittedly, computing has been applied to much more complex decision situations. The results of these applications are worth noting for the ways in which they reinforce the need to focus on the context of decision making rather than just the technology. The most notable examples of computing application to complex decision making are in the uses of large-scale computerized models for setting policy. Studies of computerized modeling in government yield fascinating insights about the potential of computing for aiding in decision making under uncertainty. The routine benefits of computing that we have noted also pertain to these circumstances, but the complicated nature of these decision situations exerts its own effect on the outcome of model use.

Briefly, large modeling systems do not result in "answers" to the larger question of what should be done. Rather, these modeling systems have important effects on the process of decision making that in turn affect the outcomes of the process. Our studies of model use in local governments (Dutton and Kraemer, 1984) and the federal government (Kraemer, Dickhoven, Fallows, and King, 1987) show that computing contributes to the decision-making process in several ways. First, computer-based models impose rigid discipline on the analytical process. This is particularly important in controversial decision situations where the opposing parties have access to the models. Models require their users to specify precisely the assumptions they are making and the basic facts of the decision situation. Omissions and changes are easy for the opposition to spot. This discipline helps make the factual bases of different positions clear to all and appears to contribute to more rapid assessment of the difference between positions taken for ideological as opposed to factual reasons.

Second, computer-based models often help bring the different parties in a decision situation together to agree on what is important and what is not. This is partially an artifact of the rigid discipline imposed by modeling, but it is also due to the fact that models can be a neutral ground for disagreement and compromise. In some cases, major progress toward a decision is made by using the model to clarify which alternatives will and will not be considered, what criteria will be used for evaluating the alternatives, and how various criteria will be weighted. It should also be noted that clarifying the issues sometimes makes compromise more difficult. Pack and Pack (1977) report that urban land use models have sometimes made political decision making more difficult because the models help clarify who wins and who loses under various land use patterns.

Finally, it appears that the use of models in decision making can serve, over time, to help educate and improve the skills of decision makers. This again is due in part to the discipline enforced by modeling. But it also comes about as decision makers gain familiarity with the processes involved in considering various factors in a methodical way. Of particular importance is the tendency of modeling to force the user to learn to discriminate between those factors that are critical to decision outcomes and those that are not. Similarly, modeling helps clarify for decision makers when there are simply insufficient facts to yield a clear preference among alternatives.

To summarize, computers tend not to drive decision making. Computing is and will continue to be only one source of information in the decision-making process. A computer analysis might tell a city that one-person patrol cars are more cost effective than two-person cars. However, the decision to go to one-person cars has to be balanced with safety concerns and union demands. At the same time, a spreadsheet analysis can show the impact of various salary structures on the budget, but it cannot tell personnel what structure unions will accept nor what structure will attract or retain the best employees. Consequently, the general rule is that the more structured or routine the decision-making situation is, such as assigning inspectors to cases, the more decisive the computer will be in the decision-making process. But as the decision-making situation becomes less structured and routine, such as projecting future revenues or deciding whether to propose tax hikes, the less decisive the computer will be. Judgment and political insight will continue to be key to the practice of public administration. It will always be necessary to keep in mind what is feasible in terms of what the organization and its social context historically have been willing and able to do.

Political Power. Characterizing computing as an instrument by which different goals might be accomplished can lead to the incorrect conclusion that computing is simply a neutral tool in organizational life, to be used as best fits the organization. In fact, computing can be politically very important. The political significance of computing arises from three features of computing use.

First is the political significance of the information processed by computers. Information is not power, but those with the best information are often most successful at accomplishing their objectives. Depending on how computing is organized and provided, various individuals and factions in organizations can gain or lose power relative to others. This is especially true in the context of the contributions of computing to decision making.

Second is what we call the "resource politics" of computing, arising from the fact that those who control computing govern a large investment of government resources. Control over organizational resources brings power, both through building a base for further increases in demands on resources and through control over capabilities that others in the organization or its clients need.

Finally, computing brings "affective power" because of its inherent attractiveness as an activity. Those who are engaged in computing are perceived by many as advanced, sophisticated, and professional. Many people are intimidated by technical jargon and computer printouts, which can be used effectively to obfuscate the underlying issues in disputes and to weaken opposition.

The fundamental question about computing and organizational politics is who gains and who loses from computing. Some have predicted that computing will alter the political profile of organizations by shifting power to technocrats (Downs, 1967; Lowi, 1972). Others have suggested that computing can strengthen pluralistic features of organizations by providing different interest groups with the ability to respond to their opposition with the tools of technology (Blum, 1972; Oettinger, 1979). Still others maintain that computing reinforces the status quo by providing the existing power elite with the tools to perpetuate and strengthen their power (Hoffman, 1973, 1977). More recent research suggest that this last is the most common outcome of computing (Danzinger, Dutton, Kling, and Kraemer, 1982; Kraemer, 1980).

This "reinforcement" of political influence is an extension of our earlier observations about computing's impacts. Computing is not in itself a powerful and influential force in organizations. But it does provide the opportunity to reinforce prevailing policy and attitudes toward larger organizational issues. These policies and attitudes are typically shaped by those already in powerful positions, and computing naturally is absorbed as a tool by this elite. The elite decide what resources will be invested in computing, what control structures will govern when and how computing is used, and what priorities will be honored in system development and implementation. This power results in the singular opportunity to decide who will benefit from computing and who will not. It is important to note that this power does not require that the elite be technically skilled in computing. It requires only that the elite control the acquisition and application of technical skill.

This finding challenges assumptions about the potential "democratizing" effects of computing. Instead of democratizing organizations, computers have been empirically determined to be a powerful tool of the status quo.

What Every Public Manager
Should Know About Computing

In the previous section we argued that, in spite of the predictions, the empirical literature indicates that computing is not an independent factor that significantly influences the nature of public administration. Rather, the impacts of computers are conditioned by the organizational and social context. Thus, computerization does not change the basic bureaucratic or political structure of a public agency, nor does it negate the all-important need for political insight and judgment on the part of public managers. Computerization can and does improve performance, but performance is still conditioned by other classic factors such as the nature of the task (Northrop and Perry, 1985), financial resources, employee skills and attitudes, and managerial leadership.

What computing does is create fear. This chapter has so far tried to dispel much of the fear for public managers that accompanies computerization. Much of the knowledge needed to effectively manage with computers is just an extension of the management theory and practice that every good public manager already knows. The practice of public administration has not significantly changed with the introduction of computers. Nevertheless, lack of knowledge of computing does hinder public managers, because they cannot communicate with those who use computers nor can they effectively avail themselves or their organization of the benefits stemming from computerization.

Because computers have permeated government, public managers must become knowledgeable about computers. First, they need to know the basic terms, concepts, and processes related to computer use. Second, they should have personal experience with at least one computer software package; they should master a spreadsheet, a statistical package, or a project management package. Familiarity with just one software package will go a long way toward dispelling the fear of computers, as well as sensitizing the manager to a vast array of computing issues for his or her employees. But public managers must realize that learning one package does not mean they can automatically use another. Each software package has its own tricks and stumbling blocks, and each requires practice to master. Third, public managers need to think about computers in terms of management use, such as reports. The manager should ask the systems analyst what the system can do or could do with the proper software. Fourth, the manager should not reinvent the wheel. Public managers should learn from others by talking to managers in other cities, states, or agencies that are automated. Also, they should talk to managers in their own level of government. Remember that computing's impact is conditioned by the organizational and social context, so managers need to translate the offered advice and insights into their own situation.

In general optimism should be the rule of thumb. Computing is here to stay and appears to have a positive effect on the work lives of public servants.

The Future of Computing: An Evaluation of Information Resource Management

Computing is here to stay, but what direction will it take? Technically, computing is always being revolutionized, making it more and more accessible in terms of cost, ease of use, and application. This trend will continue. Organizationally, computing is a reflection of the forces already guiding and shaping the organization. We believe this situation will also continue. As a consequence, such reform movements as information resource management (IRM) are highly likely to fail. Movements of this nature not only ignore several lessons about bureaucracy and cost-benefit analysis but also ignore the basic lesson of computer research that we have been emphasizing: computing impacts are conditioned by the organizational and social context.

The IRM concept is founded on the assumptions that organizations are systems amenable to systematic control, that information is a resource that can be managed in economically efficient ways, and that particular management techniques embodied under the IRM rubric will improve the efficiency and effectiveness of information management in federal agencies. These assumptions are questionable, as we will now try to argue.

Organizations as Systems. The systems view of organizations has long had utility as a way of characterizing organizational structure and function. But there is a critical difference between describing organizations as though they are systems and trying to deal with them as systems. The difference is in the limits of systematic control one can exert in real organizations. Real organizations, particularly complex organizations, exhibit behaviors that confound systems explanations. Most organizations do not have clear goals and objectives on which all organizational participants agree. Understanding of intended organizational outputs, and thus goals and objectives, vary from person to person and subgroup to subgroup.

Consider the efforts to implement planning-programming-budgeting systems (PPB) between 1955 and 1970. This approach did not work out as planned, because the systematic constructs of PPB did not cope with the political complexities of the governmental "system." The specific shortcomings were obvious. For one thing, not everyone in the vast bureaucracy of the federal government could be expected to go along with the PPB movement. Compliance was difficult to monitor, and the inertia of past practices provided a powerful incentive to give only token acknowledgment to PPB. More important, lower-level bureaucrats had agendas of their own that PPB interrupted. Those closest to the action in the mission agencies often found it easy to subvert PPB to sustaining the status quo—a very different end than PPB's creators had in mind.

IRM's most noble goals can be similarly subverted. IRM serves particular interests among federal agencies. Levitan (1982) notes that 85 percent of the approximately 200 references in her review of IRM see IRM as a substantive area, and the vast majority of those references are by people in the information systems field. Those writing in the IRM area frequently address themselves to people like themselves (Greenwood, 1979; Horton, 1979b; Synnott, 1981, Synnott and Gruber 1982, 1983). A major incentive for the IRM movement rests in the desire of information system professionals to expand their jurisdiction within the organization. These people are clearly stakeholders in the IRM concept, and IRM's implementation will benefit them directly.

This is the sort of behavior that is not readily accommodated by "systems" explanations of organizations. Thus, the systems view of organizations that underlies the IRM concept is misleading.

Information as a Resource. A major conceptual contribution of IRM is the characterization of information as a resource. A resource is a source of supply or support, and information in a theoretical sense can conform to this definition. But implementing the IRM concept of information as a resource poses a set of serious practical problems. In spite of considerable research into the economics of information, the tools available to assess the economic value of information are in their infancy (Griffiths, 1982; Rich, 1980).

The major problem is the difficulty in placing a value on information (Braunstein, 1981; Connell, 1981b; Oettinger, 1979, 1980). While this is acknowledged by IRM proponents (Horton, 1979a; Horton and Marchand, 1982; Levitan, 1982), the problem is not solved in their work. Existing economic theory does not provide guidelines for valuing information to be collected. With sufficient thought and care algorithms can be developed that inform choices on a case-by-case basis. But this always entails considerable subjective judgment, and analyses are open to attack by those who disagree with the conclusions they produce (Connell, 1981a; Dutton and Kraemer, 1985; King, 1984). Hence, the values imposed will be judgmental and case specific, making a mockery of the effort to establish objective value for information across agencies.

This problem could conceivably disappear when economists become more adept at dealing with uncertainty. But uncertainty is only one part of the problem with valuation of information. Another is that information cannot be intrinsically scarce once it is created. It can be given away to literally everyone in the world and still retain its intrinsic value, and it is not depleted through use. In sum, there is as yet no coherent body of economic theory that proves the utility of considering information as a resource.

The Efficacy of IRM. There are other reasons IRM is unlikely to enhance organizational efficiency and effectiveness. For example, it is not yet clear that traditional ways of dealing with information in the federal government, with all their flaws, are so unbearably bad and wasteful that a major reform like IRM is necessary. All aspects of information management bring costs, but are these costs "too high"? Only a small fraction of government operating budgets are spent on computerized data processing. Our recent studies of computing in local government agencies show such expenditures to be less than 2 percent, up from about 1 percent a decade ago (Kraemer, King, Dunkle, and Lane, 1986). (There are undoubtedly differences between the federal government and local governments in such expenditures, but not enough to change our observation.) Information-handling costs outside of data processing certainly add to this figure, but it is doubtful that the total costs for handling information in government agencies represent more than a small fraction of the massive sums spent directly on entitlement program payments, defense procurement, and other activities. Such costs, even if they are large in absolute terms, are probably affordable in the context of overall government operations costs. There is always room for improvement, but the shrill alarm raised by the Commission on Federal Paperwork fades in comparison to the federal government's other problems, and IRM could be a marginal solution to a marginal problem.

Another concern is with the breadth of objectives IRM is expected to achieve. IRM focuses on the big picture of organizational information use—a lofty goal but a seemingly impractical one in the context of very large and complex organizations such as the federal government. In most circumstances it is pointless to spend too much time on the "overall rationale" behind information collection and use because most organizational decisions address narrowly circumscribed issues, not organization-wide goals and objectives. The information needed for most decisions is gathered by those involved with the decision and not by a central elite. Decisions that do involve organization-wide goals usually require information that is hard to come by: strategic information about the current state, probable futures, and the likely consequences of alternative actions. Such information seldom resides in useable form in the databases of subunits. For these reasons it is usually a mistake to move from the top down in assessing organizational information management practices.

The broad array of IRM objectives also causes problems by specifying a set of control tasks so sweeping that the IRM executive would have to be superhuman or close to it to accomplish them. In addition to overseeing all existing data-processing operations, those in charge of IRM would be called on to control virtually all information that enters into organizational decisions, to change other managers' minds so they view information as a resource, and to ensure that organizational information needs are considered routinely in all aspects of the organization's enterprise. Moreover, any manager with this mandate would face formidable obstacles in overcoming the inertia of established organizational practice, not to mention the obstreperous actions of other top-level administrators attempting to contain the extraordinary power implied in the job description of the IRM executive.

A discrepancy between the larger vision of IRM and its shortcomings in practice is not surprising. Managerial reform movements often do little more than temporarily redirect people's attention from routine activities to basic issues. And in this small way they can be very useful. But IRM could bring more serious consequences by lulling government leaders into thinking information is being managed well when it is not. Again the case of PPB in the federal government proves an instructive lesson. The costs of implementing PPB turned out to be greater than the benefits of "improved management" (Merewitz and Sosnick, 1971). The administrative orders implementing PPB did not consider the actual missions of agencies, so the larger target of PPB—improved program planning at the level of the whole government—was never accomplished. The mechanics of PPB helped agency leaders select among alternative projects and make their case before the president and Congress, but PPB did not help the president or Congress decide among agency proposals. In the worst cases more attention was paid to conformance with PPB guidelines than to the substance of the proposals. Thus, PPB brought improvements to the techniques of analysis but failed to improve the functioning of the government.

Perhaps more important than IRM's contribution to an illusion of efficiency and effectiveness is the potential for deliberate manipulation of IRM-spawned controls toward ideological ends. Events of the past seven years suggest that IRM concepts are being employed to justify restricting collection or release of important data and to encourage divesting the federal government of much of its traditional data dissemination role. Under the IRM rubric, the authority of the U.S. Office of Management and Budget to approve or disapprove of federal data collection and management plans has been expanded. How should officials in OMB go about determining whether the costs of collecting data about the toxic hazards of certain products exceed the public health benefits from this knowledge? Similarly, how should they decide when efforts to ensure public access to government data have become "too expensive"? Such politically sensitive and socially important questions cannot be resolved effectively by focusing on costs and discounting other criteria.

In conclusion, it is quite possible that the passage of time will bring about for IRM the same kind of quiet death suffered by PPB seven years after it was instituted. If this happens, the shortcomings in the IRM philosophy will be made moot, and the appropriation of IRM concepts for the ideological manipulation of government information activities will cease. But this ignoble end might not come for IRM. Commentators such as Laudon (1986) suggest that modern information technologies are facilitating a drift toward increasing centralization of control over government information activity, exactly as recommended by IRM advocates. The IRM philosophy is seductive, as was the PPB philosophy. Those who seek to increase executive branch control over federal agency behavior will continue to recognize the value of control over agency data collection, handling, use, and disseminating activities.

Computing and Public Management:
General Strategies

A continuing theme of the various chapters in this book is that managers must manage. Computing, like budgeting, calls for planning and involves choices.

Neither computing nor budgeting is a skill separate from or superior to the organizational and social context. Effectiveness and efficiency are goals that we try to reach through developing new techniques, such as management by objectives, zero-base budgeting, program evaluation, privatization, IRM, and the computerization of information.

Computerization is a strategy; it is not a solution. It does not necessarily guarantee more effective service delivery, although it can, nor does it guarantee cost savings. In fact, more likely than not computing adds to budgets. But as Frank Sackton points out in Chapter Six, the country and all levels of government are growing in sheer numbers of people, sizes of budgets, and numbers of tasks performed. In effect, it is hard to sort out computing's effect on costs. Moreover, computerization has changed the nature of tasks, so to cost out computing's effect may be like comparing apples with oranges.

Computing is a strategy and one that must be managed. It should be clear from our years of experience with computing that we cannot leave computing decisions to system analysts. We have gone beyond the naive view that computing is a skill left up to its professionals and that managers need not be knowledgeable about computers given the unique specialization of jobs.

We have already spoken about how much managers need to know about computers. Our recommendation is a low level of literacy in terms of computing *practice* but a high level of literacy in terms of computing's *impacts*. This chapter has therefore dwelt on summarizing the empirical literature on the impacts of computing. We will end with some final thoughts on strategies that managers should consider in regard to computing.

First, computerization can pay off. But the most obvious payoffs have been in routine tasks. Thus, the more routine the tasks, the more likely one should automate. For example, the computerization of financial records has been wonderful on several counts, but computerization of forecasting models has been far less successful.

Second, once automated, do not ignore the task or its workers. Never presume that automation takes discretion out of decision making or that accurate data necessarily result. This is why Frank Sackton (in Chapter Six) suggests judgmental forecastings, common sense, and experience as valuable adjuncts to modeling.

Third, involve users in software design or choice of software packages to purchase. Users know their jobs, how they are structured as of now, what works, what could or could not improve the way they perform their jobs. Moreover, involvement creates commitment, which can also contribute to more successful payoffs from computers beyond those inherent in the proper choice of hardware and software.

Fourth, train your people and make it formal. Have group training sessions whenever new equipment, hard or soft, is introduced. In addition, have at least one person be a designated and knowledgeable source for answering computing questions as they crop up over time.

Finally, get a good service contract or have a good in-house service person. It may be an old adage, but nothing is worthwhile unless it works.

References

Argyris, C. "Management Information Systems: The Challenge to Rationality and Emotionality." *Management Science,* 1971, *17* (6), 275–292.

Bell, D. *The Coming of the Post-Industrial Society.* New York: Basic Books, 1973.

Bjorn-Anderson, N., and Pederson, P. "Computer-Facilitated Changes and Management Power Structures." *Accounting, Organizations, and Society,* 1977, *5* (2), 203–216.

Blau, P., and Schoenherr, R. *The Structure of Organizations.* New York: Basic Books, 1971.

Blum, E. "Municipal Services." In H. Sackman and B. W. Boehm (eds.), *Planning Community Information Utilities.* Montvale, N.J.: AFIPS Press, 1972.

Braunstein, Y. "Information as a Commodity: Public Policy Issues and Recent Research." In R. M. Mason and J. E. Creps, Jr. (eds.), *Information Services: Economics, Management and Technology.* Boulder, Colo.: Westview Press, 1981.

Braverman, H. *Labor and the Monopoly Capital: The Degradation of Work in the Twentieth Century.* New York: Monthly Review Press, 1974.

Cattela, R. C. "Information as a Corporate Asset." *Information and Management,* 1981, *4* (1), 29-37.

Connell, J. J. "The Fallacy of Information Resource Management." *Infosystems,* 1981a, *28* (5), 78-84.

Connell, J. J. "IRM vs. the Office of the Future." *Journal of Systems Management,* 1981b, *32* (5), 6-10.

Danziger, J. N., Dutton, W. H., Kling, R., and Kraemer, K. L. *The Politics of Computing: High Technology in American Local Governments.* New York: Columbia University Press, 1982.

Downs: A. "A Realistic Look at the Payoffs from Urban Data Systems." *Public Administration Review,* 1967, *27* (3), 204-210.

Driscoll, J. "Office Automation: The Dynamics of a Technological Boondoggle." In R. Landau and J. Blair (eds.), *Emerging Office Systems.* Norwood, N.J.: Ablex, 1982.

Dubnoff, S. "Interoccupational Shifts and Changes in the Quality of Working Life in the American Economy, 1900-1970." Paper presented at the Society for the Study of Social Problems, San Francisco, 1978.

Dutton, W. H., and Kraemer, K. L. "Technology and Urban Management: The Power Payoffs of Computing." *Administration and Society,* 1977, *9* (3), 304-340.

Dutton, W. H., and Kraemer, K. L. *Modeling as Negotiating: The Political Dynamics of Computer Models in the Policy Process.* Norwood, N.J.: Ablex, 1984.

Edelman, R. "Management of Information Resources." *MIS Quarterly,* 1981, *5* (1), 17-28.

Gardner, E., and others. "Human-Oriented Implementation Cures 'Cyberphobia.'" *Data Management,* November 1985, *23,* 29-32.

Giuliano, V. "The Mechanization of Office Work." *Scientific American,* 1982, *247* (3), 148-165.

Greenwood, F. "Your New Job in Information Resource Management." *Journal of Systems Management,* 1979, *30* (4), 24-27.

Griffiths, J. M. "The Value of Information and Related Systems, Products and Services." In *Annual Review of Information Science and Technology.* White Plains, N.Y.: Knowledge Industry Publications, 1982.

Hirchleifer, J., and Riley, J. G. "The Analysis of Uncertainty and Information: An Expository Survey." *Journal of Economic Literature,* 1979, *17,* (4), 1376-1421.

Hoffman, E. P. "Soviet Metapolicy: Information Processing in the Soviet Union." *Administration and Society,* 1973, *5,* 200-232.

Hoffman, E. P. "Technology, Values, and Political Power in the Soviet Union." *Technology and Communist Culture.* New York: Holt, Rinehart & Winston, 1977.

Horton, F. W., Jr. *The Information Resource.* Washington, D.C.: Information Industry Association, 1979a.

Horton, F. W., Jr. "Occupational Standard for the Information Resource Manager." *Journal of Systems Management,* 1979b, *30* (50), 35-41.

Horton, F. W., Jr., and Marchand, D. A. (eds.). *Information Management in Public Administration.* Arlington, Va.: Information Resources Press, 1982.

Jaffe, A. J., and Froomkin, J. *Technology and Jobs: Automation in Perspective.* New York: Praeger, 1966.

King, J. L. "Centralization vs. Decentralization of Computing: Organizational Considerations and Management Options." *ACM Computing Surveys,* 1983, *16* (4), 319-349.

King, J. L. "Ideology and Use of Large-Scale Decision Support Systems in National Policymaking." *Systems/Objectives/Solutions,* 1984, *4,* 81-104.

Kling, R. "Social Analyses of Computing: Theoretical Perspectives in Recent Empirical Research." *Computing Surveys,* 1980, *12* (1), 132-146.

Kraemer, K. L. "Computers, Information, and Power in Local Governments." *Human Choice and Computers,* 1980, *2,* 213-215.

Kraemer, K. L., and Danziger, J. N. "Computers and Control in the Work Environment." *Public Administration Review*, 1984, *44* (1), 32–42.

Kraemer, K. L., Dickhoven, S., Fallows, S., and King, J. L. *Datawars: Computer Models in Federal Policy Making*. New York: Columbia University Press, 1987.

Kraemer, K. L., and Dutton, W. H. "The Interests Served by Technological Reform." *Administration and Society*, 1979, *11* (1), 80–106.

Kraemer, K. L., Dutton, W. H., and Northrop, A. *The Management of Information Systems*. New York: Columbia University Press, 1981.

Kraemer, K. L., King, J. L., Dunkle, D., and Lane, J. *Municipal Information Systems Directory*. Irvine, Calif.: Public Policy Research Organization, 1986.

Kraemer, K. L., and Northrop, A. "Computers in Public Management Education: A Curriculum Proposal for the Next Ten Years." *Public Administration Quarterly*, 1984, *8* (3), 343–368.

Laudon, K. C. *Dossier Society: Value Choices in the Design of National Information Systems*. New York: Columbia University Press, 1986.

Leavitt, H., and Whisler, T. "Management in the 1980s." *Harvard Business Review*, 1958, *36*, 41–48.

Leduc, N. "Communicating Through Computers." *Telecommunications Policy*, Sept. 1979, *235*, 244.

Levitan, K. B. "Information Resource(s) Management." *Annual Review of Information Science and Technology*, 1982, *17*, 227–266.

Lippitt, M., Miller, J. P., and Lalamaj, J. "Patterns of Use and Correlates of Adoption of an Electronic Mail System." Proceedings of the American Institute of Decision Sciences, 1980.

Lowi, T. J. "Government and Politics: Blurring of Sector Lines." *Information Technology: Some Critical Implications*. New York: The Conference Board, 1972.

Machlup, J. "Uses, Value and Benefits of Knowledge." *Knowledge: Creation, Diffusion, Utilization*, 1979, *1* (1), 62–81.

Marchack, J. "Economics of Inquiring, Communicating, Deciding." *American Economic Review*, 1968, *58* (2), 1-18.

Merewitz, L., and Sosnick, S. H. *The Budget's New Clothes: A Critique of Planning-Programming-Budgeting and Benefit-Cost Analysis*. Chicago: Markham, 1971.

Mumford, E., and Banks, O. *The Computer and the Clerk*. London: Routledge and Kegan Paul, 1967.

Myers, C. *The Impact of Computers on Management*. Cambridge, Mass.: MIT Press, 1967.

Northrop, A., Dutton, W. H., and Kraemer, K. L. "The Management of Computer Applications in Local Government." *Public Administration Review*, 1982, *42* (3), 234-243.

Northrop, A., and Perry, J. "A Task Environmental Approach to Organizational Assessment." *Public Administration Review*, 1985, *45* (2), 275-281.

Oettinger, A. G. "Information Resources: Old Questions, New Choices." *Bulletin of the American Society for Information Science*, 1979, *6* (1), 1-19.

Oettinger, A. G. "Information Resources: Knowledge and Power in the 21st Century." *Science*, 1980, *209* (4), 191-198.

Pack, H., and Pack, J. R. "The Resurrection of the Urban Development Model." *Policy Analysis*, 1977, *3* (3), 407-427.

Petersohn, H. "Management of Information Resources: Basic Concepts and Principles of Organization." *Information and Records Management*, 1981, *15* (9), 65-77.

Pfeffer, J. *Power in Organizations*. Marshfield, Mass.: Pitman, 1981.

Rich, R. "The Value of Information." In E. R. Morss and R. Rich (eds.), *Government Information Management: A Counter-Report to the Commission on Federal Paperwork*. Boulder, Colo.: Westview Press, 1980.

Robey, D. "Computer Information Systems and Organizational Structure." *Communications of the ACM*, 1981, *24* (1), 679-686.

Rumberger, R. "The Changing Skill Requirements of Jobs in the U.S. Economy." *Industrial and Labor Relations Review*, 1981, *34*, 578-590.

Synnott, W. R. "Changing Roles for Information Managers." *Computerworld*, 1981, *15* (38), 19-28.

Synnott, W. R., and Gruber, W. H. "Information Resource Management: Opportunities and Strategies for the 1980s." *Online Review,* 1982, *6* (3), 269–270.

Synnott, W. R., and Gruber, W. H. "User Involvement Strategies for IRM Professionals." *Data Management,* 1983, *21* (1), 34–39.

Withington, F. *The Real Computer: Its Influences, Uses and Effects.* Reading, Mass.: Addison-Wesley, 1969.

8

᠁᠁᠁᠁᠁᠁᠁᠁᠁᠁᠁᠁᠁᠁

Making the Most of Strategic Planning and Management

Jerry L. Mc Caffery

From a planning perspective, government seems overly political, short term, bounded from one election to the next, and vulnerable to interest-group pressures and the need for politicians to do something to get reelected. As a result, public sector decisions seem incremental, reactive, and opportunistic. Conversely, administrators tend to characterize strategic planning as unrealistically rational, formalistic, and dominated by lengthy planning documents written by planners who have never faced an operational necessity, a revenue shortfall, or an angry citizen. Little wonder, then, that as late as 1979 scholars commented that while strategic planning and management were well accepted concepts in the private sector, they were virtually "unexplored territory" for the public sector researcher (Wortman, 1979), or that formal long-range planning in the public sector had been judged a failure (Eadie, 1983) because of its projection of internal knowledge about current activities into a static future (Eadie and Steinbacher, 1985). This kind of planning was clearly of little help to an organization whose issues did not fit neatly into a single department or whose environment was changing dramatically.

The critique of strategic planning led to the explosive growth in the public sector of the concept of strategic management, perhaps as a result of the critique of strategic planning, as a response to fiscal hardships and program shortcomings, or simply as a result of unimplementable strategies (Eadie and Steinbacher, 1985). The movement from strategic planning to strategic management is a movement away from controlling the future toward managing the present (Eadie, 1988). It leads to a focus on flexibility and the ability to be more responsive to the organization's environment. It emphasizes a continuous rather than cyclical process and the importance of processing information to select issues and formulate and implement strategies to deal with them.

Could your organization benefit from strategic management? If you agree with one or more of the statements in this Strategic Diagnostic Checklist, it could (Eadie, 1988).

1. We do not have a sufficiently clear vision or set of priorities to guide our planning and management.
2. We are too often caught off guard by unanticipated issues that have serious consequences.
3. Our environment is changing so rapidly that we feel overwhelmed and cannot seem to exert control over events.
4. Our policy body is increasingly frustrated by what some members perceive as a role that is too vague or weak in policymaking.
5. The policy body–administration relationship is becoming frayed, making it increasingly difficult to deal with important issues.
6. Our senior managers spend very little time collectively identifying strategic issues and formulating strategies to deal with them.
7. Our annual budget-preparation process basically involves adjusting objects of expenditure and provides little opportunity for creative policymaking.

Strategic management includes strategic planning, but it is a more inclusive concept, emphasizing dynamic interaction with the environment and an incremental methodology that allows for scanning the environment to choose the target that will yield the most benefit for the effort expended. It operates out of a full knowledge that time is a limiting variable and that leaders cannot attack all problems and must be able to achieve solid accomplishments for the expenditure of their vital resources.

The emphasis on stakeholders is very different from the narrower concept of strategic planning; stakeholders are decision makers within the organization and its environment who have an interest in organizational performance and can help or hinder the choice and implementation of strategies. Stakeholders must be brought along for a strategy to succeed. Strategic management also has a shorter timeframe than strategic planning in that it looks to the near-term future to accomplish realistic strategic implementations and not to some arbitrary five-year plan.

The technical tools of strategic planning are found in the environmental scanning process of strategic management where various organizational, economic, and political factors are considered, but they are only part of a process that seeks to provide co-alignment of internal and external variables for the agency and its environment. The concept of balance with the environment is another vital explicit difference between strategic management and strategic planning. Performance gaps—the acknowledgment that something is going wrong with the agency's programs—as a catalyst for the strategic management process is also a difference from the cyclical routine nature of strategic planning. Boschken and Shumaker (1988) suggest that where an organizational or political crisis is not apparent "the agency is unlikely to perceive the need for strategic planning, preferring instead an unanalyzed continuation of existing policies and programs" (p. 8).

The focus on the external environment rather than on improving agency operations is another crucial change in emphasis with strategic management. The thrust of strategic planning was to put the environment in a dependent position; if the agency allocated resources correctly, program delivery would take care of itself. Another important thread of strategic management is the deliberate effort to attack problems that cross departmental lines in order to manage complex programs and policy areas.

Where private sector strategic planning tends to operate from market competition, profit, and market share, public sector organizations are part of an interweaving of "multi-lateral power, influence, bargaining, voting and exchange relationships" (Wechsler and Backoff, 1986, p. 321). This complexity has consequences for the way the organization does strategic management and for the skills that are necessary to do it.

A final important differences lies in the choice of who does strategic management. While planning staffs can do technical work supporting the intelligence-gathering functions in scanning the environment of the organization, the strategic management function has to be closely associated with the top management group. It has to be supported by that group. One technique of strategic management is to convene the top management group away from the workplace under the guidance of a facilitator to reaffirm the organization's mission and discover what the group identifies as the crucial issues facing the organization as well as which of these issues should receive priority attention. Eadie (1988) calls this "the right people around the right table for the right amount of time applying the right methodology to the right information." The attention to the human factor and teamwork is a critical difference between strategic planning and strategic management.

The sense of operating at the margin is important to strategic management. Most resources are fixed and there is little slack to reprogram to attack problems; consequently, the manager has to be sure that the reapplication of scarce resources to issue A rather than issue B is going to pay off in real results. This sense of getting something done in the near future and paying for it out of scarce resources is a recognition of limits—limits to people, to the organization, and of the possible, which is very different from the old sense of strategic planning where resources and time constraints and the necessity to do something soon were lost in long-range planning. The involvement of operators rather than planners in deciding what has to be done is different, as is the emphasis on pulling operators out of their normal work profile and, with a facilitator, out of the normal authority structure to do strategic issue identification.

One way that the product of this process is reintegrated into the organization's normal operating routines is by adding an "anteroom" to the budget process, wherein top management meets to identify the crucial issues facing the organization in the next budget process before the formal process begins. The normal budget process then proceeds, but departments also have to address the crucial strategic issues as identified in the preliminary strategic management session. Thus, two budget agendas are created, one business-as-usual and one strategic (Eadie, 1988). This keeps the attention of the organization focused on the big picture, on the crucial issues, and on the balance between the organization and its environment in the budget process as well as costing out how much more is needed for office supplies.

This chapter will consider the issue of strategic management in government. The importance of the techniques of strategic management lies in their use of available human capital to focus organizational resources on imbalances between the organization and its environment and to find ways to rebalance the organization and its environment.

Defining Strategic Management

Definitions of strategic management range from the organizational to the communal. Wechsler and Backoff (1986) observe that common usage invokes such words as adaptation, learning, evolution, and co-alignment. These researchers suggest that at the agency level strategic management involves the joining together of external demands, constraints, and mandates with agency-specific goals, objectives, and operational procedures. This involves strategies for implementing policy, for the internal and external management of the agency, and for the establishment of organizational purpose and character. Schendel and Hofer (1979) describe strategic management as a process that deals with the entrepreneurial work of the organization, with organizational renewal and growth, and with the development and use of the strategy that is to guide the organization's operations. The human dimension is critical: "Involved people, not rigid controls, are viewed as the key both to productivity and to strategic response'' (Eadie and Steinbacher, 1985, p. 430).

Ellen Chaffee (1985) finds three models of strategy in the literature. The first type is linear. This strategy consists of integrated actions that will set and achieve long-term goals. The focus for linear strategy is means and ends. The aim of the strategy is goal achievement.

The second type of strategy is adaptive. An adaptive strategy seeks a viable match between the opportunities and risks in the external environment and the organization's capabilities and resources for exploiting those resources. This model relies on simultaneous adaptation, while the linear model assumes some time lags. In the adaptive model the focus is on the means, and the goal is the alignment of the organization with its environment. Advance planning is relatively unimportant. The boundary between the organization and its environment is highly permeable, and the environment is seen as highly complex, with trends, events, competitors, and stakeholders interacting in a rich tapestry of actions. The aim of adaptive strategy is co-alignment with the environment.

The third model of strategy is interpretive. This is a social contract model that rests on the ability to persuade individuals to cooperate in mutually beneficial exchanges. Reality is seen as not external to the perceiver but rather something that can be defined through a process of social interchange in which perceptions are affirmed, modified, or replaced according to their apparent congruence with the perceptions of others.

The goal of this strategy is not changing with the environment as in the adaptive model but rather dealing with the environment through symbolic action and communication. The aim of the strategy is legitimacy. Its focus is on participants and potential participants in the organization.

Chaffee concludes that although no consensus exists on a definition of strategy since it is multidimensional and situational, these three themes are clearly separable. Nevertheless, all three rest on the inseparability of the organization and its environment, and they focus on the use of strategy by the organization to deal with a changing environment. Strategy includes both the actions taken and the process by which those actions are discovered and decided upon. Strategies can be divided into the intended strategy, the emergent strategy—that which occurs when plans meet realities—and the realized strategy—the final outcome. Ring and Perry (1985) call emergent strategies a key feature of public sector management: "Strategy in the public sector tends toward the emergent rather than the deliberate" (p. 283). Since the public sector inclines toward emergent strategies, the public sector manager must maintain flexibility, be ready to bridge conflicting worlds—such as efficiency versus equity in program delivery—and wield influence, not authority. The public sector manager also has to minimize discontinuities caused by unstable coalitions, brief electoral tenures, and changing political agendas. The administrator has to know the environment and the political climate, define the management task clearly, and cultivate skills for both allocating resources and caring for coalitions.

Doing Strategic Management

Strategic management can be used to improve the management of a governmental department or agency. It can be used for the collective management of a strategic agenda that changes as the organization's problems and opportunities change. It can also be used as a vehicle to identify and manage issues related both to the content and direction of programs and services and to the management process itself. This latter use is a conscious organizational development tool.

It is interesting to trace the development of strategic planning to strategic management. In 1972, Charles Mottley suggested that seven steps were fundamental to the strategic planning process in any subject matter area:

1. Diagnosing needs
2. Identifying and describing issues
3. Formulating proposed courses of action to settle the issues
4. Eliminating inappropriate proposals and retaining the appropriate proposals

5. Preparing the retained proposals as options for policy decisions
6. Attaining agreement on policy and the proposal or proposals necessary to implement that policy
7. Transforming policy into a preferred course of action as a basis for program and budget planning

Eadie (1988) describes strategic management as a six-step process:

1. *Confirmation of mission.* A review of the fundamental purposes of the organization, often done when leadership changes or when major environmental changes occur. This is a top leadership function and is often done in a group. Clarity at this stage keeps the organization from diluting its strengths, doing things it should not, and eroding task capability.

2. *Scan of the external environment.* Identification of the scope of the environment and the demographic, economic, technological, political, and cultural factors in it, along with their implications for the organization, including trends and projections. This may be done by staff or consultants for the top leadership. Different organizations have different environments; for example, the environment of a school board is different from that of the city council. Different environments call for different solutions. The fundamental question here is "What do I need to know about my environment to stay in balance with it?"

3. *Identification of strategic issues.* Again, a top leadership function, often done in a group setting by people sitting around a table. This is a top-down people-oriented function. The purpose is to construct a short agenda of issues to be addressed, since the organization has only the time or talent to address a limited number of issues. Some will be departmental; others will be cross-cutting. An important criterion is the future cost of forgoing action now.

4. *Assessment of organizational resources.* An assessment of the human, financial, and technical resources that the organization may apply to an issue. The issue of human resources is often the most difficult to address. This may mean retraining current employees or hiring new people.

5. *Formulation of strategies.* Using cost-benefit analysis of some type to select a course of action. This includes the target for change, implementation plans, milestones, assignment of accountability, and cost estimates. Projects are essentially developed around issues. These projects constitute a portfolio of action strategies to deal with particular strategic issues.

6. *Execution of strategies.* Implementation and adaptation of strategies. As strategies are implemented, new issues may emerge, and the process is then repeated. The manager has to be prepared to adapt to emergent strategies, since few intended strategies are realized. Execution should also be tied to the organization's budget process to ensure that resource starvation does not undercut the implementation process.

Montanari and Bracker (1986) suggest that a state strategic planning unit would follow these steps in a strategic management process:

1. Find the relevant publics.
2. Scan for competition in acquiring scarce resources.
3. Do an analysis of strengths, weaknesses, advocates, and adversaries.
4. Audit strengths and weaknesses, to prevent undertaking projects on the basis of wishful thinking.
5. Locate programs in a policy matrix and formulate appropriate strategies.
6. Formulate a budget to support the program.

Both of the latter approaches rely on the budget to link the output of the strategic management system to continued operational outputs. With these approaches it is obvious that the larger environment has become much more prominent for strategic management and planning since Mottley's 1972 formulation.

Using Policy Matrices to Manage Strategic Issues

The policy matrix is a concept that has been borrowed from the portfolio management literature in the private sector, where research indicates that the largest competitor in a market tends to be the most profitable. For the business management group, then, the imperative is to become the largest competitor in a market. If the company has the largest share, the objective is to hold on to it.

Products have life cycles, however, and the task of business leadership is to have a basket of products in different life cycle stages so that as market preferences change, different products will be available to take advantage of those changes. The basic task of the private sector manager is to respond to changing tastes in the market and to competitor attempts to gain market share.

At least nine different portfolio models have been identified (Wind and Mahajan, 1981), but the most widely known and used in the private sector is the market growth/market share cash-flow model where the long-run health of the firm depends on having some products that generate cash and others that use that cash to support growth. This model is usually presented in a four-cell matrix with market growth on one axis and market share on the other. The cell containing a product or products with high market share and high market growth rates is called a superstar; conversely low growth, low market share is the territory of dogs.

Products that have a dominant share of the market but a low growth rate are called cash cows—they throw off cash but their future is limited and as a result investing in them to drive up market growth rate is unwarranted, usually because the product is technically obsolescent or because tastes are moving away from it. The last cell, in which the growth rate of market share is high but market share compared to the share of the largest competitor is low, is the area of the problem child. Astute marketing or slightly improved technology resulting from research and development may turn problem children into superstars. Or perhaps a wiser decision might be to abandon the market and the product altogether. Since there can only be one market leader and because most markets are mature, most products fall into the dog category: low growth and not the dominant product in the market.

The point of this strategic planning tool is to map out product planning strategies for the commitment of scarce resources. Products are located in the matrix on the basis of market share and growth potential. Then appropriate strategies are pursued by the management depending on assessments of the size and vulnerability of the cash cows, the prospects for superstars, and the number of problem children or dogs.

The portfolio model is a two-dimensional matrix for producing strategies to increase market share by moving products from the dog to the superstar category. Fig. 8.1 is a composite public sector adaptation of this model with public sector programs replacing razor blades and radios. In this matrix a potential public sector star would enjoy high funding attractiveness because it enjoys high public support and is open to policy intervention. Since it also is at the high end of the scale for the unit's ability to serve it, the potential for an excellent

Figure 8.1. Program Policy Matrix.

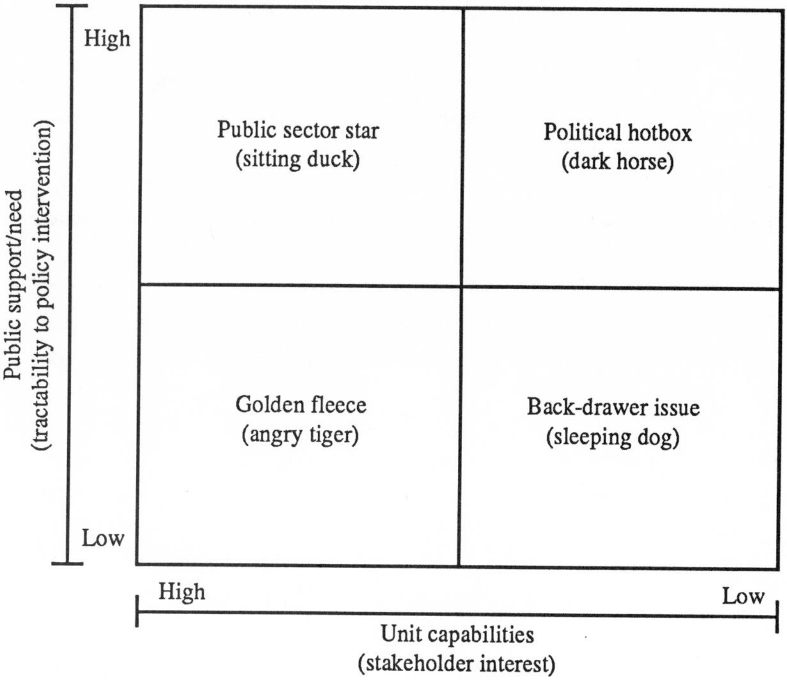

Source: Adapted from Montanari and Bracker (1986).

match of need to ability exits. A "back-drawer issue" is one
that rates low on public need and support and low on the unit's
capabilities. A "political hotbox" rates high in public need and
support but low in unit capability. Thus, like the problem child,
it presents the administrator with a problem in investment of
time and resources. At the opposite corner is the "golden fleece,"
a program that the unit has high capability to serve but that
ranks low in public need. The administrator who attacks this
problem may be accused of overinvesting.

Another version of this matrix offers up programs as a
variety of fauna (Ring and Perry, 1985) with the horizontal axis
representing stakeholder interest and the vertical axis the tractability of the program to policy intervention. For example, the
"sitting duck" has high stakeholder interest and rates high on
tractability—hence its name. The "sleeping dog" rates low on
stakeholder interest and low on tractability—hence it is best to
let sleeping dogs lie. The "angry tiger" rates high on stakeholder
interest but low on tractability. The administrator who attacks
such a problem may have a tiger by the tail. The "dark horse"
is one that rates low on stakeholder interest but high on tractability. In this conceptualization, notice that stakeholders broaden
the concept of who plays in the decision. Stakeholders are not
only internal to the organization but clients, pressure groups,
and other interested parties who have a stake in the issue.

The dilemma of the public sector manager is that there
are few sitting ducks and stars. An ethical dilemma also exists
when letting sleeping dogs lie may be the best strategic response
but not the best long-term professional behavior. Moreover, a
newspaper or a public interest group can suddenly become an
important and vocal stakeholder and move the issue to the
political hotbox or angry tiger quadrant, with the outcome of
the issue depending on how the agency is able to boost its capabilities.

Matrix Management Outcomes

The State of Oregon Department of Human Services used
a variation of this matrix system in the early 1980s. Programs

were rated on three matrices: need, effectiveness, and efficiency. Then the matrix documents were used in a series of negotiations at several levels within the department. The outcome of the process was very successful.

An internal review of the Oregon matrix system disclosed various benefits. First, not only was the system used to produce a budget under stringent resource conditions, but subsequent changes in departmental operating patterns were made as a result of the rating process, the questions it provoked, and the audit trail it left. In one program, the case workload was decreased in order to increase program effectiveness. In another, supervision was increased in order to improve the targeting on high-risk families. In a third, a close count was made on the number of hours of service delivered in an attempt to cut costs. The department also found that in this particular program contracting out with agencies would be more costly than continuing to contract out with individuals. In this instance, the idea generated by the matrix was not accepted but served as a working hypothesis and was tested and found wanting. In protective services for children, one of the criticisms that came out of the matrix rating process was that there was initial overinvestigation of child abuse. Following a study, coordination with law enforcement agencies was increased for the initial investigation and determination, before referral to the department.

Criticisms of the Oregon matrix system tended to revolve around the subjectivity of the definitions and the difficulty in separating out the in-between programs. However, even the critics lauded the process of routinized negotiation that the Oregon system demanded, whatever its technical inadequacies. During this process administrators developed priority rankings for programs, but, in addition, they identified critical program components and weak administrative routines that threatened the whole program. These "weak links" then became the targets for analytic efforts, additional resources, reorganization, or, if all else failed, termination. An additional benefit was definition or redefinition of the purpose of a program and getting consensus on that definition vertically and horizontally, among line and staff, and between social service administrators and top management in the department. The matrix form itself became a policy audit trail for future reference during policy discussions. One administrator observed that at meetings a year later when discussion became heated, ''we have seen the director and administrators go back to the matrix rating forms and say how did we evaluate this?'' The matrix forms became a historical record. Moreover, they also served as a perceptual record of how administrators perceived issues and outcomes: ''The things people have said in the matrix and things they say and do now tend to be the same'' (Mc Caffery, 1982).

The dialogues produced during matrix rating for budgeting carried over into ongoing administrative routines. For example, one administrator commented that the matrix rating process demonstrated that putting someone in a nursing home was a cut-and-dried routine as opposed to arranging a community-based care program that required complex administrative processes; consequently, a predilection toward the nursing home decision existed just because it was easier. Following this revelation, the department took steps to screen forms in order to prevent a decision from being taken simply because it was administratively easier for the department to do, irrespective of the welfare of its client.

Decreased cost, ranking of programs, better service to the clientele, and administration of programs within the boundaries of the resources available all seem to be worthwhile outcomes for a strategic planning system and, indeed, for government.

Public Sector Constraints

Since strategic management is being done in the public sector in a variety of types and levels of governments, no one can argue that it cannot be done. Nonetheless, the public sector does have constraints that private sector managers do not have to grapple with. Most obvious are those flowing from constitutional origins separating policy formulation from policy implementation. Another constraint lies in those aspects of civil service reform that give administrators a high degree of independence from political executives. A third lies in the openness of public organizations to their external environment. Strategic management is a team-building concept resting on top-down decision making. The inherent adversarial nature of the Constitution and separation of powers establishes a barrier for strategic management. Civil servant status means that leaders must be more persuasive than authoritarian, unlike their private sector counterparts. Additionally, stockholders do not participate in most key corporation meetings, but citizens have many routes of access to government and a citizen who chooses to do so can often become an important stakeholder in an issue for a public organization. Ring and Perry (1985) suggest that public sector managers generally confront a greater number of interest groups, cope with more ambiguously defined policy directives, and are faced with different time constraints than their private sector counterparts. The typical pattern in the public sector is to tackle a "twenty-year problem with a five-year plan, staffed with two-year personnel funded by a one-year appropriation" (p. 291). Moreover, policy legitimation coalitions are less stable and are more prone to disintegrate during policy implementation. This increases the difficulty of strategic management in the public sector and requires that the public sector manager be able to take advantage of emergent strategy rather than intended strategy, since patterns in the public sector tend toward the emergent rather than the deliberate and depend more on ecological factors than managerial intention (Ring and Perry, 1985).

Public sector constraints range from constitutional arrangements to legislative and judicial mandates, to government-wide rules and regulations, to jurisdictional boundaries, to scarce resources, to political climate factors, to client and constituent interests. Time is a particularly difficult issue. Public sector policymakers typically have a short attention span because of electoral cycles, fiscal crises, and a history of ineffective long-range planning. Moreover, the strategic management process is complex, difficult to master, and time-consuming. However, it is a good tool for keeping the organization in balance with its environment; for determining an agency's critical tasks, operational policies, and programs; and for making optimal use of its human capital and resources. Given the turbulent environment of government, these benefits are extremely important and cannot be expected to be cheap in time, effort, or money.

Conclusion

Governments that aspire toward excellence should use strategic planning techniques. Governments faced with great environmental change will benefit from strategic management. Governments faced with severe fiscal constraints may find that program survival depends on the environmental balance part of the strategic management process.

Top management must be committed to the strategic management process and to paying its cost, in terms of both dollars and their own time. The adversarial nature of many of our governmental relationships is a problem but one that can be overcome by managers dedicated to leading by persuading, rather than by ordering.

In a powerful metaphor, Bryson and Hostager (1988) compare strategic management to the theater. The plan is likened to writing the text for a play, while implementation is likened to the final performance. The power of the metaphor is its ability to indicate how much has to go on from creation of the text to presentation of the play: casting, producing, directing, lighting, props, financial arrangements, site selection, dress rehearsal, and finally opening night. Until that instant, no one knows for sure what the final product will be, nor does anyone know how the audience will receive it. Public sector managers must also deal with the host of details in writing the text and bringing the play to opening night. Then if the critics roast the performance, the program must be rewritten, recast, and restaged. The point is that a multitude of details have to be managed, even for the smash hit, between the text writing and the performance, and all are important. Moreover, the theatrical metaphor leaves a place for emotion in organizational life; the theater is rife with emotion, but then so is organizational life. Bryson and Hostager suggest that students learn to express and handle emotions, for they will have to do so in organizations.

Thus, while strategic management demands analytic skills, it also demands a variety of additional skills. Bryson and Hostager cite the abilities to synthesize, interpret, speak, write, lead, persuade, present, "direct," "act," watch, listen, and critique constructively. Creative power, analytic thinking, and interpersonal negotiation skills are demanded by a strategic management system. But the public sector has these talents; it needs to ensure that it is not acting in isolation or against its relevant environments but rather in harmony with them.

References

Boschken, H. L., and Shumaker, S. L. "Strategic Management and Entrepreneurship: Conditions of Appropriateness for Public Sector Application." Paper presented at the National Conference of the American Society for Public Administration, Portland, Oregon, 1988.

Bryson, J. M. *Strategic Planning for Public and Non-Profit Organizations.* San Francisco: Jossey-Bass, 1988.

Bryson, J. M., and Hostager, T. J. "Strategic Management and Organization." Paper presented at the National Conference of the American Society for Public Administration, Portland, Oregon, 1988.

Chaffee, E. E. "Three Models of Strategy." *Academy of Management Review,* 1985, *10* (1), 89–98.

Eadie, D. C. "Putting a Powerful Tool to Practical Use: The Application of Strategic Planning in the Public Sector." *Public Administration Review,* 1983, *43,* 447–452.

Eadie, D. C. "Developing the Strategic Capability of Public Organizations." Workshop materials compiled by Strategic Development Consulting, Inc., preconference workshop, National Conference of the American Society for Public Administration, Portland, Oregon, 1988.

Eadie, D. C., and Steinbacher, R. "Strategic Agenda Management: A Marriage of Organizational Development and Strategic Planning." *Public Administration Review,* 1985, *45,* 424–430.

Freeman, R. E. *Strategic Management: A Stakeholder Approach.* Boston: Pitman, 1984.

Korten, D. C. "Strategic Organization for People-Centered Management." *Public Administration Review,* 1984, *44,* 341–352.

Mc Caffery, J. "The Return of Strategic Planning: Matrix Budgeting for Cutback Management in the Human Services." Working paper in public finance and budgeting, School of Public and Environmental Affairs, Indiana University, 1982.

Montanari, J. R., and Bracker, J. S. "The Strategic Management Process at the Public Planning Unit Level." *Strategic Management Journal*, 1986, *7*, 251–265.

Mottley, C. M. "Strategic Planning." In F. J. Lyden and E. G. Miller (eds.), *Planning-Programming-Budgeting.* (2nd ed.) Chicago: Markham, 1972.

Ring, P. S., and Perry, J. L. "Strategic Management in Public and Private Organizations: Implications of Distinctive Contexts and Constraints." *Academy of Management Review*, 1985, *10*, 276–296.

Schendel, D., and Hofer, C. W. *Strategic Management: A New View of Business Policy and Planning.* Boston: Little, Brown, 1979.

Wechsler, B., and Backoff, R. W. "Policy Making and Administration in State Agencies: Strategic Management Approaches." *Public Administration Review*, 1986, *46*, 321–327.

Wechsler, B., and Backoff, R. W. "The Dynamics of Strategy in Public Organizations." *Journal of the American Planning Association*, 1987, *53*, 34–43.

Wind, Y., and Mahajan, V. "Designing Product and Business Portfolios." *Harvard Business Review*, 1981, *59*, 155–165.

Wortman, M. S. "Strategic Management: Not-for-Profit Organizations." In D. Schendel and C. Hofer (eds.), *Strategic Management: A New View of Business Policy and Planning.* Boston: Little, Brown, 1979.

9

𝍗𝍗𝍗𝍗𝍗𝍗𝍗𝍗𝍗𝍗𝍗𝍗𝍗𝍗𝍗𝍗𝍗𝍗𝍗𝍗𝍗𝍗𝍗𝍗

Maintaining Quality and Accountability in a Period of Privatization

John Rehfuss

Why Are Governments Contracting Out?

Contracting out is a traditional means of providing a range of public services. Governments have been contracting out for decades—the Pentagon to Lockheed and General Dynamics for military hardware, state agencies to nonprofit firms and hospitals for human services, and cities to engineers for design and construction of streets. In recent years, however, the number of government jurisdictions doing such contracting has increased. Many units are contracting more intensively: federal contract expenditures, mostly in the Defense Department, grew 10 percent from 1983 to 1984 (Congressional Budget Office, 1987). Many different types of services are being contracted out; for example, the percentage of local units contracting out recreational facilities increased eightfold between 1972 and 1982 (International City Management Association, 1986). In short, contracting out, an established practice, has a new look and has become more popular. Let's examine the major reasons for this increase in popularity.

Fiscal Stress. The major force behind the increase in contracting out is that governments at all levels are trying to cut costs.

Federal managers face severe pressures resulting from Gramm-
Hollings-Rudman cutbacks. Federal grants to states and localities dropped 34 percent in real terms between 1980 and 1987
(Gleason, 1988). This decline accompanied the loss of federal
revenue sharing. It came when many state and local economies,
particularly in energy-producing areas, were weak. Even strong
state and local economies were often just recovering from voter-
imposed limitations such as California's Proposition 13 and
Massachusetts's Proposition 2½.

Financial needs will continue into the foreseeable future.
Basic public needs such as roads, water treatment plants, and
sewage disposal systems will require perhaps a trillion dollars
by the year 2000 (Touche Ross, 1987). As a result, managers
at all levels face enormous future needs while operating under
severe budget restrictions. Small wonder that they are looking
for means to reduce costs. Contracting out appears to offer one
such means.

The Privatization Movement. Fiscal stress provides the pragmatic
reason for interest in contracting out, while privatization provides additional ideological support. Privatization, legitimizing
less reliance on government, has become a major intellectual
force, based on scholarly works, the fervent support of the Reagan administration, and the apparent success of the Thatcher
administration in Great Britain (Poole, 1980; Savas, 1987). This
at least partially explains why fiscally hard-pressed governments
are increasingly turning to contracting out (the most common
form of privatization) to deliver services, rather than making
more traditional kinds of cutbacks or economies with in-house
workforces.

Privatization consists of four components: loadshedding,
expanding competition, increasing use of fees and charges, and
turning to alternate service delivery systems such as contracting out.

In loadshedding the government simply abandons a number of its functions, letting private parties provide them if there
is any particular citizen demand for them.

The second aspect of the privatization movement is an attempt to develop competition in the provision of public services. Competition reduces prices and provides consumer choice. In Minneapolis, both private contractors and public employees compete to provide refuse collection services in different areas. City collectors have gradually reduced costs to match private collectors. Competition provides a yardstick for measuring the cost and quality of public services. Standards can be set for acceptable expenditure levels for a given service. Most public services cannot be measured as precisely as refuse collection, but it is still desirable to obtain benchmark figures for services whenever possible so that contracting-out cost comparisons can be made and acceptable standards set.

The third element in the privatization movement is increased emphasis on fees and user charges. Fees and charges have been used more heavily in recent years because they bring in additional revenue, regardless of the economic merit claimed for them by privatization advocates. Between 1957 and 1977, the national share of state and local revenue from user charges increased from 12.7 percent to 18.6 percent (Coleman, 1983).

The final privatization component is use of alternate service delivery systems designed to reduce the scope of government action. Contracting out is the most commonly used alternative service delivery system; others include franchising, self-help, and volunteering. Contracting out is such a common and traditional way to deliver services that its linkages to privatization are overlooked, yet much of the current emphasis on contracting out is tied to the increasing popularity of privatization.

Ideological commitment to privatization has been the driving force behind contracting out in Great Britain. England's public sector, under the Conservative administration since 1979, has been privatized substantially, with contracting out being a major emphasis (S. Young, 1986). Local authorities, for example, now contract out school meals and park maintenance (P. Young, 1986) while London Regional Transit began to contract out in 1984, with contracts 20 percent below prebid costs ("Privatization Jolts London Bus Transit," 1987).

Elsewhere abroad, contracting exists, although not necessarily for ideological reasons. In Denmark, a private company, Falck, offers a range of both public and private services. Falck's ambulance service covers 98 percent of all Danes and its fire services cover 62 percent of all municipalities (Stewart, 1982).

An Overview of Contracting Out

Contracting out in the United States is much more complex than it is abroad. Contracting varies by functional area (garbage collection is contracted more often than sanitary inspections) and by level of government. All levels of government contract out different functions and vary in the degree to which they rely on contracting. Service delivery systems are also complex. Human services may be contracted to a private or nonprofit firm by a county operating under state guidelines using state, federal, and local funds, and the contractor may be subject to requirements by both state and county. All levels of government contract out and may share jurisdictions over any one contract.

Who Contracts Out—For What? The greatest available information about contracting out is at the local level. Here contracting is increasing. The services being contracted out are diverse (personnel, snow plowing, insect control, traffic control) and now are more frequently privately contracted (International City Management Association, 1986). However, the services increasingly contracted out are not necessarily the most often contracted out in total. In 1982 the city and county services most often contracted out were vehicle towing, day care, cultural programs, hospital operations, and legal services. The least common were traffic control, secretarial, and police/fire communications (Shulman, 1982). A more recent survey found that building and ground maintenance, vehicle towing, and solid-waste collection and disposal were most commonly contracted (Touche Ross, 1987).

Local government contracting may be increasing but is by no means the dominant form of service delivery. An earlier study of cities under 50,000 found that most services were not provided by private contractors. Those services provided by contractors were internal, such as janitorial, rather than direct, such as street sweeping (Florestano and Gordon, 1981).

Although comparative figures are not available, the federal government is probably much more reliant on contracting than local governments. In 1982 a quarter of all federal expenditures were for contracts (American Federation of State, County, and Municipal Officials, 1983), although the Defense Department, where most federal contracting takes place, far exceeded this ratio. In 1984, the Defense Department spent $133 billion of the $183 billion for federal contracts (Chi, 1985). In 1976, 80,000 federal employees were involved in contract management, but by 1987 the Defense Department alone had 150,000 acquisition officers, arranging 15 million contracts worthy nearly $200 billion (Melloan, 1987). These contracts were for an incredibly wide range of items; spare parts, for example, made up 15 percent of defense procurement in 1984 (Comptroller General, 1986).

Other federal agencies were busy contracting out, too. The Department of Health, Education, and Welfare (now Health and Human Services) back in the 1970s had 157,000 federal employees, whose numbers were dwarfed by the 750,000 people who worked under HEW contracts (Sharkansky, 1980). There is no indication that this one-to-five ratio has changed.

Information on state government is less comprehensive than on the federal government. Although some detailed information is available, data on state contracting out tend to be scattered and episodic. States are moving from traditional contracting for services such as highway building and building maintenance toward becoming more involved in privatization in general and contracting out in specific. There is, of course, considerable variation among states.

State and local spending on services from private sources tripled from $27 billion in 1975 to $81 billion in 1982. Much of this spending was for economic development, transportation, social services, and welfare, and spending in these functional areas is likely to increase (Chi, 1985, 1986). In 1982 the majority of Minnesota's contracts were for transportation (2,178 for $454 million), followed by economic security (1,720 contracts) and energy and economic development (694). In the same year, the majority of Virginia's contracts were for individual and family services (including health care), while social services and welfare were the most common contracts in Wisconsin (Chi, 1986).

Specific contracts in the various states are as diverse as the programs operated in states. Two specific areas of state contracts are employment training and health care. Several states are using private partnerships for employment training. For example, Ohio and Connecticut have contracted with American Works to place welfare recipients in unsubsidized jobs. The company operates a program in Dayton and Cleveland, Ohio, and in the Hartford–New Britain area in Connecticut. In health care, nineteen states use private health maintenance providers for Medicaid, while another thirty-five states contract with private fiscal agents to operate and manage Medicaid (Chi, 1986).

Nontraditional Contracting. Each level of government contracts out for somewhat traditional services, but many nontraditional services at all levels of government are being contracted out or otherwise privatized. Such nontraditional areas include the provision of human services and the financing and managing of prisons or corrections institutions. The following discussion indicates the degree to which contracting out for such services is making or may make inroads into traditional in-house government provision of services.

Contracting Out for Social (Human) Services. Contracting for social services is a good example of some of the diversity in contracting out, for human or social services are somewhat different from traditional services delivered to citizens. Human services involve personal services intimately related to the physical well-being of the recipient. They involve crucial individual relationships with clients that require high levels of commitment. When contracted out, however, human services are subject to the pressure for efficiency found in a normally contracted service. This concern for efficiency without losing individual concern for clients marks social service contracting.

Individual human service programs are contracted more often with nonprofit than profit organizations. For example, at the local level, 29 percent of elderly programs are contracted with nonprofit providers, compared to 4 percent with for-profit firms. In a similar human service program, 41 percent of drug/alcohol treatment programs are contracted with nonprofit providers, compared to 6 percent with for-profit firms. However, contracting with private operators occurs often in specific cases for provision of human services. Philadelphia County's Children and Youth Agency, for example, contracts out 78 percent of its budget ($80 million) to private contractors for direct services ("Handling Children and Youth Services Through Contracting," 1987).

Contracting out for social services occurs for several reasons: Nonprofit organizations are viewed as placing the client's interest foremost; they can often recruit higher-quality volunteer help; they have strong community support; they often have more expertise; and they can more flexibly handle the personnel changes necessitated by changing state or federal mandates (DeHoog, 1984; Valente and Manchester, 1984).

Contracting for social services is no panacea, however. Whitcomb (1984) cautions that public agencies have to be ready to make emergency infusions of funds, must monitor the contract heavily, and must shift clients frequently if the providers reject them as too difficult. She argues that formal contracts should be based on competitive proposals, rather than client-by-client arrangements, that contract cost savings should equal at least 15 percent, and that agencies be wary of contracting. Furthermore, effective social service contracting requires competition among providers, strong monitoring, clear contract authority, and complete freedom from the hint of political influence (DeHoog, 1984; Straussman and Fairie, 1981).

Prison and Corrections Contracting. Prison and corrections contracting is a much more recent phenomenon than social services contracting. Historically, private contractors have been involved with prisons through prison industries. Firms have contracted with some states for prisoner labor, while other states have allowed private operators to manage the entire prison industry. An example is Minnesota's Stillwater State Prison, where Control Data Corporation trains inmates to program software and assemble component parts (National Institute of Justice, 1985).

Now, however, private contractors are financing and managing prison and correctional facilities at all levels of government. Financially hard-pressed units of government sometimes rely on private funds to build such facilities. Private investors are finding these to be good investments, although their tax advantages were reduced somewhat by the 1986 Tax Reform Act. Most of the arrangements are through leases or lease-purchase arrangements. Eighteen states were using straight leases for halfway house or community service center construction by 1984, with half the beds being in Pennsylvania and Michigan. Jefferson County, Colorado, and Los Angeles have used even more exotic financing arrangements (National Institute of Justice, 1985).

Across the nation thirty detention centers for illegal aliens, juvenile offenders, and mental patients are privately owned. Other states are examining legislation to authorize private ownership. In California, the La Honda prison facility is operated by a private firm. In two other states, Florida and Pennsylvania, private and nonprofit parties operate juvenile facilities ("Some States Lock in Private Prisons, Others Worry—Is It Legal?" 1987).

Private operation of prison facilities has kicked off a bitter debate. Advocates see private operation as the only alternative to gaining more space and as a means to preserving flexibility in prison management by using private employees. They argue that standards will be maintained because contractors want to keep their contracts. Opponents counter that the state's power should not be turned over to private parties. They also worry that private operators will cut corners and will bring pressure for harsher sentences to fill prisons for profit margins. Indeed, liability and security questions are still unresolved ("Supporters, Opponents Locked into Private Prison Debate," 1987).

It seems but a short time until prisons will be privatized. Local jurisdictions are becoming experienced in the use of private financing for major infrastructure facilities, including waste-to-energy facilities, sewage disposal plants, and waste-water plants. The private party, depending on the financing arrangement, may own and operate as well as finance the facility. A 1986 survey indicated that 3 percent of local governments used privatization financing, 64 percent of them for waste-water facilities (International City Management Association, 1986).

Accountability Under Contracting Out

A host of political and management questions surround contracting out. Political questions, especially in regards to the quantity and quality of public services, should be settled first. These political issues, as they involve the decision of whether to contract out, are discussed later in this chapter.

Administrative issues often receive a good deal of attention, even before basic political decisions are settled. Administrative and technical questions involve such matters as drafting the contract, meeting legal requirements for bidding, creating adequate performance specifications, monitoring the contract properly, encouraging competition, and avoiding excessive dependence on contractors. In some cases, these administrative matters involving how to contract become more important than the basic policy question of whether to contract. This occurs most often when contracting out is not particularly controversial.

Management Issues Before Signing the Contract. Administrative details can make the difference between a successful and an unsuccessful contract. They often occur before the contract is actually signed. These details include carefully analyzing existing services, preparing detailed performance standards, making adequate feasibility studies, observing strict bidding procedures, and carefully selecting the contractor. Effectively managing these technical issues will do much to eliminate hasty, badly written contracts. Mastery of these issues will also reduce mistakes in choosing contractors.

A careful analysis of existing services helps determine which services might be contracted out and which should be done in house. For example, the Highway Patrol dispatches officers, patrols with helicopters, monitors with radar, maintains vehicles, and investigates accidents. Some of these activities can be contracted out, while others cannot. To the extent possible, cost centers should be created for each major service so that managers will know more about costs before the issue of contracting arises. Performance measures should be developed for each activity. Helicopter patrol might include the number of miles flown and the number of speeders radioed to the patrol. These measures can be part of the contract document to specify performance levels.

Feasibility studies have to be completed for each activity or set of activities being considered for contracting out. Feasibility studies are often not done or are done improperly, either because of ideological commitments for or against contracting or because of inadequate information about the contractor's or the agency's costs. However, contractor information is usually easily available for the asking. Likewise, it is simple to calculate the agency costs if only unavoidable costs, direct and indirect (indirect costs may have to be estimates), are used.

Once the feasibility study favors contracting, the bidding process is next. The agency can use a formal bidding process, called invitation to bid (ITB), or can negotiate a contract, using a request for proposal (RFP). ITBs are used when the contract can be precisely defined. Here is where clear performance specifications are important, preferably as specific as how high the grass is to be mowed or how often rugs are to be shampooed. RFPs are used for experimental programs, for emergencies, for sole source suppliers when necessary, and for personal service contracts. The ITB process emphasizes cost and minimum qualifications, while the RFP process emphasizes the comparative evaluation of bidders (except for sole source or emergency providers). A formal procedure for ranking RFPs should be in place, and it should be known in advance. This process can formally weight a contractor's experience, the quality of the proposal, and the cost. RFP bidding is often suspect, because many individuals believe that the contractor has been preselected. Thus, the bidding and awarding of contracts should be carried out as openly as possible to reduce such suspicions (Marlin, 1983).

An important issue in increasing the probability of a successful, or at least a less expensive, contract is the extent to which competition between potential contractors exists. Efforts to expand competition pay enormous dividends, and effective managers work hard to assure competing bids. Competition reveals unrealistically low "buy-in" bids, focuses attention on whether the entire contract process is workable, lowers costs for contract work (or establishes realistic prices), and assures that alternate providers are available should the contractor perform unsatisfactorily.

Nevertheless, lack of competition plagues many agencies. Techniques to encourage private competition include dividing a contract into geographic areas for garbage pickup to encourage more vendors and hence more bids; having city forces bid against private contractors for the contract, as the cities of Phoenix and Minneapolis do; and encouraging or even forming neighborhood or nonprofit groups to bid on contracts.

Other techniques can remove impediments to competition. Excessive bid or performance bonds shut out many bidders and should be reduced. Agencies can pay their contractors promptly (many pay late or unpredictably). The bidding process can be handled professionally and aboveboard to reduce contractor fears of having the contract become unnecessarily controversial.

Contract Provisions. Contract provisions can play a major role in protecting the agency against loss of control over contractors. One threat agencies face is contract interruption, when the contractor goes bankrupt or when a major strike against the contractor occurs. (Despite horror stories to the contrary, these events rarely occur.) The agency can require performance bonds or have the contractor purchase service interruption insurance, naming the agency as beneficiary. It is more important, however, to be able to replace the service. There are three general methods for doing so. Contingency contracts bind a secondary contractor (or government agency) to provide the service. Another alternative is to provide partial service contracts, dividing the contract, usually by geographic areas, among different contractors so that one can step in when interruptions occur with another. A third alternative is to share the contract between contractors and city staff, so that city staff can replace an interrupted contract.

Failure to perform adequately can be a major problem. The agency should require reasonable performance bonds to cover poor performance. The contract should also provide for reduced or suspended payments, depending on how far contractor performance falls below contract standards. As in the case of contract interruptions, contingency contracts or partial service contracts with other providers are highly desirable. Finally, contracts should provide for termination under specific conditions by the agency in the event that the contractor fails to perform.

Occasionally, agencies must suddenly change service levels. Contract clauses should give the agency the option to change service levels or to establish alternate levels or service. Since many programs are based on subsidies or grants, the agency must be able to terminate the contract if its subsidy or grant is terminated.

Emergency response is another major problem, particularly in public works services such as snow removal or emergency street repairs. Contracts should have provisions for contractor emergency response, usually as an extra work item. More protection can be obtained by arrangements with other contractors or agencies, such as making partial or contingency contracts.

"Lowballing" is the final threat to losing control of the contract. Lowballing occurs when a contractor wins the contract by an artificially low bid, then increases the bid substantially for subsequent bidding when there is no competition. The agency, with no alternative, must deal with him or her. Strategies to protect against lowballing include (1) inserting contract provisions that allow the agency to unilaterally extend the contract, (2) frequently rebidding contracts to maintain competition, and (3) using short-term contracts to maintain competition. Long-term strategies include partial contracting or agency competition (Wesemann, 1981).

The above provisions, designed to prevent specific problems, are not without cost. They drive bids up by making contracting potentially less profitable. A contract with all these provisions might be prohibitively expensive. There are tradeoffs between complete security from contract interruption and the expense that such security involves. The long-term answer is to promote competition by partial contracts, contingency contracts, or shared contracts. Agencies need better choices than being forced to heavyhandedly enforce a punitive contract provision.

Monitoring Contracts and Measuring Performance

Contract provisions can be devised to guard against contract interruption or failure to perform, but assuring the overall quality of the contracted service generally depends on effective monitoring. Unfortunately, monitoring is the Achilles heel of contracting out. Most of the Defense Department procurement horror stories of quality shortcomings are about, or are caused by, weak or nonexistent monitoring (American Federation of State, County, and Municipal Officials, 1983). At other government levels, several observers echo similar comments about monitoring (Aleshire, 1986; California Tax Foundation, 1981; Whitcomb, 1984).

The purpose of monitoring contracts is to assure adherence to legal provisions and to assure that acceptable levels of performance are maintained. There are three general methods of monitoring contracts. First, periodic, comprehensive reports should be due from the contractor indicating performance to date. These reports should be verified. A second method is a system of inspections and observations. These vary from impressionistic glances to formal records of visual ratings. Finally, a complaint system must be created, along with a formal tracking system to follow up those complaints. Complaints are key feedback measures of quality, but by themselves they cannot guarantee quality. Unfortunately, monitoring often relies on citizen complaints alone, on the assumption that complaints will identify poor service. Such identification may not always occur.

A good monitoring program has four elements. First, good contractor relations include prebid and postbid conferences, a specific complaint handling system, and effective feedback to and from the contractor. The second element requires a comprehensive and clearly understood set of duties for the contract manager, from verifying quantities of materials to checking invoices. Third, the contract has to specify penalties for nonperformance and, ideally, spell out performance standards. Finally, an effective complaint system involves citizens, both as complaint initiators and as formal judges of contractor performance for services that affect the citizens (Marlin, 1983; Wesemann, 1981).

Sometimes, monitoring systems do not work very well, as this report from a Wisconsin director of a retarded nursing home points out: "Their work on the whole is almost entirely unacceptable. I'm sure that most of us as private citizens wouldn't tolerate for one minute sending out laundry and getting it back like this without complaining and demanding immediate remedial action. Many of the items sent to the laundry are never returned. . . . Laundry received in the cottage is often not for that cottage and must be resorted. It isn't at all unusual to find laundry from such places as Lake Geneva Bunny Club, Marriott Inn, Holiday Inn, etc. Laundry comes back wet and mildewy-smelly" (Sharkansky, 1980).

Precise standards for judging contractor performance undergird an effective monitoring system. There are three types of standards: performance, efficiency, and effectiveness. Performance measures are largely measures of effort; efficiency measures compare input to output; and effectiveness measures measure the impact of the service on the citizen. In the case of park mowing, a performance measure would be weekly mowing, an efficiency measure would be the cost per acre mowed, and an effectiveness measure would be citizen satisfaction, as measured by formal evaluations or a citizen survey (these are becoming more popular). In the case of a library, a performance measure would be hours open, an efficiency measure would be cost per volume circulated, and an effectiveness measure would be client usage.

When and When Not to Contract Out

Political questions involve such policy issues as (1) whether governments should contract out at all, (2) the extent to which private parties should supply public goods, (3) whether the level of service will decline, (4) whether the government's political life-style and taste for public goods permit contracting, (5) whether the unit owes any obligation to displaced employees, and (6) whether money is saved and if so, whether the projected savings warrant contracting.

A great deal has been written about the pros and cons of contracting out. Advocates of contracting stress the cost savings that occur, the desirability of limitations on government activity, and the acquisition of managerial skills, financing, and advanced technology (Poole, 1980; Savas, 1987; Seader, 1986). Contracting out opponents cite declines in service after contracting, the loss of agency capacity, the likelihood that savings will not occur, and the likelihood of corruption (American Federation of State, County, and Municipal Officials, 1983; Hanrahan, 1983; Levenson, 1980).

When to Contract. A careful review of these arguments and of a number of less ideological works (California Tax Foundation, 1981; Marlin, 1983; Valente and Manchester, 1984, Wesemann, 1981) suggests that contracting out is a useful tool when it:

1. *Cuts costs.* Contracting out usually saves money. When it results in savings, it does so because workforces are used more efficiently, often because salary levels are lower (this may mean that public employees are too highly graded), because of economies of scale, or because of advanced technology (California Tax Foundation, 1981; Comptroller General, 1981; Marlin, 1983; Stevens, 1984).
2. *Can be monitored.* If contracting-out programs cannot be effectively monitored, the contractor, not the agency, is in command. In most cases, poor contractor performance is associated with weak monitoring. In some cases, contractors take advantage of weak monitoring; in other cases, weak monitoring simply demonstrates weak agency management.
3. *Obtains otherwise unavailable technical expertise.* Expertise comes from specialists such as petrochemical engineers or from use of modern equipment such as expensive hoists for trimming

tall trees. No one objects to this principle, only to its application. However, agencies can rely too much on outside expertise. Continuing contracts for outside expertise indicate that the agency should probably develop in-house capacity.

4. *Avoids policy and management constraints.* Some agencies want to avoid civil service requirements and the problems of managing large workforces. Large workforces may draw scarce management attention to supervision rather than policy issues. Newly incorporated cities, enmeshed in birth pangs, are in such a situation.

5. *Achieves other goals.* Miscellaneous goals include setting benchmark costs for either public or private provision of services and avoiding expanding too rapidly after assuming new functions.

When Not to Contract. Contracting out is often done for the wrong reasons. It is bad public and managerial policy to contract out when the contract:

1. *Disguises service reductions as cost savings.* This primarily occurs when cost reductions are sought desperately at any price. A Milwaukee County food supervisor charged that "Food vendors underestimate the cost to the hospitals for their services and then compromise quality in order to approximate their estimated budget" (American Federation of State, County, and Municipal Officials, 1983, p. 29). Disguising reductions is at best deceptive; it is simply better to announce service-level declines along with the reasons for them.

2. *Engenders strong employee resistance.* Contracts facing strong employee resistance are likely to be controversial and less likely to be judged on their merits. In addition, employee opposition often becomes general political opposition, particularly in small cities (Shulman, 1982). Opposition also often spills over into areas such as general labor management relations and may cause some damage to overall employee morale. Employee layoffs are particularly painful, although private contractors can frequently be required to hire any displaced employees. Good contracts should not be avoided just because of employee opposition, but agencies should be aware of the dangers such opposition presents.

The Twin Problems of Corruption and Ideology

In a discussion of contracting out, the problems of corruption and ideology require special attention.

Corruption. Some experts believe that the risk of corruption is the major objection to contracting out (Wesemann, 1981). Potential areas of corruption include illegal acts by contractors, payoffs to unscrupulous public officials, and prebid selection of favored contractors. It also includes legal but unethical acts such as artificially low bids, sub rosa agreements to ignore violations or to not monitor the contract, and contracting to avoid unpopular employee unions. These acts destroy citizen confidence in government and give contracting out a bad name.

Stamping out corruption entirely is probably an unrealistic goal. A more realistic goal is to improve the contracting-out process. Most of the ideas discussed earlier, such as more effective contracts or stronger monitoring, would improve contracting out where it is ineffective and would have the further benefit of making corruption less likely. However, improving techniques such as monitoring will not necessarily make contracting out more palatable to opponents. Further expansion of contracting out or even significant improvement in its techniques is limited by existing ideological attitudes for and against contracting out. These attitudes keep contracting from being a neutral management tool for improving public services.

Contracting-Out Ideologies. Ideological attitudes cover a wide range of convictions. These attitudes include beliefs in contracting out because "public services have grown too large" or against contracting out because "private firms don't understand public problems." They include management attitudes that "contracting out always saves money" (without a specific feasibility study) and "contracting out loses control of services" (from those who have never experienced contracting out). They include political attitudes ranging from "employee unions object so much that contracting isn't worth it" to "contracting keep unions out."

These attitudes make contracting out a value-laden concept that either attracts or repels individuals, regardless of its merits in any specific situation. What is needed is an objective, unbiased look at the pros and cons of contracting out in each situation. Unfortunately, ideological commitments for and against contracting out make an unbiased view difficult if not impossible.

Contracting out gives public managers another tool for providing public services efficiently and effectively. It is an alternative that the public manager may be able to adopt in a specific case. Using it blindly and ideologically invites unnecessary controversy, while ignoring it reduces alternatives for improving services.

References

Aleshire, F., City Manager of Carlsbad, California. Interview. Oct. 1986.

American Federation of State, County, and Municipal Officials. *Passing the Bucks.* Washington, D.C.: American Federation of State, City, and Municipal Employees, 1983.

California Tax Foundation. *Contracting Out Local Government Services in California.* Sacramento: California Tax Foundation, May 1981.

Chi, K. "Privatization: The Public Option?" *State Government News,* June 1985, pp. 7–11.

Chi, K. "Public-Private Alliances Grow." *State Government News,* Jan. 1986, pp. 10–13.

Coleman, W. *A Quiet Revolution in Local Government Finance: Policy and Administrative Challenges in Expanding the Role of User Charges in Financing State and Local Government.* Washington, D.C.: National Academy of Public Administration, Nov. 1983.

Comptroller General of the United States. *Civil Servants and Contract Employees: Who Should Do What for the Federal Government?* Washington, D.C.: General Accounting Office, June 19, 1981. Report FPCD-81-43.

Comptroller General of the United States. *DOD Initiatives to Improve the Acquisition of Spare Parts.* Washington, D.C.: General Accounting Office, Mar. 1986. Report GAO/NSIAD-86-52.

Congressional Budget Office. *Contracting Out: Potential for Reducing Federal Costs.* Washington, D.C.: Congressional Budget Office, 1987.

DeHoog, R. *Contracting Out for Human Services.* Albany: State University of New York, 1984.

Ferris, J., and Graddy, E. "Contracting Out: For What? With Whom?" *Public Administration Review,* 1986, *46,* 332–339.

Florestano, P., and Gordon, S. "A Survey of City and County Use of Private Contracting." *The Urban Interest,* 1981, *3,* 222–229.

Gleason, R. "Federalism 1986–87." *Intergovernmental Perspective,* Winter 1988, *14,* 9–14.

"Handling Children and Youth Services Through Contracting." *Privatization,* Oct. 7, 1987, pp. 6–8.

Hanrahan, J. *Government by Contract.* New York: Norton, 1983.

International City Management Association. *Municipal Yearbook 1985.* Washington, D.C.: International City Management Association, 1986.

Levenson, R. "Public Use of Private Service Contracts in Local Government: A Plea for Caution." In *Public-Private Collaboration in the Provision of Local Public Services.* Workshop proceedings, Institute of Governmental Affairs and the UCD Kellogg Program, University of California, Davis, Apr. 11, 1980.

Marlin, J. *Contracting Municipal Services.* New York: Wiley, 1983.

Melloan, G. "Even Generals Get the Arms Procurement Blues." *Wall Street Journal,* June 23, 1987, p. 31.

National Institute of Justice. *The Privatization of Corrections.* Washington, D.C.: U.S. Department of Justice, Feb. 1985.

Poole, R. *Cutting Back City Hall.* New York: Universe Books, 1980.

"Privatization Jolts London Bus Transit: Public Provider Pushed by Competition." *Privatization Newsletter,* March 7, 1987, p. 8.

Savas, E. S. *Privatization: The Key to Better Government.* Chatham, N.J.: Chatham House, 1987.

Seader, D. "Privatization and America's Cities." *Public Management,* 1986, *52,* 6–7.

Sharkansky, I. "Policy Making and Service Delivery on the Margins of Government: The Case of Contractors." *Public Administration Review,* 1980, *40,* 116–124.

Shulman, M. "Alternative Approaches for Delivering Public Services." *Urban Data Services,* Oct. 1982, *14,* 8-9.

"Some States Lock in Private Prisons, Others Worry—Is It Legal?" *Privatization,* April 7, 1987, 1-6.

Stevens, B. *Delivering Municipal Services Efficiently: A Comparison of Municipal and Private Service Delivery.* New York: Ecodata Services, June 1984.

Stewart, J. "The Falck Organization: A New Model for Delivering Social Services." *Transatlantic Perspectives,* Feb. 1982, *6,* 10-14.

Straussman, J., and Fairie, J. "Contracting for Local Services." *The Urban Interest,* Spring, 1981, *2,* 43-50.

"Supporters, Opponents Locked into Private Prison Debate." *Privatization,* June 7, 1987, p. 17.

Touche Ross. *Privatization in America.* Washington, D.C.: Touche Ross, 1987.

Valente, C., and Manchester, L. *Rethinking Social Services: Examining Alternative Delivery Systems.* Washington, D.C.: International City Management Association, Special Report, 1984.

Wesemann, E. *Contracting for City Services.* Pittsburgh, Penn.: Innovations Press, 1981.

Whitcomb, C. *Checklist for Preparing Requests for Proposals Tailored to Human Service Programs.* McLean, Va.: Community Services Manual, 1984.

Young, P. "Privatization in Great Britain." *Government Union Review,* Spring 1986, *7,* 1-23.

Young, S. "The Nature of Privatization in Great Britain, 1979-85." *Western European Politics,* 1986, *9,* 235-252.

10

🮲🮲🮲🮲🮲🮲🮲🮲🮲🮲🮲🮲🮲🮲🮲🮲🮲🮲🮲🮲🮲🮲🮲🮲🮲

Evaluating Program Results and Success

Sharon L. Caudle

Evaluation is a word most public managers tuck away under such headings as "trouble," and "no-win situation." Political and career managers, caught as they are between performance expectations, administrative constraints, and conflicting public policy objectives, many times find the positive aspects of the evaluation process less helpful than they find the negative aspects to be damaging.

An evaluation is planned, conducted, and disseminated in a political environment and is influenced by and influences the political process that results in policies and implementing programs. Evaluation happens in a public administration context that stresses better performance, is pushed by resource constraints and past failures in public policies, and, as Palumbo (1987) notes, examines policies and programs that are the result of diverse and multiple-interest negotiations and accommodations among many decision makers. The evaluation findings, positive and negative, serve as inputs to a political process, accessible by executive, legislative, and judicial decision makers and managers; public interest groups; the media; central management and oversight agency personnel; and program clients.

In its broadest sense, evaluation determines political accountability and effectiveness as it judges the worth or quality of programs—not just the policy but how well the programs are run within policy parameters. An evaluation can focus on program efforts designed to achieve program results such as the number of clients served, on program effectiveness in actually achieving results, and on program efficiency in productively using resources to meet policy and program objectives (Austin and others, 1982).

Many evaluations are required by legislation or regulation. Other evaluations are initiated at the behest of external or internal parties. The evaluative mandates can attempt to cover questions that could be directed at a multitude of diverse programs after their implementation or can require evaluation planning before implementation (Berry, 1987). While the evaluation mandate can be couched in program effectiveness language, accountability concerns often underlie evaluation requirements. Anderson and Ball (1987) suggest that these concerns are likely based on the belief that improving information and service delivery will lead to better resource utilization.

In some cases, hidden agendas accompany the evaluation mandate. Some requesting an evaluation may want a vote of confidence regardless of how effective a program really is. They may want to embarrass the program or the support managers and staff, to use evaluation to garner additional funding or derail plans for an externally requested evaluation, or to use evaluation as a delaying tactic so that already-determined needed changes are further postponed.

At one time or another, a manager will be involved in an evaluation of policy or programs. The policy or programs may or may not be under the manager's jurisdiction, and the manager may not be a key decision maker. Even though the manager may not have requested an evaluation, probably resents the process, and may fear an evaluation's outcome, "care and feeding" of an evaluation may be one of the most important roles the manager undertakes. This chapter approaches evaluation as an activity that public managers must *manage,* just as they must manage direct service delivery or policy formulation.

The evaluation's acceptance and input into the political process can be greatly strengthened by how well a manager serves as a key facilitator in determining how an evaluation is planned, conducted, and reported. The chapter provides comments and suggestions in evaluation areas for the public manager's special attention in constructively facilitating the evaluation effort. These areas include the purposes and types of evaluation, the politics of evaluation, preparation for the evaluator's questions, research methodology and decision rules, evaluation of performance, options in choosing the evaluator, and manager input for evaluation presentations.

Evaluation Basics: Purposes and Types

Managing evaluation requires a knowledge of evaluation basics. Chelimsky (1985, p. 7) defines evaluation as "the application of systematic research methods to the assessment of program design, implementation, and effectiveness." Rossi and Freeman (1982, p. 20) have a similar definition: "Evaluation research is the systematic application of social research procedures in assessing the conceptualization and design, implementation, and utility of social intervention programs." Nay and Kay (1982) say that evaluation can be synthesized to the three words of measurement, comparison, and use—what is going on in the program, how what is going on compares with a standard, and what is going to be done with the comparison.

Measurement, comparison, and use—these are the evaluative watchwords for the program manager. They form the framework to address the evaluation purpose. Anderson and Ball (1987) highlight the main purposes of evaluation as:

1. To contribute to decisions about program installation. The evaluation would likely cover the need for a particular policy or program, provide cost estimates, and explore anticipated operational difficulties.
2. To contribute to decisions about program continuation, expansion or contraction, or certification such as licensing or accreditation. The evaluation can look to actual program operations, costs, and impacts.
3. To contribute to decisions about program modification. The evaluation could serve to improve the program by examining program content, methodology, context, and practices.

4. To obtain evidence favoring a program to rally support, or to obtain evidence against a program to rally opposition. An evaluation's advocacy purpose in this instance would be overtly declared.
5. To contribute to the understanding of basic social or economic processes, thus serving a pure research agenda.

Although there are many types of evaluation designed to meet these purposes, the public manager will normally be concerned with a small number, described by Chelimsky (1985) and Anderson and Ball (1987). *Front-end analysis* considers policy formulation in terms of the likelihood of success of a proposed program. This evaluation considers need assessment, costs, and operational feasibility. *Evaluability assessment* matches program assumptions against objectives, questioning how reasonable the assumptions are and whether program activities will achieve program objectives. *Process evaluation,* also known as formative evaluation, aims at improving the program activity processes. This type of evaluation emphasizes such process variables as client acceptance and benefits, program methodology, and personnel policies and practices.

In contrast, *impact evaluation* (summative evaluation) studies how effective a policy or program has been in achieving its objectives. It takes a broad view and generally considers potential side effects as well as program variability. *Program and problem monitoring* examines many areas of a program or problem continuously for action and reaction. Finally, *metaevaluation* synthesizes the results of other evaluations for answering evaluative questions.

For the manager, the impact, process, and program-monitoring evaluations may have the greatest political and professional significance. Impact evaluations decide the future of a policy or program, whether it continues, expands, or contracts. Process evaluations judge the internal workings of the program (Anderson and Ball, 1987). Program monitoring continuously evaluates activities.

The Politics of Evaluation

From developing the questions the evaluator is to answer to completing the evaluation and generating new policy and programmatic questions, program evaluation is embroiled in politics (Chelimsky, 1987). As the purposes of evaluation show, there are many ways an evaluation can be used, and managers generally know of the politics inherent in any evaluation. In a political environment, an evaluation can be both positive and negative. For example, an evaluation designed to gather support for a program can also provide ammunition for its enemies, either through the evaluation's overt findings or by challenges to the research methodology and overall credibility of the "positive" evaluation.

Evaluators are trained to be objective and fair, to do rigorous research, and to perform as "change agents" where that is appropriate. Frequently, however, evaluators do not give serious thought to the political considerations in any evaluation. Patton (1978) suggests that evaluators tend to describe as "political" those issues that seem to have a global impact and not the routine day-to-day activities in which programs and evaluations evolve. The end evaluative result may not be usable, especially if the evaluator does not understand the preimplementation political program or policy development, how the implemented program and policy adapt to changing political conditions, and how political forces respond to programs and policies that are flawed.

Weiss (1975) concludes that evaluators must understand the political context in which they work and consider political tradeoffs and not just the official program or policy goals. Because programs and policies are the result of compromise, stated goals may conflict and some may even be merely symbolic. Multiple values of equity, efficiency, and effectiveness may thread through the program or policy objectives, and factors outside the program or policy may have more than a passing significance. "How well a program is doing may be less important than the position of congressional committee chairmen, the political clout of its supporters, or other demands on the budget," says Weiss (1975, p. 17).

The difficulty is finding a comfortable common ground for both the evaluator and the manager charged with facilitating an evaluation, from the research design through the feasibility of evaluation recommendations, given these political dynamics.

Public managers, crafting program operations within many practical constraints, can find themselves in what seems a very vulnerable position. The evaluator should be told about those accommodations made in the practical administration of the program that might have strayed from formal mandates. In turn, the evaluator must judge whether those accommodations fit the spirit, if not the letter, of the program and policy goals.

Good evaluation comes from a relationship of cautious trust and relative honesty between the evaluator and the facilitating manager. If the manager knows that a program or policy in practice has strayed from legislative intent, he or she should be honest about it. These compromises must also be justified for the evaluative record. If the straying has been egregious—for example, if the policy or program was never implemented—it is better to be up front with the evaluator than to hope the evaluation will not be rigorous enough to catch the fact it is evaluating something that is not there.

Finally, the politics of evaluation must recognize that wholesale changes recommended in an evaluation do not play well in a political environment. Steiss (1982, p. 190) captures the reality by saying, "The real art of program improvement is not the bold guillotining of unpromising programs but rather is the reconstruction or renegotiation of the program-developing process." Instead of program terminations, Steiss explains, managers and decision makers are more likely to opt for program modification, for several reasons.

Policies and programs are designed initially to endure. Managers and decision makers also try to ensure that policies and programs adapt to emerging conditions so that they avoid death. In addition, since the policy or program is the result of major battles in the initiation stage, termination is a difficult alternative for officials to consider. The clientele and other supporters of the program or policy also rarely withdraw their support after the program is no longer effective. Termination requires "due process" that further delays actual death of a program or policy. In addition, those who wish to terminate a program or policy find that leading the opposition is costly both monetarily and politically.

The sections that follow highlight important issues for the manager involved in an evaluation effort, underscoring political implications.

Preparing for the Evaluator: Basic Questions

A good place to start reflecting on managing evaluation involvement is to consider why evaluation results are not used. Chelimsky (1985) summarizes the major problems as misunderstandings about how evaluation results may be used, evaluation's threatening nature, and the relevance, timeliness, and presentation of evaluation findings. Horst and his colleagues (1985) stress that breakdowns between the evaluators and those who will use the results are many: evaluations may not be intended to support decision making; the timing, format, and precision of the evaluation do not meet user needs; and findings are not communicated well to decision makers.

These problems should be the facilitating manager's "pressure points" in preparing for the evaluation. What strategies will direct the evaluation so that the design, timing, and findings are what the manager believes are needed? A large part of the answer lies in thinking through the program or policy objectives, understanding the many decision makers involved, and then preparing for the specific questions the evaluator will ask.

Managers, caught in the day-to-day operation of a program or interpretation of policies, rarely step back and reflect on concepts and objectives, but these will surely be the beginning point of the evaluation. A useful reflective tool is Suchman's (1967) list of questions that form objectives for evaluative research. Evaluators will tend to ask policy and program managers virtually the same questions:

> What is the nature of the policy or program objective? That is, is the intent to change knowledge, attitudes, or behavior, or to produce exposure, awareness, interest, or action?
> Who is the target of the policy or program? That is, is

the policy or program aimed at individuals or groups, and is the policy or program intended to work indirectly or directly on the targets?

When is the desired change to take place? That is, is this change to be immediate or incremental, and how long should the policy or program impacts remain?

Are the objectives unitary or multiple? That is, should the policy or program produce several changes or one change, and do the changes differ for different targets?

What is the desired magnitude of effect? That is, what expected level of effectiveness or standards must be met for the policy or program to be considered a success?

How is the policy or program objective to be attained? That is, what are the policy or program practices, and who will carry them out?

To Suchman's listing could be added others that might be especially important in a political environment. For example, are the goals clearly stated in legislation or regulatory documents? Here, the evaluator and manager confront the legislative intent of the program and policy. Another question could be: Is the product or the service measurable in an understandable way? Achieving an expected level of effectiveness or certain standards implies measurement and comparisons.

These questions lead to statements of *expectations* concerning policy or program objectives, target populations, implementation, measurement, and performance standards. For each question, the manager might then answer from knowledge about the program or policy *in practice*. After reflecting on these questions, the manager should marshal his or her thoughts to answer the following anticipated questions the evaluator should pose.

What Is the Purpose of the Evaluation? The evaluation purpose determines the evaluation framework geared to inform certain types of decisions. The purpose might simply be to decide whether a policy or program should be continued or terminated, calling perhaps for an impact evaluation methodology. The questions and their answers can decide a program or policy's fate.

With the program hanging in the balance, the temptation is to ask a broad range of questions, hoping there will be enough evidence (or evaluation report volume) to sustain the program. Naturally, there is a cost to this approach. Nay and Kay (1982) list three types of evaluation questions: those that can be answered at reasonable cost, those that can be answered only at unreasonable cost, and those that cannot be answered at any cost. When formulating evaluation questions, the manager should stop and think about the cost implications and focus on those questions that should obtain the evidence needed for the evaluation's purpose.

Decision makers at different levels may have questions that have very different purposes, a possibility that the manager should consider and explicitly resolve before the evaluation begins. In a pilot program managed by this author, the National Commodity Processing Program (NCP), operational program managers wanted a process evaluation that could provide guidance in improving program design. These managers were anticipating that the political reality might dictate program extension. Senior managers and policymakers, on the other hand, wanted a strictly impact evaluation that they hoped would convince Congress and the U.S. Office of Management and Budget that the program should be terminated. The process evaluation information, including state agency data on alternative recommendations, never made it to the evaluation report. As a result, when the program was extended, operational program managers found it difficult to obtain the objective evaluation data to improve current program operations or pose policy alternatives. Because the data were not in the formal evaluation findings, it was as if they had never existed.

Who Is the Audience? The primary audience can make a difference in how questions are phrased, how rigorous the methodology must be, and how comprehensive the recommendations and alternatives must be. In sum, this question is asking who cares about the evaluation findings. For example, the NCP evaluation, while requested by agency managers and promised in regulations governing the pilot program, was really meant for the eyes of Congress and the Office of Management and Budget officials. As a result, the evaluation report became almost an executive summary for political negotiating. As a practical matter, though, state agency groups, private companies, local recipient agencies, and others who were primary stakeholders became part of the audience. The evaluation results were applauded by those who agreed and challenged by those who did not. The important lesson for the manager facilitating the evaluation effort is to make sure that the evaluator understands who is likely to read the report and what uses the readers will make of it.

What Are the Policy or Program Objectives? This question considers program or policy goals and the objectives that will attain the goals. As Suchman's (1967) list of questions suggest, this topic covers the intent and timing of the program, as well as the targets.

　　In the case of the NCP program, there were several program objectives and multiple targets of the program intervention, causing evaluation difficulties. For example, the primary goal of NCP was to help reduce massive surplus stocks of government-owned dairy and other agricultural products. But the stated objectives to accomplish this goal were very general, relied on program intervention linkages between the public and private sector that did not exist, and did not provide "effectiveness" details so that standards could be developed.

What Are the Performance Standards? The standards are the comparison for outputs and outcomes. While at the bright beginning of the policy or program the standards might have been quite clear, as Anderson and Ball (1987, p. 293) remark, "We are all well aware that standards change with circumstances, expectations, and who is setting them." However, unless the manager educates the evaluators, the standards will likely come from the formally stated goals; the evaluation questions will be posed in terms of how well the policy or program meets the stated goals. Performance standards also determine measurement criteria, so the manager should make sure that the performance standards and actual objectives match.

Where Is the Information on Inputs, Outputs, and Outcomes and How Good Is It? Here the manager is best served by being clear on the reliability, validity, and availability of the information the evaluator is using. As Northrop, Kraemer, and King point out in Chapter Seven, computer-based information can be very helpful if the information system is designed and operated to contribute to the decision-making process. For example, in the NCP case the management information system on paper appeared to be well designed and operating in "real time." However, lack of edit checks on reported data resulted in duplicate and missing information. Because of constrained keypunching resources, the data that should have been entered into the system were woefully late. While the operational program managers warned the evaluators that the data were marginal at best, the data were still used. Of course when the time came to challenge the evaluation results, opponents used the data unreliability to maximum political effect.

What Comparisons Are Desired? Comparisons are the lifeblood of evaluation. Cost factors are important in comparison decisions. The manager may want comparisons of his or her program with others in other locations or perhaps site comparisons that are before and after the fact. The comparisons requested will be a major feature of the research design. As a practical matter, the manager should also consider how the comparisons will, as some federal managers say, "play on the front page of the *Washington Post.*" Are the comparisons subject to challenge on any front?

The temptation in giving advice to the evaluator as to what parts of the program to study is to steer him or her to a program unit that the manager knows is managed well and/or where the results seem to match what was intended by the policy or program in the first place. This does a disservice for two reasons. First, it obviously does not answer the question of whether the policy or program is effective in different environments or whether there are other ways a program could be implemented (Bickman, 1987). It is valuable to know why the program is not effective and what recommendations might result in management improvement or policy redesign. What caused the variability from place to place, and what might be learned to improve the program across all areas? Second, someone will always find out that the deck has been stacked in selecting the evaluation targets. The credibility of the evaluation is then immediately lost, and the manager's reputation becomes an issue.

What Are the Priorities for Each of These Questions? Invariably the evaluation wish list either will cost too much or could not be performed in the time allotted. The facilitating manager should be prepared to tell the evaluator which questions or requests must be answered and which questions can be dropped if the need arises. The priorities should follow from decisions on the evaluation framework and report expectations agreed on by the manager and the evaluator.

When Are the Results Needed? Timeliness of an evaluation's findings is absolutely vital. All too often an evaluation gathers dust because it was not ready in time to fit into a decision-making process timeframe. The evaluator may never have been told of the due date or, if told, may have assumed some slippage was permitted. The manager has the responsibility to think through how the report will be used and thus what the timing should be of not only the final report but also any interim drafts on which the evaluator needs comments. If the evaluation should be ready for a major agency conference or legislative hearing, the evaluator should know the timing constraints. If funding is affected, the timing of the budget cycle is likely to create the evaluation results' timing. If the results are to affect program reauthorization, the legislative staff will need lead time to begin the reauthorization process.

Research Methodology and Decision Rules

Many managers spend little, if any, time discussing the research methodology (including measurement) and decision rules with evaluators. If there is any area where the manager will get hurt in political skirmishing over the evaluation results, it will be here. The seemingly boring evaluation technicalities can be hidden time bombs. The research approach is literally the evaluation map. If the manager does not care where he or she is going, then the adage that any evaluation road will take him or her there is true. Unfortunately, the ride and final destination may be unpleasant. The manager should give special attention to the research design, planned measures, and difficulties in performance evaluation, painful though the process might be.

Research Design. The basic designs used in evaluation are before and after the program comparisons, time-trend data projections (with and without the program comparisons), planned versus actual performance comparisons, and controlled experiments (Steiss, 1982). For each, there are advantages and disadvantages for the evaluation. The manager should ask the evaluator, once an evaluation question is posed, what research design, or perhaps what combination of designs, best suits the question. The manager should also ask about the tradeoffs and weaknesses inherent in choosing a specific design.

Measurement. Evaluation explicitly implies measurement, so it is appropriate that Nay and Kay (1982) make measurement the first word that describes the essence of evaluation. Without measures, comparisons cannot be made, and that is the heart of evaluation. Measurement can be defined as "an operation for capturing some characteristic of reality and assigning a value (usually a number) to it so that the characteristic can be moved about, discussed, replicated, and so on without taking the entire reality along" (Nay and Kay, 1982, p. 60).

Measurement almost necessarily dictates the use of quantitative data. But that is problematic, as program effectiveness and quality are difficult to quantify in the public arena. Wholey and others (1986) find that program management information systems are likely to capture information on inputs or outputs such as the number of clients served or the tons of garbage collected—efficiency measures—but not on effectiveness and quality outcomes. Questions such as "Are clients rehabilitated within a certain level of quality service?" or "Are the streets clean?" speak to effectiveness and quality, but measuring them is a methodological challenge.

One of the manager's measurement difficulties is deciding whether obtaining policy and program outcome data is worth the time and effort. In particular, impact evaluations generally require well-defined goals that can be measured. Outputs compared to inputs form an efficiency measure, generally associated with workload. But if effectiveness is to be measured, program results must be examined. Quality requires a different focus, such as measuring an agency's responsiveness to clients' needs. And if equity is a value, then service distribution is important (Buntz, 1981).

Nay and Kay (1982) provide some observations useful for considering manager reaction to measurement that go beyond the technical difficulties. These observations can help the manager narrow the options for measures. First, they note that people being judged, as program managers might be, will try to influence the selection of measures that are favorable to them. Second, if the evaluator is going to use simplistic measures and comparisons, then those being evaluated might not cooperate with the evaluator in assisting in the evaluation study. Third, those involved in the program might prefer measures they control wholly or in part and will lobby for comparisons that are likely to be favorable to them. Fourth, they will want measures and comparisons that their superiors or others, such as legislative committees that influence program resources and management rewards, will accept. Hatry (1980) provides prescriptions for selecting similar performance measurement criteria, including considering the measurement's validity and accuracy, its understandability, its timeliness, data collection costs, controllability, and comprehensiveness.

The key factor, Nay and Kay (1982) suggest, is the degree of certainty involved in measuring program cause and effect. If the linkage between cause and effect seems relatively straightforward, those in charge of programs should be comfortable with effectiveness measures. If not, those in charge might prefer comparisons such as performance in different time periods or with other organizations running the same program.

Decision Rules. The facilitating manager should consider formulating with the evaluator "decision rules" for the research approach. Decision rules are simply rules the evaluator should use in deciding various courses of action (Ross, 1980). For example, the manager may say that if at least a certain number of the policy or program objectives are met within a certain level of effectiveness, then he or she considers the policy or program to be a success. Or if statistics are used, the decision rules might specify the level of statistical significance desired. Some of the decision rules, of course, may be mandated by legislation.

Ross (1980) notes that decision rules have several advantages from both the manager's and the evaluator's standpoints. Decision rules first of all organize the evaluation and ensure that important questions are addressed. Decision rules also force the evaluator to collect only data that will be used and to use this data as intended, with decision rules actually linked to anticipated decisions. The rules provide the framework for reporting results to the decision makers, increasing the likelihood of use.

Decision rules further attempt to maintain objectivity, preventing ad hoc interpretations after the data are collected. As Ross (1980, p. 67) notes, "Unstated and unexamined prior preferences are enormously powerful influences in data analysis; the evaluator and data user are both anchored in their expectations so as to bias their interpretation of findings. The formulation of explicit decision rules in advance of examining the data forces evaluators and decision makers to overtly examine their preferences, thereby reducing their arbitrary power."

Finally, decision rules reduce later conflict, since the rules must be worked out, and the battles fought, before the actual evaluation begins. Some of the rules will be changed during data analysis, but these changes should be mutually agreed upon. An example is changing the level of statistical significance needed for generalizability because of sampling problems.

If there are many participants deciding on the decision rules, a problem will be achieving consensus, compounded if there is a lack of program goal consensus among them. Early identification of a team to provide input to the evaluation and to participate in decision rule discussions can ease some of the difficulties.

Policy and Administrative Performance

Most often, evaluation pops up in *policy performance*. Here, evaluation considers whether the policy and its implementing program are producing the outcomes expected by policymakers. This is the primary focus of impact evaluations—did the policy and program produce the expected results, and is this the best policy or program to do so (Rosen, 1984)?

Increasingly, however, *administrative performance* is receiving more management attention, usually couched in productivity terms. The policy or program is taken for granted, and the evaluation focuses on how efficiently inputs such as staff resources are used in producing goods and services (Rosen, 1984). Evaluation of administrative performance examines how well the policy and program are being operationally managed. For example, administrative performance measures can include workflow, volume, and productivity, stated in terms of client and worker time, number of clients served, and cost ratios (Austin and others, 1982). Effectiveness, or outcome measures, does not come into play.

Performance evaluations (or audits, as they are sometimes called), generally examine financial accounting and other compliance elements and the efficiency and economy of policy and program support activities such as management information systems and organization structure. In Chapter Six Frank Sackton covers performance auditing as one of the tools used in budgeting decisions. However, performance evaluations may also cover program effectiveness. The evaluation of greatest value would consider how well a policy or program is implemented in compliance with guidelines, as well as the policy or program's impact in achieving objectives (Steiss and Daneke, 1980).

According to Bickman (1985), key policymakers and program managers are often more interested initially in resource allocation and distribution than in the effectiveness of projects. Later, after a policy and program are described in measures such as worker time and clients served—service delivery—questions about effectiveness may be asked. However, the danger is that many evaluations may not get beyond process to impact. Evaluation recommendations may mean findings are presented in efficiency, and not effectiveness, terms. Unfortunately, it is possible to be operationally efficient and have little impact on program effectiveness.

Despite the possible attractiveness of efficiency measures, Downs and Larkey (1986) point out that there are difficulties even here. Measures that are meaningful over time are hard to find. With changing agency tasks and technology innovations, the outputs can be different each year. Also, there is a general lack of appreciation of the direct utility for program managers. Fear of misuse of the measured efficiency results in another difficulty. A drop in productivity, for whatever reason, is hard to explain in a political environment. Finally, managers tend to view performance improvement programs as just one more fad and a fad that encroaches on their already strained time and resources. Downs and Larkey (1986) conclude that efficiency measures make sense only when goals are relatively simple and where measures have an inherent integrity compared to the task. Because of poor understanding of how agency actions relate to effectiveness, productivity findings are difficult to translate into program and policy recommendations.

However, that is not to say that administrative performance evaluation is impossible or worthless. There are resources that evaluators can tap for a quantitative approach to evaluating government programs that provide sophisticated measures of inputs, outputs, and outcomes in the public sector. For example, the General Accounting Office, the Bureau of Labor Statistics, and the Urban Institute have all demonstrated how to measure efficiency and effectiveness (Holzer, 1984).

Steiss (1982) suggests that to get around measurement problems, evaluators should use comprehensive indicators. These indicators can include effectiveness, efficiency, and the relationship between goals and services. For example, he cites California's past use of contracts with service recipients that built in an assessment of agency performance, client satisfaction, and productivity. Evaluators can also use sources of information such as employee surveys, client surveys, and productivity data.

Choosing the Evaluator

Managers have two basic options in choosing who is going to conduct the evaluation: going outside with a request for proposals (RFP) or using internal resources. In some cases, they may have parts of the evaluation done by an external evaluator and the remainder done in house. The internal resource may be a separate evaluation staff or may be program analysts under the manager's direct supervision.

Internal evaluators are likely to be more familiar, and sympathetic, with the practical accommodations of policy implementation and program operations. However, they also owe their livelihood to the organization that houses the program under evaluation. That automatically builds in some issues for the manager to consider. Adams (1985) sees these issues as pressure on the internal evaluator to downplay the negative and stress the positive results, to undertake nonthreatening evaluation activities, and to assume a symbolic role and not a substantive evaluation function. On the other hand, internal evaluators are knowledgeable about programs and political implications as a result of being involved in the organization on a day-to-day basis. They can thus undertake specific program questions with the full cooperation of program personnel.

Whether to go with internal evaluators depends on how the evaluation results are to be used and who has asked for the evaluation. A helpful rule of thumb is: If the evaluation has been requested by someone outside the organization and the results are to secure internal or external support or to kill the program, go with an external evaluator, since an outside evaluation may increase the objectivity and credibility of the findings (Kennedy, 1983).

A practical concern with going outside for the evaluative team is writing an explicit RFP. Weidman (1985) suggests that the RFP be explicit about important constraints such as comparison sites, avoid unnecessary constraints such as defining sample size before determining output measures, limit evaluation expectations to those that can be met with available, reliable data, and keep questions relatively few in number and in a priority order.

Once a contract has been awarded to an evaluator, the manager finds his or her wishes held time and time again to the understandings stated in the RFP. Control of the evaluation is virtually in the hands of the evaluator, not the manager. Unlike the case with internal evaluators, changing evaluation parameters is a sticky proposition. Here, objectivity and credibility of evaluative efforts derive from the RFP, so the manager should find the time spent on the RFP well worth the effort in the long run.

The Presentation of Evaluation Results

From the time the evaluator discusses decision rules and does the data collection and analysis, the facilitating manager is not normally involved in the evaluation routine. However, the manager should ensure some liaison mechanism so that he or she can stay informed about progress and potential problems. The manager can in many ways serve a quality-control function during the evaluation, imposing a political and operational reality check on the evaluator. The manager can further serve a valuable role in keeping the evaluator informed about the changing program and policy context during the evaluation.

In any event, the manager does not want any surprises at the conclusion of the evaluation and expects the findings and mode of presentation to be relevant to the needs of the multiple decision makers and interests served by the findings. Liaison will help keep the manager informed, and an early agreement on how the manager wants the findings presented, such as in a formal report or an executive briefing, should help.

But perhaps more important, the manager must also educate the evaluator about the political and administrative capability to carry out possible recommendations. The search for effective alternatives in the public sector, say Steiss and Daneke (1980), runs up against the incremental nature of decision making, the focus on efficiency rather than effectiveness, and the fairly low risk threshold most public officials will tolerate. For example, Steiss (1982) notes that improving efficiency is the easiest alternative for the manager, as this generally does not require major program strategy or policy changes. Effectiveness improvement does. That is one reason, says Steiss, that evaluations stressing effectiveness are not used. The manager simply does not have the resources or opportunities to make radical program changes or must rely on legislative or regulatory changes, difficult at any time. If a program is already established, most decision makers prefer modification rather than proposal of new programs.

Hendricks (1985) notes that the evaluator's recommendations may require legislation or administrative action to change regulations or other procedures. Administrative action is much easier to accomplish compared to the uncertainty of legislative action or outcomes. Even so, the manager has, as Hendricks points out, little incentive even to take administrative action, given the lack of rewards for innovative management and public examination of any program changes. More important, administrative action cannot redefine flawed program objectives, and managers will not stray willingly from the letter of the law.

In sum, the manager facilitating the evaluation should ensure that the recommendations that make it to the final report can be adequately implemented. Hendricks (1985) provides some good guidelines for the evaluator as to how that should occur. Some are particularly important for the manager to stress in research design and analysis discussions with the evaluator. One guideline is to ask the evaluator to get different perspectives from sources such as program critics, legislators, and program participants. Another is to review and approve the evaluation design before any data are collected. A third is to have the evaluator provide documentation (such as case studies and quotes) of any findings of inappropriateness and, in any case, to include any information that might be contrary to the recommendations in the report. This ensures that decision makers and other audiences get a balanced view of what is occurring. Managers should also request evaluators to set priorities for implementation of the recommendations. Which ones, in the evaluator's opinion, are key?

Hendricks also suggests the evaluator provide different sets of recommendations for different program assumptions, interim steps for immediate action on the part of the decision makers, and implementation suggestions for each recommendation.

The manager should also share with evaluators how decision makers will evaluate the implementation feasibility of the formal recommendations. Steiss and Daneke (1980) list six basic questions managers, other decision makers, and certainly the evaluator might use in evaluating the implementation feasibility of recommendations within political, social, and organizational constraints:

> Whose ox is likely to be gored (political and economic climate)?
>
> What qualitative and quantitative resources are required for successful implementation (resource climate)?
>
> How well does the recommendation fit in with existing agency missions (organizational climate)?
>
> What factors of community or client disposition may affect implementation (social climate)?
>
> How have proposed implementing agencies or similar agencies performed in the past, and what difficulties are they likely to encounter in the future (climate of agency competency)?
>
> What are the innovative aspects of the recommendation that may require major attitudinal shifts among the participants (climate of innovation)?

Managers and Program Evaluation

As Kennedy (1983) reminds us, evaluation is perhaps inherently contradictory. Evaluation is to promote change, but the clients tend to resist change. Evaluation is to assist goal achievement, but different goals may conflict. And, evaluation is to provide information for decisions, yet decision makers rarely produce decision options in time for evaluations to be of use. That is the nature of the beast in public administration's political context.

The political perspective is needed for good evaluations. The facilitating manager's strong involvement in the evaluation process and decision making can ensure that this perspective is not forgotten. The guidelines in this chapter are fairly simple: plan for the evaluation by thinking through major questions and problems, be clear on absolute evaluation needs, educate the evaluator about the political context, keep the evaluator informed and insist on being kept informed in turn, make sure all the important aspects of the evaluation are covered by mutually agreed on decision rules, and work to ensure that the evaluation recommendations are ones that have a good chance to be discussed and considered for adoption.

Weiss (1988) cautions that those involved in evaluation should remember that multiple actions by multiple actors result in program and policy decisions. Decision making, being a negotiative process, will not result in a single correct decision. No evaluation can supply all the answers. Sometimes, she says, decisions are made in a process that is not clear-cut or that lacks complete information. The status quo, she concludes, sometimes is the most comfortable outcome. What is important in her view is remembering that evaluation findings do infiltrate the policy-making process. They can serve as warnings of problems, as guidance in the policy process, as offering new approaches to old issues, and as help in mobilizing support.

Sometimes the mutual influence between evaluation and the policy process that Weiss describes can take years to unfold. A good lesson for public managers, policymakers, and evaluators comes from airline deregulation, where evaluation findings slowly infiltrated a policy process and finally resulted in a policy and program change when political and operational feasibility was assured (Behrman, 1980).

In the foreseeable future, effectiveness of public policies and programs will continue as a visible public issue. When the evaluation results are presented, they should provide decision makers with a ''window of opportunity'' formed around how the policy or program is fulfilling its intent. If the manager does not manage evaluation involvement, the likely result is an opportunity for ''damage control'' or continuation of the status quo, alternatives that rarely lead to long-term program policy and administrative performance gains.

References

Adams, K. A. "Gamesmanship for Internal Evaluators." *Evaluation and Program Planning,* 1985, *8,* 53–57.

Anderson, S. B., and Ball, S. "Evaluation Purposes." In L. Bickman (ed.), *Using Program Theory in Evaluation.* New Directions for Program Evaluation, no. 33. San Francisco: Jossey-Bass, 1987.

Austin, M. J., and others. *Evaluating Your Agency's Programs.* Beverly Hills, Calif.: Sage, 1982.

Behrman, B. "Civil Aeronautics Board." In J. Q. Wilson (ed.), *The Politics of Regulation.* New York: Basic Books, 1980.

Berry, L. "Providing Guidance for Program Evaluations: Sunset Reviews Versus Evaluation Plans." *Evaluation Review,* 1987, *10* (6), 757–775.

Bickman, L. "Improving Established Statewide Programs." *Evaluation Review,* 1985, *9,* 189–208.

Bickman, L. "The Functions of Program Theory." In L. Bickman (ed.), *Using Program Theory in Evaluation.* New Directions for Program Evaluation, no. 33. San Francisco: Jossey-Bass, 1987.

Buntz, C. G. "Problems and Issues in Human Service Productivity Improvement." *Public Productivity Review,* 1981, *4,* 299–320.

Chelimsky, E. "Old Patterns and New Directions in Program Evaluation." In E. Chelimsky (ed.), *Program Evaluation: Patterns and Directions.* Washington, D.C.: American Society for Public Administration, 1985.

Chelimsky, E. "What Have We Learned About the Politics of Program Evaluation?" *Evaluation Practice,* 1987, *8* (1), 5–21.

Downs, G. W., and Larkey, P. D. *The Search for Government Efficiency.* Philadelphia: Temple University Press, 1986.

Hatry, H. P. "Performance Measurement Principles and Techniques." *Public Productivity Review,* 1980, *4,* 312–339.

Hendricks, M. "Should Evaluators Judge Whether Services Are Appropriate?" *Evaluation and Program Planning,* 1985, *8,* 37–44.

Holzer, M. "Public Administration Under Pressure." In M. Holzer and S. S. Nagel (eds.), *Productivity and Public Policy.* Beverly Hills, Calif.: Sage, 1984.

Horst, P., Nay, J. N., Scanlon, J. W., and Wholey, J. S. "Program Management and the Federal Evaluator." In E. Chelimsky (ed.), *Program Evaluation: Patterns and Directions*. Washington, D.C.: American Society for Public Administration, 1985.

Kennedy, M. M. "The Role of the In-House Evaluator." *Evaluation Review,* 1983, *7* (4), 519–541.

Nay, J. N., and Kay, P. *Government Oversight and Evaluability Assessment.* Lexington, Mass.: Lexington Books, 1982.

Palumbo, D. J. "Politics and Evaluation." In D. J. Palumbo (ed.), *The Politics of Program Evaluation.* Beverly Hills, Calif.: Sage, 1987.

Patton, M. Q. *Utilization-Focused Evaluation.* Beverly Hills, Calif.: Sage, 1978.

Rosen, E. D. "Productivity: Concepts and Measurements." In M. Holzer and S. S. Nagel (eds.), *Productivity and Public Policy.* Beverly Hills, Calif.: Sage, 1984.

Ross, J. A. "Decision Rules in Program Evaluation." *Evaluation Review,* 1980, *4* (1), 59–74.

Rossi, P. H., and Freeman, H. E. *Evaluation: A Systematic Approach.* (2nd ed.) Beverly Hills, Calif.: Sage, 1982.

Steiss, A. W. *Management Control in Government.* Lexington, Mass.: Lexington Books, 1982.

Steiss, A. W., and Daneke, G. A. *Performance Administration.* Lexington, Mass.: Lexington Books, 1980.

Suchman, E. A. *Evaluation Research.* New York: Russell Sage Foundation, 1967.

Weidman, D. R. "Writing a Better RFP: Ten Hints for Obtaining More Successful Studies." In E. Chelimsky (ed.), *Program Evaluation: Patterns and Directions.* Washington, D.C.: American Society for Public Administration, 1985.

Weiss, C. H. "Evaluation Research in the Political Context." In E. L. Struening and M. Guttentag (eds.), *Handbook of Evaluation Research,* Vol. 1. Beverly Hills, Calif.: Sage, 1975.

Weiss, C. H. "Evaluation for Decisions: Is Anybody There? Does Anybody Care?" *Evaluation Practice,* 1988, *9* (1), 5–19.

Wholey, J. S., Abramson, M. A., and Bellavita, C. "Managing for High Performance: Roles for Evaluators." In J. S. Wholey, M. A. Abramson, and C. Bellavita (eds.), *Performance and Credibility.* Lexington, Mass.: Lexington Books, 1986.

Conclusion:
Strategies for Managing
Public Programs Effectively

Robert E. Cleary
Nicholas Henry

The Environment Within Which
the Public Manager Lives

Today's public managers must make special efforts to learn how to do a better job, not only in their programmatic functions but, given the involved nature of modern government, as *managers*. They need to ask themselves, how does one manage public programs effectively in a complex political context? *Managing Public Programs* is intended to assist public managers in answering this question as they carry out their managerial tasks, tasks that are crucial in the delivery of programs and services to the public.

Our world is inordinately complicated. The convoluted nature of American society results in a tangled web in government. Our public responses to societal problems have at times furthered the complexity, which results in an extremely intricate task of management for government administrators.

A prime example lies in intergovernmental relations in the United States, where, as David B. Walker observes (in Chapter Two), the typical manager—federal, state, or local—

is more deeply bound by a complicated network of law, regulation, and politics than ever before. As a consequence, the administrator must increasingly be cognizant not only of superiors but of other authorities and managers at his or her level of government as well as in other levels of government. The expansion of intergovernmental relations and management in the last generation, the movement of IGR into new substantive areas, the development of multiple cross-cutting regulations (as, for instance, in the application of affirmative action requirements to program grants), and the growth of third-party program implementation (as, for example, in federally insured and regulated student loans) make organizational complexity the norm these days.

The fundamental issue here goes far beyond matters of management per se. Classical public administration theory rests on a dichotomy between policy and politics on the one hand and administration on the other, under which politically elected officials are to decide what programs the government will operate for what audiences and to which purposes, while administrators are to carry out these programs. On issues of any importance, though, this ideal separation of democratic decision making and administrative expertise is now more the exception than the rule.

According to classical public administration theory, the basis of bureaucratic power is the expertise and knowledge that stem from full-time attention to and specialization in a particular subject. But in many cases public administrators no longer possess the domination in expertise in government that they may have had a few years ago, for subject-matter expertise is increasingly found on executive and legislative staffs as well. Political executives are now utilizing appointed aides to specialize in a subject or a limited number of subjects and thus to help control program managers. In addition, the "issue networks" described by Hugh Heclo (1977) are more and more apparent in government as legislators work directly with administrators to influence the delivery of public programs. One result of all this is the growing requirement for program managers to interact regularly with a variety of other public officials in a political as well as an administrative context if they are to be effective in the basic performance of their duties.

Today's labyrinth of public organizations, programs, and services makes it difficult for government to function consistently on the basis of coercion, direction, and control. Public officials increasingly rely on discussion and negotiation to bring about the effective delivery of programs and services. Thus Jerry L. Mc Caffery, in discussing the public context for strategic management and planning (in Chapter Eight), catalogues an interesting set of government characteristics when he declares that government is short term, pressure-group oriented, incremental, reactive, opportunistic, and "political."

Government is certainly political. As H. George Frederickson emphasizes (in Chapter One), "public administration is embedded in politics." Managers must operate in a political context. To do so effectively, they must understand not only the larger political environment but the importance of politics in program management as well. The environment within which public managers work is double-edged—or, perhaps better described, two-faced. Frederickson observes that politics is both "a noble expression" of the human capacity to work cooperatively for the common good and an unjust use of power to advance narrow or selfish interests. He argues that "effectiveness as a public administrator is predicated on both an understanding of politics . . . and an ability to manage public programs in a political context." Consequently, modern public administration demands that managers supplement their technical skills with political knowledge and ability to properly carry out their programmatic responsibilities.

Public office is a public trust, as Frank Sackton points out (in Chapter Six) in discussing the importance of fiscal controls in government. By definition, government officials have an obligation to function in such a way as to serve the public as effectively as possible. Sackton declares that "the right things" must be "done right, without wasting valuable resources."

Robert E. Cleary notes (in Chapter Three) that this obligation of public servants to further the public good has to be understood in the context of a complex set of authority interrelationships that involve the legislature, the law, organizational superiors, and the organizational structure, as well as the public.

Our democratic system includes conflicting authorities, a situation that leads at times to unclear and overlapping responsibilities. As a result, public administrators must sort out competing obligations and even on occasion antithetical responsibilities as they manage public programs or deliver public services.

Sackton observes that American government, taken as a whole, has grown faster than the society of which it is a part. But as Walker writes, the twentieth-century expansion of the governmental role in American society has not been paralleled by a public acceptance of big government. This situation has led to a greater emphasis in recent years on contracting out and, for that matter, to intensifed growth in the overall privatization movement. John Rehfuss declares (in Chapter Nine) that one of the main purposes of this movement is to reduce the scope of government. At the same time that we have seen major increases in privatization, however, demands for governmental accountability of all types—system accountability, agency accountability, and program accountability—have increased in number and in intensity. Rehfuss, Frederickson, and Walker all note that this situation has been a major contributing factor to greatly expanded efforts by political officeholders to strengthen their control of the bureaucracy and, concomitantly, to reduce the role of program managers in policymaking and implementation.

Skills and Techniques for Public Managers

To operate effectively in today's convoluted governmental framework, public servants—managers and nonmanagers alike—have the clear obligation to use all the knowledge, techniques, and approaches available to them to improve their capabilities. This book has attempted to present the major tools for assisting in this endeavor. In addition to certain abilities and understandings, these tools include skills and techniques in the areas of:

Personnel management (Chapters Three and Five)
Financial management (Chapters Two and Six)
Computers and data processing (Chapter Seven)

Strategic management and planning (Chapter Eight)
Contracting out (Chapter Nine)
Program evaluation (Chapter Ten)

N. Joseph Cayer points out (in Chapter Five) that practical skills, people skills, political skills, and leadership skills are
necessary for good human resource management. The practical
skills embrace such matters as running a meeting, making decisions, and managing conflict. The people and political skills involve improving one's ability to deal with other actors in the
political system, including peers and subordinates. The leadership skills constitute such matters as task accomplishment and
organizational maintenance. Cleary notes (in Chapter Three)
that particular skills are required for the management of professionals, with the good manager being proficient at identifying and melding competing responsibilities, obligations, and
rewards in the larger public interest.

Financial management skills focus on developing the ability
to employ today's sophisticated fiscal tools to improve program
management. Sackton declares (in Chapter Six) that such tools
as cost-benefit analysis, performance budgeting, productivity
management, and forecasting will aid significantly in maintaining program effectiveness, equity, and organizational cohesion
in today's financially troubled times. In addition, Walker argues
(in Chapter Two) that the past generation's major expansion
of targeted grants for some programs and use of block grants
for others have substantially increased the need of financial and
program managers at all government levels to have the ability
to use a variety of fiscal tools effectively if they are to fulfill their
official responsibilities.

Computing skills involve at a minimum an understanding of the basic terms, concepts, and processes related to computer use. Alana Northrop, Kenneth L. Kraemer, and John
Leslie King note (in Chapter Seven), however, that perhaps even
more important for managers is a comprehension and appreciation of the possibilities and limits of computerization, including
the understanding that computers per se are not likely to change
the fundamental nature of their environments or organizations.
Computers can assist in improving organizational and program-

matic decision making by retrieving information more quickly, analyzing data more fully and speedily, improving discipline in the analytic process, and helping decision makers become more discriminating as to which data are important in a decisional situation. Northrop, Kraemer, and King observe that managers who have a basic understanding of the possibilities and delimitations of the computer in the organization are in a substantially better position to think knowledgeably about computers for management use. These managers can more intelligently discuss with experts the role of the computer in the office and in the organizational environment, particularly with regard to such matters as the retrieval of information, projection of data, analysis of data, and generation of reports.

Skills in the area of strategic management and planning stem from comprehension of the incremental nature of planning as a management tool. Jerry L. Mc Caffery points out (in Chapter Eight) that strategic management is essentially a way of thinking and proceeding that rests on teamwork and "involvement" to accomplish organizational goals. It emphasizes the dynamic interaction of an organization with its internal and external environments, including the political environment. Strategic management aims at relating the organizational mission to the environment in order to isolate key strategic issues; it then helps formulate strategies based on available resources. Strategic management involves choosing the strategy and the target that hold promise of maximizing benefits for the costs invested. It is a good tool for keeping the organization in balance with its environment, for determining critical tasks, and for making optimal use of human capital and resources. Strategic management is especially useful in resource allocation situations, but it is by no means limited to use as a fiscal tool. It can be employed as a programmatic decision-making aid in areas as diverse as defense, law enforcement, social work, and education.

Management skills for contracting out are a microcosm of basic public management skills. In addition to providing an explanation of when contracting out may make public sense (when it is likely to cut costs, can be monitored, avoids increasing policy or management constraints, and perhaps involves such

matters as the ability to provide a yardstick by setting benchmark
costs or the ability to avoid expanding too rapidly), John Rehfuss
explores (in Chapter Nine) such essentials of good program
management as the need for accountability, the requirement
for quality service(s), the essentiality of competent and effective management, and the need for effective program monitoring through the measurement of performance.

Managers who wish to use program evaluation as a tool
must understand that evaluation is a developmental process.
Sharon L. Caudle (in Chapter Ten) quotes Eleanor Chelimsky's
definition of evaluation as "the application of systematic research
methods to the assessment of program design, implementation,
and effectiveness" (1985, p. 7). Program evaluation involves
careful consideration of such matters as framing the evaluative
question, choosing the evaluator, preparing for the evaluation,
selecting the research design and methodology, and determining how to implement the recommendations of the evaluation.

The proper use of program evaluation as a management
aid depends on the understanding and relation of program objectives, the evaluation question, performance standards, research methodology, decision rules, and presentation of results.
Caudle declares that "good evaluation comes from a relationship of cautious trust and relative honesty between the evaluator
and the manager. If the manager has strayed from the legislative
goal path, he or she should be honest about it."

Caudle underlines the fact that program evaluation is a
political tool. She notes that evaluation can provide support for
a program or ammunition for its enemies. In any case, evaluation results are likely to become part of the political argument
immediately. Consequently, managers who wish to use evaluation as an opportunity for program improvement must take into
account the political context in which they work. What clout
do the program's major supporters have? Do these individuals
and groups want program change? What about the program's
opponents? Are there significant hidden agendas (by others or,
for that matter, on the part of the manager)? Program managers
must grapple with questions of this nature if they are to be in
a position to maximize the utility of a program evaluation.

Abilities and Understandings for Public Managers

In addition to strengthening their skills and techniques in the areas we have summarized, public managers are well advised to develop certain fundamental abilities, understandings, and perspectives, including:

1. The ability to deal fairly and competently with others, particularly subordinates and peers (Chapter Five)
2. An appreciation of the intricate nature of intergovernmental relations, and development of the capacity to operate as a manager in the framework of substantial organizational complexity (Chapter Two)
3. Understanding that program and service-delivery decisions are made in a political context and that not only should the political implications of a management decision be included in the decisional database, but the program manager should play an active role in helping form program mandates and goals (Chapter One)
4. An understanding of the importance of balancing program and organizational needs in pursuit of the public interest as mandated by law and regulation (Chapter Three)
5. The ability to act as a professional and to employ professionals in such a way as to enhance and strengthen their professionalism (Chapter Three)
6. The ability to behave in an ethical manner rooted in a recognition of the moral underpinnings of the "social contract" in order to advance the public good (Chapter Four)
7. An understanding of the civic duty inherent in public service and the consequent requirement to further the public interest while advancing the cause of effective and responsible program management (Chapters One and Three)

Cayer writes (in Chapter Five) that the development and maintenance of productive personnel in the organization is a primary managerial task. Successful organization or program management tends to be related to the development of a good organizational climate, a climate in which employees are treated fairly and with dignity. In such a climate efforts to improve performance and productivity are typically linked to a strong emphasis on communication and discussion, with subordinate personnel participating in programmatic decision making.

Cayer declares that the ability to deal fairly and competently with peers and subordinates (and, for that matter, with superiors) involves a congeries of skills and abilities, including listening skills, communication skills, and a fundamental honesty in dealing with other people. A willingness to listen to others and to empathize with their concerns (not, of course, to the point of trying to solve every personal problem) leads to a capacity for recognizing differences among individuals and a facility in relating to and drawing on their strengths. The talent of effective communication, usually both in writing and orally, is virtually essential for quality management. It is impossible for others to know an administrator's desires unless they are communicated. Finally, a manager who is not straightforward and forthright in dealing with other people is, in the long run—and at times even in the short run—bound to fail.

Walker notes (in Chapter Two) that the nature of intergovernmental relations in the United States in this generation presents public managers with a major challenge of performance, despite certain reductions in the federal role in IGR in the 1980s. Managers are frequently in an ambivalent position in a federal system that remains highly centralized despite major efforts to decentralize. In fact, the "Reagan revolution" has furthered governmental complexity in a number of ways, including its emphasis on contracting out and administration through third parties and its attention to program accountability through expanded political control of the bureaucracy. Public managers must understand and appreciate the convoluted context in which they work, and, more important, they must develop the skills and techniques necessary to function effectively within this framework.

Frederickson observes (in Chapter One) that politics and administration are now so interrelated that the cause of effective and accountable government can be appreciably furthered if managers play an active role in working with political officeholders to set mandates and goals for public programs. He argues that public administrators should even undertake a leadership role in the development of networks that will maximize agreement on program goals by all major interested parties.

Frederickson declares, "The wise program administrator will attempt to fashion a program mandate by carefully seeking support and understanding from critical elements in the legislature and in the staff of the elected executive; he or she will also try to find as much support as possible with interest groups and among the public. . . . Not only is enabling legislation fuzzy, the steps to be taken to implement that legislation are rarely clear-cut. It is, therefore, the effective administrator's responsibility to design these steps, and to make them as practical and politically feasible as possible. The administrator must clear them with key elements in the legislature, with the chief executive, and with relevant interest groups. . . . The effective program manager will, therefore, serve a bridging or transactional role, attempting to keep all the experts [wherever located] informed and working in the same policy direction."

It is in this context that Cleary emphasizes (in Chapter Three) the fact that the ultimate goal of democratic government is service to the public. As noted earlier, he describes the labyrinth of conflicting obligations that impinge on public servants—responsibilities to their programs, their organizations, political superiors, and the law, as well as to the public. He asserts that program managers and their superiors must meld programmatic and organizational needs with the requirements of law and regulation if public results are to be maximized and the public interest served. He concludes that reliance on basic ethical principles, along with attention to the various skills, techniques, and abilities discussed in this volume, will help substantially as program managers attempt to function in this framework.

The ability to act as a professional and to draw on the strengths of other professionals in public service, as Cleary also observes, is increasingly a requirement for managers in American government. Public organizations employ a large number of professionals. Professionals have learned a way of proceeding based on their professional training that must be adapted to

public organizations. It is a task of management to help maximize the strengths of the professional training within the organizational context, to meld the inner legitimacy that the professional derives from the profession with the political legitimacy
conferred on the public servant (Baena del Alcazar, 1987).

These endeavors should rest on a firm ethical base. Morality, as Ralph Clark Chandler notes (in Chapter Four), is a fundamental human characteristic, one that clearly should guide
administrative behavior. Basic ethical principles, related to a
"communal consensus" about what people should or should
not do, should lead to an underlying disposition on the part of
public officials to behave and act in certain ways. The development of the administrative state has been accompanied by sharp
conflicts with such predispositions. The public administrator is
faced with the responsibility of overcoming these conflicts. Chandler argues that today's public administrator must become a
"social partner" with citizens and citizen groups to help foster
"a culture of reciprocity, obligation, and responsibility" to advance the effective delivery of public programs and services.

The United States is a large and functioning democracy
in which rights of the individual citizen are crucial. Our country prides itself on "liberty and justice for all." The public
manager has, by definition, a civic duty to further the public
interest in the pursuit of his or her official responsibilities. The
interest of the public, nebulous as they might be, sit at the table
of decision in public policymaking. This entire book speaks to
this point, but Chapters One, Three, Four, and Six in particular
emphasize its importance and discuss how the manager may
best further this civic responsibility.

In his chapter on contracting out, Rehfuss pinpoints the
issues involved in deciding whether to contract out or to stay
in house. As noted earlier, he discusses the need for accountability, the requirement for quality service(s), the essentiality for
competent and effective management, and the need for proficient program monitoring. At bottom, these are the essentials
of good public management in house as well. A public manager
must be accountable to the public through the law and his or
her superiors. A public manager has a special obligation to provide

the public with the best possible programs or services. A public manager should be effective and competent in the performance of his or her duties. And a public manager should be proficient in monitoring programs in order to maintain and improve performance.

In addition, as Frederickson emphasizes, a public manager must be politically adept. He argues that privatization, or "government by proxy," and its effects have substantially complicated matters of public accountability. The resulting situation, taken along with the widespread efforts by political officeholders to control public administrators, presents "a significant new challenge" to public administration. Public managers cannot rely on the traditional definition and tools of public administration to do their jobs. Frederickson strongly recommends they attempt to understand and then to *influence* the intricate system of governmental power and authority that exists today. We all know that in the final analysis public administrators are politically subordinate to their elected and appointed superiors. But as the authors of this volume have amply demonstrated, discussion, bargaining, and negotiation by public managers with peers and superiors can contribute significantly nowadays to competent and effective program management in the public interest.

Public administrators certainly have enough program knowledge and expertise to be in a position to influence other participants in the modern issue network. As Frederickson notes, administrative expertise, almost by definition, is still crucial to quality public programming. Consequently, he argues, public administrators have the *responsibility* to actively assist their superiors and legislatures in the formulation of a system of feedback that will maximize coalescence on program goals and the delivery of program services on the part of all those involved. The result, he declares, will be more accountable and responsible government.

The Responsibility of the Public Manager

H. George Frederickson concludes Chapter One as follows: "Technical expertise is expected of good public administration. But it is effective political skills that make good public administration possible. . . . Working with elected officials, within the constitutional order, and with good political skills, public administration leaders are essential to democratic government.'' It is Frederickson's fundamental message that public administration today must make the reality of politics—and thus the cruciality of the administrator's leadership role in furthering program mandates and goals—central to its functioning.

Public program managers who assimilate and utilize the principles, tools, and techniques outlined in this volume have a significantly increased potential of performing their programmatic responsibilities competently and effectively. These program managers will appreciably enhance their ability to tame the "outside forces" affecting public management and thereby make a personal and a professional contribution to improving the quality of public services. The understandings and perspectives presented in this book will assist these public administrators to enhance their ability to use such tools as personnel management, financial management, data processing, strategic planning, contracting out, and program evaluation; to improve their ability to work with others; to develop their leadership skills; to advance their capacity to operate in a complex political context to further their program responsibilities; to develop their ability to behave in an ethical manner; to strengthen their understanding of the civic duty inherent in public service; and to increase their capability to meld their competing obligations in order to maximize the larger public interest.

As Chandler points out, public administrators must conceive of themselves and behave as social partners with the other members of the body politic. Steven Kelman (1987) has pointed out how America's governmental institutions are rooted in such public values as altruism, cooperation, mutual respect, participation, persuasion, and pluralism. Unfortunately, recent years have seen a decline in public support for public institutions and officials in the United States, a decline that has highly dysfunctional implications for the effective operation of the American system of government.

The furthering of the American democracy requires the efforts of all of us, including program managers who are committed to reinforcing our system of government *and* who know how to act administratively and politically as dedicated public servants in the full complexity of their positions and functions. Program managers must be able to operate in this intricate context to be fully effective as public servants. The manager who, as a conscious strategy, focuses not only on his or her program or service delivery responsibilities but also on the administrative and political context of these responsibilities and on the skills, techniques, abilities, and understandings necessary to help foster "a culture of reciprocity, obligation, and responsibility" will aid materially in strengthening the body politic. The pursuit of the American democracy, with liberty and justice for all, can demand no less.

References

Baena del Alcazar, M. "Pointers for a Discussion on the Relations Between Politicians and Higher Civil Servants." *International Review of Administrative Sciences,* 1987, *53* (1), 89–116.
Chelimsky, E. (ed.). *Program Evaluation: Patterns and Directions.* Washington, D.C.: American Society for Public Administration, 1985.
Heclo, H. *A Government of Strangers: Executive Politics in Washington.* Washington, D.C.: Brookings Institution, 1977.
Kelman, S. *Making Public Policy.* New York: Basic Books, 1987.

Index

A

Abrahamson, M., 99

Abramson, M. A., 254

Accountability: abilities for, 265–266; and contracting out, 219–223; demands for, 258; and evaluation, 231–232; and government by proxy, 31–32

Adams, K. A., 248, 253

Administration: of federal activism, 56–57; and politics, dichotomy of, 15–16, 28–29, 119, 256; values of, 29

Administrative agencies, and iron triangle, 18, 22

Administrative law judges, and federal activism, 53–54

Administrative performance, evaluation of, 246–247

Advisory Commission on Intergovernmental Relations (ACIR), 39, 42n, 47, 48, 50, 51, 58, 60, 66, 69–70

Affirmative action, as managerial challenge, 131–133

Aid to Families with Dependent Children (AFDC): and federal activism, 39; and forecasting, 162

Aleshire, F., 223, 228

American Federation of State, County, and Municipal Officials, 215, 223, 225, 226, 228

American Society for Public Administration (ASPA), code of ethics for, 83–85, 99, 106, 107, 109–112, 119

American Works, contracts for, 216

Anderson, S. B., 232, 233, 234, 240, 253

Appointments, political, 20–22, 56, 58–59

Argyris, C., 170, 187

Aristotle, 102

Arizona: and contracting out, 221; privatization in, 157

Armstrong, J. S., 160, 166

Austin, M. J., 232, 246, 253

Austria, professional education in, 96

B

Backoff, R. W., 100, 196, 197, 210

Baena del Alcazar, M., 265, 268

Bailey, S. K., 97, 99

Baker, J., 21

Ball, S., 232, 233, 234, 240, 253

Banks, O., 170, 190

Barnard, C., 127, 128, 129, 136, 141

Behrman, B., 252, 253

Bell, D., 172, 187

Bellavita, C., 254

Benn, A. W., 115

Benne, K., 128, 141

Berry, L., 232, 253

Bickman, L., 241, 246, 253

Bjorn-Anderson, N., 170, 187

Blackmun, H. A., 53

Blau, P., 136, 141, 170, 187

Blum, E., 178, 188

Boeing Aircraft: contracts for, 25; senators from, 22

Bonneville Power Administration, proposed sale of, 26

269